T0155828

Communications in Computer and Information Science 1667

More information about this series at https://link.springer.com/bookseries/7899

Péter Galambos · Erdal Kayacan ·
Kurosh Madani (Eds.)

Robotics, Computer Vision and Intelligent Systems

First International Conference, ROBOVIS 2020, Virtual Event
November 4–6, 2020, and Second International Conference
ROBOVIS 2021, Virtual Event, October 27–28, 2021
Revised Selected Papers

 Springer

Editors
Péter Galambos
Óbuda University
Budapest, Hungary

Erdal Kayacan
Aarhus University
Aarhus, Denmark

Kurosh Madani
University of Paris-EST Créteil (UPEC)
Créteil, France

ISSN 1865-0929   ISSN 1865-0937 (electronic)
Communications in Computer and Information Science
ISBN 978-3-031-19649-2   ISBN 978-3-031-19650-8 (eBook)
https://doi.org/10.1007/978-3-031-19650-8

This Springer imprint is published by the registered company Springer Nature Switzerland AG
The registered company address is: Gewerbestrasse 11, 6330 Cham, Switzerland

Preface

The present book includes extended and revised versions of a set of selected papers from the 1st and 2nd International Conference on Robotics, Computer Vision and Intelligent Systems (ROBOVIS 2020 and ROBOVIS 2021). Both editions were held online due to the COVID-19 pandemic. ROBOVIS 2020 was held during November 4–6, 2020, and ROBOVIS 2021 was held during October 27–28, 2021.

ROBOVIS 2020 received 20 paper submissions of which 20% were included in this book, and ROBOVIS 2021 received 33 paper submissions of which 21% were also included in this book. The papers were selected by the event chairs and their selection was based on a number of criteria that included the classifications and comments provided by the Program Committee members, the session chairs' assessment, and also the program chairs' global view of all papers included in the technical program. The authors of selected papers were then invited to submit revised and extended versions of their papers having at least 30% innovative material.

Robotics is a field that is closely connected to computer vision and intelligent systems. Research and development of robots require technologies originating from these other two areas. The research work in computer vision has often been driven by needs in robotics, while intelligent systems models and software have often been developed aiming at applications in the areas of physical agents, i.e. robots, or in areas related to scene understanding, video and image processing, and many other aspects of computer vision. There was a need for a venue where these three research communities, often isolated, could meet and discuss innovation possibilities driven by the intersection of these highly synergetic fields.

We would like to thank all the authors for their contributions and also the reviewers who have helped in ensuring the quality of this publication.

October 2021

Péter Galambos
Erdal Kayacan
Kurosh Madani

Organization

Conference Chair in 2020

Kurosh Madani   University of Paris-Est Créteil, France

Conference Chair in 2021

Erdal Kayacan   Aarhus University, Denmark

Program Chair in 2020 and 2021

Péter Galambos   Óbuda University, Hungary

Program Committee in 2020

Barry Weitzner	Boston Scientific, USA
Benjamin Aribisala	Lagos State University, Nigeria
Christian Balkenius	Lund University, Sweden
Ezio Malis	Robocortex, France
Faiz Ben Amar	Sorbonne Université, France
Filippo Cavallo	University of Florence, Italy
Guanghui Wang	University of Kansas, USA
Ismael García-Varea	Universidad de Castilla-La Mancha, Spain
Jan Faigl	Czech Technical University in Prague, Czech Republic
Jan Siebert	University of Glasgow, UK
Kao-shing Hwang	National Sun Yat-sen University, Taiwan, Republic of China
Leonardo Trujillo	Instituto Tecnolgico de Tijuana, Mexico
Liyuan Li	Institute for Infocomm Research, Singapore
Martinet Philippe	Inria, France
Mehdi Khamassi	Sorbonne University, France
Michael Cree	University of Waikato, New Zealand
Michael Defoort	University of Valenciennes and Hainaut-Cambrésis, France
Michael Jenkin	York University, Canada
Ming C. Leu	Missouri University of Science and Technology, USA
Nicholas Patrikalakis	Massachusetts Institute of Technology, USA

Simon Parsons	University of Lincoln, UK
Sio Hoi Ieng	Sorbonne University, France
Stefano Borgo	ISTC-CNR, Italy
Stephan Weiss	University of Klagenfurt, Austria
Sule Yildirim Yayilgan	Norwegian University of Science and Technology, Norway
Xiaoyi Jiang	University of Münster, Germany
Yang Liu	Harbin Institute of Technology, Shenzhen, China
Yangmin Li	Hong Kong Polytechnic University, Hong Kong
Yannick Aoustin	University of Nantes, France
Yimin Zhang	Intel Corporation, China

Program Committee in 2021

Aiguo Song	Southeast University, China
Andriy Sarabakha	Nanyang Technological University, Singapore
Clark Olson	University of Washington, USA
Devrim Ünay	Izmir Demokrasi University, Turkey
Emmanuel Dellandréa	Ecole Centrale de Lyon, France
Eric Baumgartner	Milwaukee School of Engineering, USA
Fabio Morbidi	University of Picardie Jules Verne, France
Giuseppe Carbone	University of Calabria, Italy
Luigi Biagiotti	University Modena and Reggio Emilia, Italy
Luis Miguel Bergasa	University of Alcala, Spain
Marco Buzzelli	University of Milano-Bicocca, Italy
Mohit Mehndiratta	Sensible 4, Finland
Nobuyuki Kita	National Institute of Advanced Industrial Science and Technology, Japan
Norbert Kruger	University of Southern Denmark, Denmark
Primo Zingaretti	Università Politecnica delle Marche, Italy
Ryszard Tadeusiewicz	AGH University of Science and Technology, Poland
Udo Frese	University of Bremen, Germany
Yoshinori Kuno	Saitama University, Japan

Program Committee in 2020 and 2021

Amir Shafie	International Islamic University Malaysia, Malaysia
António Moniz	Universidade Nova Lisboa, Portugal
Changming Sun	Commonwealth Scientific and Industrial Research Organization, Australia
Chao Liu	Laboratory of Informatics, Robotics, and Microelectronics Montpellier, France

Christine Chevallereau	CNRS, France
David Fofi	Université de Bourgogne, France
Enrique Moltó	IVIA, Spain
Fernando Osorio	University of São Paulo, Brazil
Frieder Stolzenburg	Harz University of Applied Sciences, Germany
Jamshed Iqbal	University of Hull, UK
Juha Röning	University of Oulu, Finland
Kristinn Andersen	University of Iceland, Iceland
Oya Celiktutan	King's College London, UK
Qingsong Xu	University of Macau, Macau
Rashid Shariff	Universiti Putra Malaysia, Malaysia
Roberto Vezzani	University of Modena and Reggio Emilia, Italy
Rui Yang	InterDigital, Inc., USA
Salvatore Pirozzi	Università degli Studi della Campania Luigi Vanvitelli, Italy
Shih-Hung Wu	Chaoyang University of Technology, Taiwan, Republic of China
Takashi Yoshimi	Shibaura Institute of Technology, Japan
Yakup Genc	Gebze Technical University, Turkey

Additional Reviewer in 2020

Ana Fred	Instituto de Telecomunicações and University of Lisbon, Portugal

Additional Reviewer in 2021

Jesse Richter-Klug	Universität Bremen, Germany

Invited Speakers in 2020

Krzysztof Kozlowski	Poznan University of Technology, Poland
Sanaz Mostaghim	Otto-von-Guericke-Universität Magdeburg, Germany
Csaba Benedek	Institute for Computer Science and Control, Hungary
Erdal Kayacan	Aarhus University, Denmark

Invited Speakers in 2021

Kostas Alexis	Norwegian University of Science and Technology, Norway
Roland Siegwart	ETH Zurich, Switzerland

Contents

Multi-sensorial Environment Perception in Urban Environment

Csaba Benedek[1,2,3]($\boxtimes$)

[1] Institute for Computer Science and Control (SZTAKI),
Budapest H-1111, Hungary
[2] Faculty of Information Technology and Bionics, Péter Pázmány Catholic
University, Budapest H-1083, Hungary
[3] Faculty of Informatics, University of Debrecen, Kassai út 26,
Debrecen 4028, Hungary
benedek.csaba@sztaki.hu

Abstract. In this paper various new solutions are introduced for the analysis of the dynamic 3D environment using up-do-date sensor configurations. The paper begins with an overview on current challenges of environment perception and the opportunities provided by the latest sensor developments. Thereafter we propose a workflow and several new algorithms for real time environment perception relying on a moving car-mounted Rotating Multi-beam (RMB) Lidar sensor, where as reference background map we use very dense 3D point clouds of the environment obtained by mobile laser scanning by Mobile Laser Scanning (MLS) technology in urban environment. First real time methods are presented for moving object detection and recognition in RMB Lidar sequences. Thereafter we introduce a new 3D convolutional neural network (CNN) based approach to segment dense MLS point clouds into nine different semantic classes, which can be used for high definition city map generation. Next, we propose a RMB Lidar based real time and accurate self-localization approach for self-driving vehicles in high resolution MLS point cloud maps of the environment. Finally, we propose an end-to-end, automatic, online camera-Lidar calibration approach, for application in self driving vehicle perception and navigation.

Keywords: Perception · Lidar · Sensor fusion

1 Introduction

Automated perception and interpretation of the surrounding environment are key issues in intelligent city management, traffic monitoring, security surveillance, or autonomous driving. Critical tasks involve detection, recognition, localization and tracking of various moving and static objects, environmental change detection and change classification. Nowadays a standard expectation is that the localization and tracking must be performed in the real 3D world coordinate system of the observed environment, which requirement, considering the temporal dimension of the measurements, implies 4D perception problems [4].

© Springer Nature Switzerland AG 2022
P. Galambos et al. (Eds.): ROBOVIS 2020/ROBOVIS 2021, CCIS 1667, pp. 1–24, 2022.
https://doi.org/10.1007/978-3-031-19650-8_1

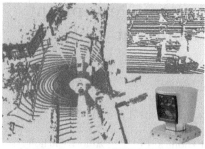
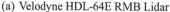

(a) Velodyne HDL-64E RMB Lidar   (b) Riegl VMX-450 MLS

Fig. 1. Data comparison of two different Lidar sensors: **a** a time frame from a dynamic RMB Lidar sequence and **b** static point cloud scene obtained by Mobile Laser Scanning (MLS).

A significant part of the existing environment monitoring systems use electro-optical cameras as perception sensors, due to their established technologies, wide choices of the available properties and scalable prices. Nevertheless, despite the well explored literature of the topic, event analysis in optical image sequences may be still challenging in cases of crowded outdoor scenes due to uncontrolled illumination conditions, irrelevant background motion, and occlusions caused by various moving and static scene objects [17,40]. In such situations multi-camera configurations can provide better solutions, since they monitor a dynamic scene from multiple viewpoints by taking the advantages of stereo-vision to exploit depth information for 3D localization and tracking [14,18]. However, both mono and multi-camera systems suffer from a number of basic problems, such as artifacts due to moving shadows and low contrast between different objects in the color domain [27,38], which issues raise still open research challenges in the topic.

As alternative solutions of conventional optical video cameras, range sensors offer significant advantages for scene analysis, since direct geometrical information is provided by them [10]. Using infra light based Time-of-Flight (ToF) cameras [37] or laser based Light Detection and Ranging (Lidar) sensors [23] enable recording directly measured range images, where we can avoid artifacts of the stereo vision based depth map calculation. From the point of view of data analysis, ToF cameras record depth image sequences over a regular 2D pixel lattice, where established image processing approaches, such as Markov Random Fields (MRFs) can be adopted for smooth and observation consistent segmentation and recognition [5]. However, such cameras can only be reliably used indoors, due to limitations of current infra-based sensing technologies, and usually they have a limited Field of View (FoV), which fact can be a drawback for surveillance and monitoring applications.

Rotating Multi-beam (RMB) Lidar systems provide a 360° FoV of the scene, with a vertical resolution equal to the number of the sensors, while the horizontal angle resolution depends on the speed of rotation (see Fig. 1a). Each laser point of the output point cloud is associated with 3D spatial coordinates, and possibly with auxiliary channels such as reflection number or an intensity value of laser reflection. RMB Lidars can produce high frame-rate *point cloud videos* enabling dynamic event analysis in the 3D space. On the other hand, the measurements have a low spatial density, which quickly decreases as a function of the distance from the sensor, and the point clouds may exhibit particular patterns typical to sensor characteristic (such as ring patterns in Fig. 1a). Although the 3D measurements are quite accurate (up to few *cm*s) in the sensor's local coordinate system, the global positioning error of the vehicles may reach several meters due to limitations of the availability of external navigation signals.

Mobile laser scanning (MLS) platforms equipped with time synchronized Lidar sensors and navigation units can rapidly provide very dense and accurate point clouds from large environments (see Fig. 1b), where the 3D spatial measurements are accurately registered to a geo-referenced global coordinate system [39,41,44]. These point clouds may act as a basis for detailed and up-to-date 3D High Definition (HD) maps of the cities, which can be be utilized by self driving vehicles for navigation, or by city authorities for road network management and surveillance, architecture or urban planning. While the high speed of point cloud acquisition is a clear advantage of MLS, due to the huge data size yielded by each daily mission, applying efficient automated data filtering and analyzing algorithms in the processing side is crucially needed.

In this paper, we introduce various contributions in the Lidar based 4D environment perception topic. More detailed, we propose a new workflow and introduce various new specific algorithms for dynamic urban scene analysis with a car-mounted moving RMB Lidar sensor, exploiting MLS data as a HD background map.

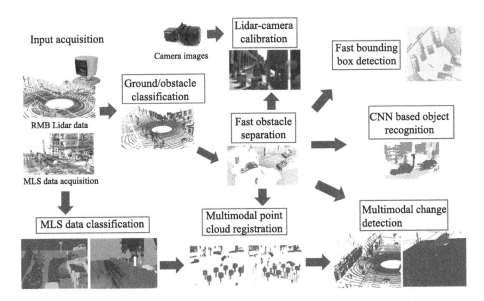

Fig. 2. Workflow of instant environment perception, composed of the proposed algorithms. Publications serving as basis of this section are noted above the algorithm boxes.

2   Lidar Based Urban Scene Analysis

This paper introduces various new algorithms related to real time perception of dynamic urban environments with a car-mounted RMB Lidar scanner. As high resolution 3D background map, we utilize dense point clouds obtained by mobile laser scanning (MLS).

The workflow of the conducted research work is briefly summarized in Fig. 2. The first four steps work solely on the RMB Lidar streams. The process starts with *ground-obstacle separation*, which must be performed in real time and robustly, dealing also with lower quality (non-planar) road surfaces often appearing in minor roads of cities [6,22]. Within the obstacle class, we distinguish *low foreground* and *high foreground* regions, which will help the subsequent steps. Then, we perform *fast object separation* in the foreground areas of the sparse and inhomogeneous RMB Lidar point clouds [9], while a quick bounding box estimation algorithm will also be presented to support the analysis of field objects [7]. Thereafter, the separated object blobs in the *low foreground* are classified via a deep neural network into vehicle, pedestrian, street furniture, and wall component classes, with the help of tall anchor objects of the scene [8,11].

The remaining steps in Fig. 2 aim at the efficient joint utilization of the dynamic RMB Lidar based and static MLS measurements. First we perform a 3D CNN-based semantic classification of the dense MLS point clouds [30], which enables filtering out all moving and movable objects from the high resolution background map. Then, using a coarse Global Positioning System (GPS) based initial positioning of the vehicle, we propose a fast and accurate registration algorithm between sparse RMB Lidar frames and the dense MLS point clouds [16], which facilitates centimeter-accuracy localization of the vehicle in the HD map [31]. Finally, we construct a *multimodal change detection* approach [15] to identify regions of the actual RMB Lidar point cloud frames, which are not present in the MLS background model.

To enable the fusion of the onboard Lidar measurements and optical camera image sequences, a new automatic target-less Lidar-camera calibration technique [32] is also introduced at the end of the section.

2.1 Ground-Obstacle Classification

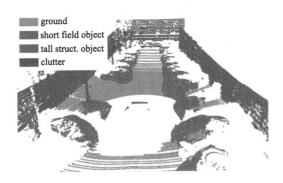

Fig. 3. Segmented frame of the Velodyne point cloud stream.

In this step, the input point cloud is segmented into four regions: *ground, short field objects* (also called *short foreground*), *tall structural objects* (or *high foreground*) and *sparse areas*. By our definition, *short field objects* include cars, pedestrians, benches, mail boxes, billboards etc, while *tall structural objects* cover among others building walls, trees, traffic signs and lamp posts.

Point cloud segmentation is achieved by a grid based approach [22]. We fit a regular 2D grid S with fixed rectangle side length onto the $P_{z=0}$ plane (using the RMB Lidar sensor's vertical axis as the z direction), where $s \in S$ denotes a single cell. We assign each $p \in \mathcal{P}$ point of the point cloud to the corresponding cell s_p, which contains the projection of p to $P_{z=0}$.

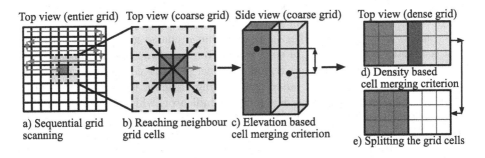

Fig. 4. The step by step demonstration of the object detection algorithm.

We use point height information for assigning each grid cell to the corresponding cell class. Before that, we detect and remove *sparse* grid cells which contains less points than a predefined threshold (used 8 points). After clutter removal all the points in a cell are classified as *ground*, if the difference of the minimal and maximal point elevations in the cell is smaller than a threshold (used $25cm$), and the average elevation in the neighboring cells does not exceed an allowed height range. A cell belongs to the class *tall structural object*, if either the maximal point height within the cell is larger than a predefined value (used 140cm above the car top), or the observed point height difference is larger than a threshold (used 310cm). The rest of the points in the cloud are assigned to class *short field object*. A segmented frame is shown in Fig. 3.

Due to the limited vertical view angle of the RMB Lidars (for Velodyne HDL-64E: $+2°$ up to $-24.8°$ down), the defined elevation criteria may fail near to the sensor position. In narrow streets where road sides located closely to the measurement position, several nearby grid cells can be misclassified regularly e.g. some parts of the walls and the building facades are classified to *short field object* cell class instead of the *tall structure object* cell class. By definition, we will refer to these misclassified wall segments henceforward as *short facades*, which should be detected and filtered out at a later step by the object detector.

2.2   Fast Object Separation and Bounding Box Estimation

After the point cloud segmentation step, our aim is to find distinct groups of points which belong to different urban objects within the *short field* and *tall structural object* regions, respectively. For this task we introduced a hierarchical grid model [9]: On one hand, the coarse grid resolution is appropriate for a rough estimation of the 3D blobs in the scene, thus we can roughly estimate the size and location of the possible object candidates. On the other hand, using a dense grid resolution, it is efficient to calculate point cloud features from smaller subvolumes of the scene, therefore we can refine the detection result derived from the coarse grid resolution.

The following two-level grid based connected component algorithm is separately applied for the sets of grid cells labeled as short and tall objects, respectively. *First*, we visit every cell of the coarse grid and for each cell s we consider the cells in its 3×3 neighborhood (see Fig. 4a, b). We visit the neighbor cells one after the other in order to calculate two different point cloud features: (i) the maximal elevation value $Z_{max}(s)$ within a coarse grid cell and (ii) the point cardinality in a dense grid cell. *Second*, our intention is to find connected 3D blobs within the foreground regions, by merging the coarse level grid cells together. We use an elevation-based cell merging criterion to perform this step. $\psi(s, s_r) = |Z_{max}(s) - Z_{max}(s_r)|$ is a merging indicator, which measures the difference between the maximal point elevation within cell s and its neighboring cell s_r. If the ψ indicator is smaller than a predefined value, we assume that s and s_r belong to the same 3D object (see Fig. 4c). *Third*, we perform a detection refinement step on the dense grid level (Fig. 4c, d). The elevation based cell merging criterion on the coarse grid level often yields that nearby and self-occluded objects are merged into a same blob. We handle this issue by measuring the point density in each sub-cell s'_d at the dense grid level. A super-cell is divided into different parts, if we find a separator line composed of low density sub-cells at the fine resolution. As shown in Fig. 5, experiments confirm that using this approach, nearby objects, which were erroneously merged at the coarse level, could be often appropriately separated at the fine level [9].

We also proposed a fast 2D bounding box fitting algorithm for cluttered and partially incomplete objects [7]. It is highly challenging to fit precise bounding boxes around the objects in RMB Lidar range data streams, since we should expect various artifacts of self-occlusion, occlusion by other objects, measurement noise, inhomogeneous point density and mirroring effects. These factors drastically change the appearances of the objects, and the conventional principal component analysis (PCA) based techniques [2,20] may not give sufficient results (see Fig. 6). Therefore we calculate the 2D convex hull of the top-view projection of the objects, and we derive the 2D bounding boxes directly from the convex hull, which procedure is implemented by Algorithm 1. As shown in Fig. 7, this strategy is less sensitive to the inhomogeneous point density and the presence of missing/occluded object segments, since instead of calculating spatial point distributions for the entire object's point set, we capture here the local shape characteristics of the visible object parts, and fit appropriate 2D bounding boxes with partial matching.

2.3 Deep Learning Based Object Recognition in the RMB Lidar Data

Our next main goal is to identify the vehicle and pedestrian objects among the set of connected point cloud segments extracted in Sect. 2.2. Our general assumption is that the focused two object classes are part of the short field object regions, therefore we start with an appearance based classification of the previously obtained object candidates.

Our labeling considers four object classes. Apart from the *vehicle* and *pedestrian* classes, we create a separate label for the *short facades*, which appear in the low foreground due to the limitations of the height measurement. The remaining short street objects (benches, short columns, bushes etc.) are categorized as *street clutter*. Object recognition is performed in a supervised approach: 2D range images are derived from the object candidates, which are classified by a deep neural network. The classification output for each input point cloud sample consists of four confidence values estimating the class membership probabilities for vehicles, pedestrians, short facades and street clutter, respectively.

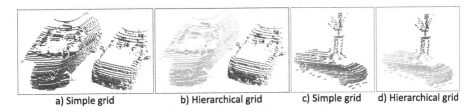

a) Simple grid   b) Hierarchical grid   c) Simple grid   d) Hierarchical grid

Fig. 5. Object separation for a case of nearby objects. Comparison of the *Simple Grid Model* Fig. (**a**), (**c**) and the *Hierarchical Grid Model* Fig. (**b**), (**d**).

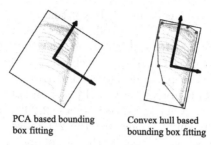

PCA based bounding   Convex hull based
box fitting   bounding box fitting

Fig. 6. Demonstrating the limitations of PCA based bounding box approximation, and the advantages of the proposed convex hull based bounding box fitting technique on the top-view projection of a selected vehicle in the point cloud.

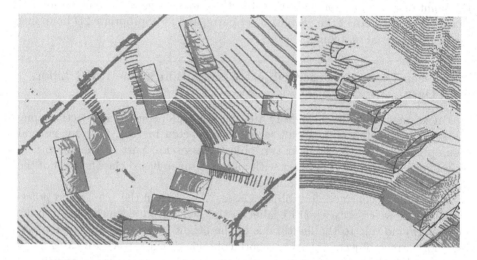

Fig. 7. Qualitative results of vehicle detection with displaying the top-view bounding boxes (by red) and the side view concave hulls (blue) extracted by the algorithm. (Color figure online)

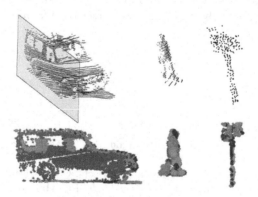

Fig. 8. Range image formation of the RMB Lidar frames for object detection.

Algorithm 1. Fast bounding box estimation for partially detected objects.

Input: 2D ground projection of the objects extracted at the coarse level of the two-level grid based algorithm

Step 1. Estimate the boundary cells of the objects, and construct the convex hull from the boundary using the monotone chain algorithm [1]. Let be $i = 1$.

Step 2. Visit the consecutive point pairs of the hull P_i and P_{i+1}, one after another ($i = 1, 2, \ldots, i_{max}$):

- Consider the line I_i between point P_i and P_{i+1}, as a side candidate of the bounding box rectangle.

- Find the $P_\star$ point of the hull, whose distance is maximal from l_i, and draw a $I_\star$ parallel line with I_i which intersects $P_\star$. We consider $I_\star$ as the second side candidate of the bounding box.

- Project all the points of the convex hull to the line I_i, and find the two extreme ones P' and P''. The remaining two sides of the bounding box candidate will be constructed by taking perpendicular lines to I_i, which intersect P' and P'' respectively.

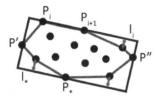

Step 3. Chose the optimal bounding box from the above generated rectangle set by minimizing the average distance between the points of the convex hull and the fitted rectangle.

To obtain the feature maps, we convert the object point clouds into regularly sampled depth images, using a similar principle to [13], but with implementing a number of differences. *First*, we attempt to ensure side-view projections of the objects, by estimating the longitudinal cross section of the object shapes, using the bounding box estimation algorithm from Sect. 2.2. *Second*, we calculate the distance between the estimated plane and the points of the object candidate, which can be interpreted here as a depth value. In order the avoid occlusions between overlapping regions i.e. multiple 3D point projections into a same pixel of an image plane with different depth values, we sort the depth values in an ascending order, and we project them to the image plane starting from the closest to the farthest. As demonstrated in Fig. 8 this projection strategy ensures that object points in the front side do not become occluded by the object points in the back.

For object recognition, we trained a *Convolutional Neural Network (CNN)* based feature learning framework called *Theano* firstly introduced by [3]. The CNN framework receives the previously extracted depth images as an input layer scaled for the size of 96 × 96, and the outputs are four confidence values from the [0,1] range, describing the fitness of match to the four considered classes: vehicle, pedestrian, short facade and street clutter. In this way, we can later utilize not only the index of the winner class, but also describe how sure the CNN module was about its decision for a given test sample. After testing various different layer configurations, we experienced that four pairs of convolution-pooling layers followed by a fully connected dense layer give us the most efficient results [11]. Finally, in post processing, we extended our approach with a contextual refinement step, exploiting topological constraints between various scene objects using specific *tall structure* objects, called *anchor facades*, as landmarks. Results of object detection on a sample Lidar frame are shown in Fig. 9.

2.4   Semantic MLS Point Cloud Classification with a 3D CNN Model

We have proposed in [30] a new 3D CNN based semantic point cloud segmentation approach, which is adopted to dense point clouds of large scale urban environments, assuming the presence of high variety of objects, with strong and diverse *phantom* effects caused by scene objects moving concurrently with the MLS platform [29]. Our technique is based on a sparse voxel based representation of the scene (with fine 0.1m voxel resolution), and classifies each voxel into one of the following nine semantic classes: *phantom, tram/bus, pedestrian, car, vegetation, column, street furniture, ground* and *facade*.

During the data mapping, we assign two feature channels to the voxels based on the input cloud: point *density*, taken as the number of included points, and *mean elevation*, calculated as the average of the point height values in the voxel. The unit of training and recognition in our network is a $K \times K \times K$ voxel neigborhood (used $K = 23$), called hereafter training volume. To classify each voxel v, we consider the point density and elevation features in all voxels in the v-centered training volume, thus a given voxel is labeled based on a 2-channel 3D array derived from K^3 local voxels. Our 3D CNN network contains a feature extractor part using a combination of several 3D convolution, max-pooling and dropout layers, and a second part with fully connected dense layers, which learn the different class models. To segment a scene, we move a sliding volume across the voxelized input point cloud, and capture the $K \times K \times K$ neighborhood around each voxel. Each neighborhood volume is separately taken as input by the two channel CNN classifier, which predicts a label for the central voxel only. We have validated the efficiency of the approach in diverse and real test data from various urban environments, sample results are shown in Fig. 10.

Fig. 9. Object classification results in the RMB Lidar frames.

2.5   Multimodal Point Cloud Registration

We have developed a solution [16] to robustly register the sparse point clouds of the RMB Lidar sensor mounted on a moving platform to the dense MLS point cloud data, starting from a GPS based initial position estimation of the vehicle (see Fig. 11). Although we can find in the bibliography widely used general point cloud registration techniques, such as variants of the Iterative Closest Point (ICP) [43], and the Normal Distribution Transform (NDT) [26], they all need as initial condition a sufficiently accurate preliminary alignment between the input point clouds. Expecting that in our application field significant translation (up to 10m) and large orientation difference must be compensated by the registration method, we have constructed a two-step approach: first, we estimate a coarse transform between the point cloud frames at object level, which step is followed by accurate registration refinement using the standard NDT algorithm.

Our process begins with abstract object extraction both in the RMB Lidar frame and in the MLS point cloud segment, using the fast object separation algorithm introduced in Sect. 2.1, which provides two sets of object centers $C1$ and $C2$. Similarly to the fingerprint minutia matching approach by [34], we estimate the optimal transformation parameters between $C1$ and $C2$ using the generalized Hough transform: we discretize the set of all allowed transformations, then for each transformation we calculate a matching *fitness* score. Finally the transformation with the highest score is taken as result.

Since the Lidar point clouds reflect the true object distances from the 3D world, we can consider the transformation as a composition of translation and rotation only. Note as well that since the vehicles carrying the sensors are moving on urban roads, which rarely contain sudden steep slopes, orientation difference is mainly expected around the vertical z axis of the captured point cloud's local coordinate system, while translation in the x and y direction, along the $P_{z=0}$ horizontal plane. Exploiting that this object level step only aims to find an approximate solution for the matching, we project the point clouds to their $P_{z=0}$ plane, and estimate the 2D translation and scalar rotation in this image plane. In this way, the searched transformation takes the following form:

$$\mathcal{T}_{dx,dy,\alpha}\begin{pmatrix} x \\ y \end{pmatrix} = \begin{bmatrix} \cos\alpha & \sin\alpha \\ -\sin\alpha & \cos\alpha \end{bmatrix}\begin{bmatrix} x \\ y \end{bmatrix} + \begin{bmatrix} dx \\ dy \end{bmatrix}$$

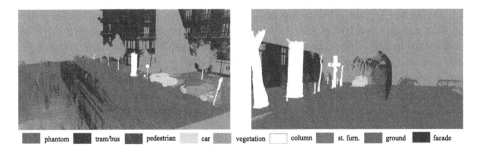

phantom   tram/bus   pedestrian   car   vegetation   column   st. furn.   ground   facade

Fig. 10. Point cloud segmentation result with a 3D CNN.

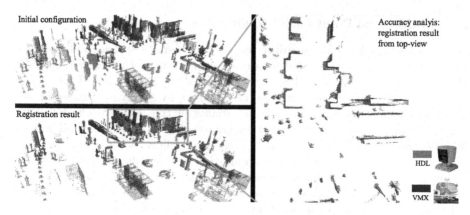

Fig. 11. Multimodal Velodyne HDL-64E to Riegl VMX-450 registration results using our proposed method (Fővám tér, Budapest).

The space of transformation consists of triplets (dx, dy, α), where each parameter is discretized into a finite set of values.

Fitness scores for the transformation candidates are collected in the accumulator array A, where the $A[dx, dy, \alpha]$ element counts the evidence for the concerning $\mathfrak{T}_{dx,dy,\alpha}$ transformation. The A array can be filled in an iterative way. For each object pair $(o1, o2)$ where $o1 = (x_1, y_1)$ is a point in the set $C1$ and $o2$ is a point in the set $C2$ we determine all possible $\mathfrak{T}_{dx,dy,\alpha}$ transformations that map $o1$ to $o2$ and we increment the evidence for these transformations in the array. Here we exploit that for every possible rotation value α there is a unique translation vector $[dx, dy]^\top$ such that $\mathfrak{T}_{dx,dy,\alpha}(o1) = o2$, and it can be calculated as:

$$\begin{bmatrix} dx \\ dy \end{bmatrix} = o2 - \begin{bmatrix} \cos\alpha & \sin\alpha \\ -\sin\alpha & \cos\alpha \end{bmatrix} o1$$

The obtained dx and dy values need to be quantized to the nearest bins for appointing the actually increaseable element of the A array. The complete pseudo code of the scan alignment method is given by Algorithm 2.

Although the above object based scan matching process proved to be largely robust for the considered urban point cloud scenes, its accuracy is limited by the considered planar translation and rotation transformation constraints, and the inaccuracies of object center estimation from the different point clouds. As we detailed in [22], due to the special data acquisition technology used in mobile laser scanning, the ground-less *obstacle* cloud can be efficiently used for automated scene matching with the Normal Distribution Transform (NDT) [26] in case of a high quality initial transformation estimation, which is available in our case by taking the output of the object-level step. Therefore in the proposed

Algorithm 2. The cloud alignment algorithm. Takes two clouds as inputs and calculates the transformation between them. $Rot(\alpha)$ represents the rotational matrix along z axis.

```
 1: procedure SCANALIGNMENT(F1, F2, T)
 2:    C1 ← ObjectDetect(F1)
 3:    C2 ← ObjectDetect(F2)
 4:    Initialize 3D accumulator A
 5:    for all o1 ∈ C1 do
 6:       for all o2 ∈ C2 do
 7:          for α ∈ [0, 359] do
 8:             o1' ← Rot(α) * o1
 9:             (dx, dy) ← o2 − o1'
10:             A[dx, dy, α] ← A[dx, dy, α] + 1
11:          end for
12:       end for
13:    end for
14:    α, dx, dy ← FindMaximum(A)
15:    F1, T1 ← TransformCloud(F1, α, dx, dy)
16:    F1, T2 ← NDT(F1, F2)
17:    T ← T2 * T1
18: end procedure
```

registration approach, we transform first the *obstacles* cloud according to the obtained optimal $\mathcal{T}_{dx,dy,\alpha}$, thereafter we apply NDT for the resulting clouds (see line 16 of Algorithm 2). A sample result of the registration process is shown in Fig. 11.

Color codes: road   static objects based on the MLS reference model   moving objects and changes compared to the reference cloud

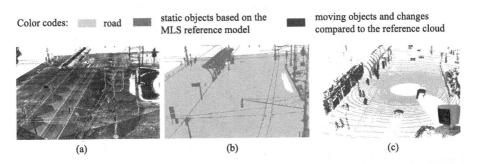

(a)   (b)   (c)

Fig. 12. Change detection between reference MLS data (**a**, **b**) and instant RMB Lidar frames (**c**).

2.6   Frame Level Cross-modal Change Detection

The *change detection* module receives a co-registered pair of RMB Lidar and MLS point clouds. Since the MLS data acts here as a detailed 3D background model, as shown in Fig. 12, we eliminate all moving our movable elements (such as pedestrians, vehicles, phantoms) from the MLS point cloud using the semantic labeling module of Sect. 2.4.

Our solution proposed in [15] extracts changes in the range image domain. The range image $I_{\mathrm{RMB}} : \{d_s | s \in S\}$ over a 64×1024 pixel lattice S is generated from the RMB Lidar's point stream, where missing pixel values are interpolated from their 8-neighborhood. The reference background range image $I_{\mathrm{MLS}} : \{a_s | s \in S\}$ is generated from the 3D MLS point cloud with ray tracing, exploiting that the current position and orientation of the RMB Lidar platform are available in the reference coordinate system as a result of the point cloud registration step. Thereafter simulated rays are emitted into the MLS cloud from the moving platform's center position with the same vertical and horizontal resolution as the RMB Lidar scanner. To handle minor registration issues and sensor noise, each range image pixel value is interpolated from MLS points lying inside a pyramid around the simulated RMB Lidar ray [15,45]. A sample range image pair generated by the above process is shown in Fig. 13a and b.

In the next step, the calculated RMB Lidar-based I_{RMB}, and MLS-based I_{MLS} range images are compared using a Markov Random Field (MRF) model, which classifies each pixel of the range image lattice s as foreground (fg) or background (fg). Foreground pixels represent either moving/mobile objects in the RMB Lidar scan, or various environmental changes appeared since the capturing date of the MLS point cloud.

To formally define the range image segmentation task, we assign to each s pixel of the pixel lattice S a $\varsigma_s \in \{\mathrm{fg}, \mathrm{bg}\}$ class label so that we aim to minimize the following energy function:

$$E = \sum_{s \in S} V_D(d_s, a_s | \varsigma_s) + \sum_{s \in S} \sum_{r \in \mathcal{N}_s} \beta \cdot \mathbf{1}\{\varsigma_s \neq \varsigma_r\}, \tag{1}$$

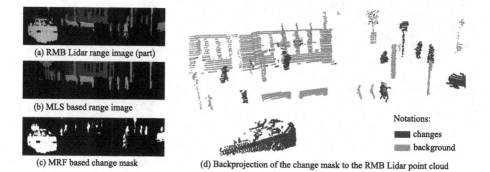

(a) RMB Lidar range image (part)

(b) MLS based range image

(c) MRF based change mask

(d) Backprojection of the change mask to the RMB Lidar point cloud

Notations:
■ changes
■ background

Fig. 13. Demonstration of the proposed MRF based change detection process in the range image domain, and result of label backprojection to the 3D point cloud.

where we used a $\beta = 0.5$ smoothness parameter. The data terms are derived as:

$$V_D(d_s, a_s|\text{bg}) = -\log\left(1 - \sigma(-d_s + a_s)\right), \quad V_D(d_s, a_s|\text{fg}) = -\log\left(1 - \sigma(d_s - a_s)\right)$$

where $\sigma()$ denotes the sigmoid function:

$$\sigma(x) = \frac{1}{1 + e^{-x}}.$$

The MRF energy (1) is minimized via the fast graph-cut based optimization algorithm [12], which process results in a binary change mask in the range image domain, as shown in Fig. 13c. The final step is *label backprojection* from the range image to the 3D point cloud (see Fig. 13d), which can be performed in a straightforward manner, since in our I_{RMB} range image formation process, each pixel represents only one RMB Lidar point.

2.7 Automatic Targetless Lidar-Camera Calibration

Sensor fusion is one of the main challenges in self driving and robotics applications. In [32] we proposed an automatic, online and target-less camera-Lidar extrinsic calibration approach. As demonstrated in Fig. 14, we adopt a structure from motion (SfM) method to generate 3D point clouds from the camera data which can be matched to the Lidar point clouds; thus, we address the extrinsic calibration problem as a registration task in the 3D domain. The core step of the approach is a two-stage transformation estimation: First, we introduce an object level coarse alignment algorithm operating in the Hough space to transform the SfM-based and the Lidar point clouds into a common coordinate system. Thereafter, we apply a control point based nonrigid transformation refinement step to register the point clouds more precisely. Finally, we calculate the correspondences between the 3D Lidar points and the pixels in the 2D camera domain. We evaluated the method in various real-life traffic scenarios in Budapest, Hungary. The results (see Fig. 15) show that our proposed extrinsic calibration approach is able to provide accurate and robust parameter settings on-the-fly.

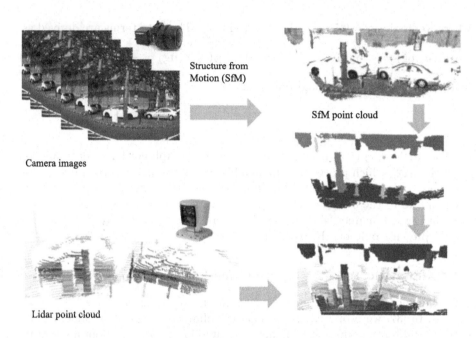

Structure from
Motion (SfM)

SfM point cloud

Camera images

Lidar point cloud

Fig. 14. Workflow of the proposed Lidar-camera registration algorithms.

Fig. 15. Sample results of our Lidar-camera calibration method.

3   Evaluation of the Proposed Algorithms

The new algorithms and methods proposed in this paper have been evaluated versus state-of-the art solutions one by one.

3.1   Experiments on RMB Lidar Based Object Perception

For testing the improvements in object separation and classification (Sects. 2.1–2.3), we created a new hand labeled dataset, called SZTAKI Velo64Road, based mainly on point cloud sequences recorded by our car-mounted Velodyne

Table 1. Numerical comparison of the detection results obtained by the Connected Component Analysis [35] and the proposed *Hierarchal Grid Model*. The number of objects (NO) are listed for each data set, and also in aggregate.

Point cloud dataset	NO	Conn. comp. analysis [35]		Prop. hierarchical grid	
		F-rate(%)	Avg. processing speed (fps)	F-rate(%)	Avg. processing speed (fps)
Budapest dataset #1	669	77	0.38	89	29
Budapest dataset #2	429	64	0.22	79	25
KITTI dataset [19]	496	75	0.46	82	29
Overall	1594	72	0.35	83	28

HDL-64E Lidar scanner in the streets of Budapest.[1] First we run the segmentation (Sect. 2.1) and object extraction (Sect. 2.2) steps of our model on the raw data, thereafter we annotated all the automatically extracted short objects (2063 objects alltogether) without any further modification with the labels *vehicle, pedestrian, short facade* and *street clutter*. To demonstrate that the training results are suitable for various urban scenes, we have also validated the performance of our trained model in the `Washington` dataset [24].

First, the object separation module (Sect. 2.2) was evaluated, by comparing the automatically extracted object blobs to a manually labeled Ground Truth configuration. As described in [9], we counted the true positives, missing objects and false objects, thereafter we calculated the *F-score* of the detection at object level. As reference of the proposed 2-level grid based model we used a 3D connected component analysis (3D-CCA) approach implemented in [35]. While in *F-score* the proposed approach presented a 13% performance gain versus CCA (84% versus 71%), it decreased the running speed by two orders of magnitude due to eliminating the kd-tree building step at each frame (27 fps versus 0.30 fps in average, measured over 1800 sample frames), details are shown in Table 1.

Next, we examined the object classification step (Sect. 2.3), by evaluating the appearance based labeling, and also the context based refinement. For training the CNN classifier we separated 904 objects from our dataset, which was completed with 434 selected samples Sydney Urban Object Dataset [13]. The test data was composed of the remaining 1159 objects of the `SZTAKI Velo64` dataset. During the evaluation object level *precision, recall* and *F-score* values of the detection for each class separately and cumulatively as well. As an independent reference technique, we considered a similar object matching algorithm to [42] based on a corresponding grouping (CG) technique [35]. Comparative results (Table 2a) showed a 89% overall performance of the proposed approach, and a 15% gain versus the CG reference, while the contextual refinement caused around 5% improvement. Among the different classes, pedestrian detection proved to be the most challenging one with a 78% *F-score*.

---

[1] Url: http://mplab.sztaki.hu/geocomp/SZTAKI-Velo64Road-DB.html.

Table 2. Evaluation of the object classification and change detection steps. Notations: Precision (Pr), Recall (Rc), F-score (Fs), in %.

(a) Object classification

Object cat.	Correspond. grouping [35]			Proposed method [11]		
	Pr	Rc	Fs	Pr	Rc	Fs
Vehicle	71	84	77	98	99	99
Short facade	79	52	62	93	77	84
Street clutter	87	93	90	92	97	94
Pedestrian	66	57	61	78	78	78
Overall	76	72	74	90	87	89

(b) Change detection in sidewalk areas

Scene	Voxel based method [25]			Proposed method [15]		
	Pr	Rc	Fs	Pr	Rc	Fs
Deák	81	71	76	87	89	88
Astoria	88	81	84	84	100	91
Kálvin	89	96	92	98	87	99
Fővám	84	64	73	81	97	88
Overall	86	78	81	90	93	92

3.2   Evaluation of Semantic MLS Point Cloud Segmentation

We evaluated our 3D CNN-based semantic point cloud classification technique (Sect. 2.4) on a new dataset called SZTAKI-CityMLS, which consists of real MLS data captured with a Riegl VMX-450 system in Budapest.[2] The available measurement set contained in total around 300 Million points from various urban scenes, including main roads with both heavy and solid traffic, public squares, parks, and sidewalk regions, containing various types of cars, trams and buses, several pedestrians and diverse vegetation. As reference technique, we trained a single channel 3D CNN model [21], referred as OG-CNN, which used a 3D voxel occupancy grid as input feature. As metrics we calculated the voxel level *precision*, *recall* and *F-score* for each class separately as well as the overall performance. By analyzing the results, we could conclude that the proposed two-channel 3D CNN can classify all classes of interest with an *F-score* larger than 83%. The overall results of the reference OG-CNN technique fall behind our proposed method with 13%.

3.3   Experiments on Point Cloud Registration

We evaluated the proposed multimodal registration process with matching the measurements of Velodyne sensors to the MLS point clouds. Quantitative analysis result of the matching process is given in Table 3. Since *Ground Truth* transformation was not available, we calculated first the asymmetric Modified Hausdorff Distance (MHD) between the $\mathcal{P}_{\text{RMB}}$ Velodyne and $\mathcal{P}_{\text{MLS}}$ MLS clouds:

$$\text{MHD}(\mathcal{P}_{\text{RMB}}, \mathcal{P}_{\text{MLS}}) = \frac{1}{\#\mathcal{P}_{\text{RMB}}} \sum_{p \in \mathcal{P}_{\text{RMB}}} \min_{q \in \mathcal{P}_{\text{MLS}}} dist(p,q)$$

where $\#\mathcal{P}$ denotes set cardinality. Columns 5–7 of Table 3 contain the obtained MHD values initially, after the object based Hough matching step, and in the

---

[2] Url: http://mplab.sztaki.hu/geocomp/SZTAKI-CityMLS-DB.html.

final stage following NDT-based registration refinement. We can observe that both steps significantly decrease the distances between the scans in almost all data sets. However, the absolute MHD values do not reflect properly the accuracy of the algorithm, since the presence of several moving objects, especially large trams or tracks, mislead (increase) the calculated average distances. For this reason, we also used a modified error metrics called Median Point Distance (MPD), where we sort the points in $\mathcal{P}_{RMB}$ from the lowest to the highest value of $\min_q dist(p, q)$, and take the median of the distances among all $p \in \mathcal{P}_{RMB}$. As shown in the 8–10th columns of Table 3 the MPD values are also significantly decreased during the registration process, and in seven out of the eight scenes the resulting MPD errors are below 3cm, which fact was also confirmed by visual verification. Only the test scene Bajcsy yielded erroneous registration result both by visual and quantitative (MHD, MPD) analysis. In this sample both RMB point clouds contained several moving vehicles, including large buses which occluded various relevant scene structure elements. The 11th (last) column of Table 3 lists for each scene the computational time of the complete matching process (varying between 0.3 and 2.2 s), which confirms that the approach is close to online usability.

3.4 Experiments on Multimodal Change Detection

Since we have not found any similar RMB Lidar-MLS multimodal change detection approaches in the literature to our one presented in Sect. 2.6, we adopted a voxel based technique [25] as reference, which was originally constructed for already registered MLS/TLS point clouds. We used a voxel size of 0.3 m for [25], which choice yielded approximately the same computational cost as our proposed MRF-range image based model (around 80 msec/frame on a desktop computer, with CPU implementation). Comparative tests showed that the proposed method had an efficient overall performance, and it outperformed the voxel based method in general with 1–6% *F-score* in the different scenes. We have experienced that the main advantage of the proposed technique was the high accuracy of change detection in cluttered street regions, such as sidewalks with several nearby moving and static objects, where our method surpassed the voxel based approach with 7–15% gaps in the test scenes (see Table 2b).

3.5 Evaluation of Lidar-Camera Calibration

We evaluated the proposed target-less automatic Lidar-camera calibration method on a new manually annotated dataset (with ground truth) and we compared it with a semi automatic target based calibration method [33] and with two further automatic reference techniques [28, 36].

Table 3. Results of multimodal RMB Lidar and MLS point cloud registration (Velo-dyne HDL-64E/VLP-16 to Riegl-VMX scan matching).

Scene	Sensor	Initial offset, Rotation	MHD (m)			MPD (m)			Comput Time
			Init	Hough	Final†	Init	Hough	Final	
Astoria	HDL	2.2 m, 62°	3.641	0.773	0.415	1.587	0.511	0.022	1.923
hub	VLP	2.2 m, 99°	5.045	0.582	0.221	3.623	0.231	0.008	0.665
Bajcsy	HDL	2.0 m, 92°	5.657	11.441	10.105	1.177	2.702	4.539	0.992
Road	VLP	10.3 m, 72°	6.971	20.115	17.796	4.179	17.319	14.341	0.329
Deák	HDL	1.4 m, 32°	3.638	0.717	0.338	1.516	0.345	0.004	1.960
Square	VLP	3.6 m, 127°	7.348	0.870	0.911	5.502	0.143	0.101	0.769
Fővám	HDL	2.0 m, 134°	8.404	3.494	2.870	6.143	1.339	0.008	3.796
Square	VLP	0.1 m, 20°	5.143	1.849	1.431	3.393	0.216	0.010	1.182
Kálvin	HDL	1.4 m, 118°	9.891	0.774	0.205	5.808	0.469	0.005	1.159
Square1	VLP	2.0 m, 42°	11.427	7.016	8.178	5.007	0.752	0.014	0.573
Kálvin	HDL	5.8 m, 104°	19.445	2.252	2.002	4.968	0.437	0.023	0.288
Square2	VLP	6.1 m, 56°	19.663	2.901	5.909	16.826	0.817	0.065	0.221
Múzeum	HDL	2.2 m, 70°	14.911	3.358	1.373	12.354	1.315	0.009	2.574
boulevard	VLP	5.0 m, 91°	6.970	2.489	3.412	1.477	0.312	0.018	1.403
Gellért	HDL	1.0 m, 125°	3.180	0.949	1.046	1.238	0.224	0.014	1.045
Square	VLP	0.0 m, 34°	5.241	2.438	1.574	4.037	1.173	0.029	0.852
Average	HDL	2.3 m, 92°	9.016	1.760	1.178	4.802	0.663	0.012	1.821
Values‡	VLP	3.7 m, 68°	8.691	2.592	3.091	5.695	0.521	0.035	0.809

Error measures: MHD: Modified Hausdorff distance, MPD: median point distance. †Final result refers to the Hough+NDT cascade, ‡Bajcsy was excluded from averaging, due to unsuccessful registration

Since using the rotating multi-beam Lidar technology, the speed of the moving platform influences the shape of the recorded point cloud, we separately evaluated the results for measurements captured by *slow* and *fast* vehicle motion, respectively. Therefore we defined two test sets: set *Slow* contains sensor data captured at speed level between *5–30* km/h, while set *Fast* includes test data captured at a speed above *30* km/h.

As shown in Table 4, both in the *Slow* and *Fast* test sets our proposed approach outperforms the two target-less reference methods [28, 36] with around $1-2$ pixels in mean error, and it also exhibits lower deviation values which indicates a more robust performance. The results also show that in the *Slow* test set—in terms of accuracy—the proposed approach is sightly outperformed by the considered *offline target-based calibration* technique [33]. However it should be emphasized that to calibrate the Lidar-camera system using [33] takes more than 2 hours with several manual interaction steps, furthermore if any sensor displacement occur during the driving, they need to stop the measuring platform and re-calibrate the system. On the contrary, our proposed approach is able to calibrate the camera and Lidar on-the-fly and in a fully automatic way i.e. during the driving without stopping the car.

Table 4. Performance comparison of the target-less proposed method with two state-of-the-art target-less reference methods and with a target-based (supervised) reference technique. Notes: *Test set names *Slow* and *Fast* refer to the speed of the data acquisition platform. #Error values are measured in pixels.

Set*	Method	x-error[#]		y-error[#]	
		Avg	Dev	Avg	Dev
Slow	Target-based ref. [33]	1.13	0.27	1.75	0.37
	Bearing angle [36]	4.56	2.15	4.58	1.74
	Line based [28]	3.36	1.45	3.47	0.98
	Proposed [32]	2.58	0.73	2.82	0.88
Fast	Target-based ref. [33]	3.04	0.74	2.74	0.41
	Bearing angle [36]	4.87	2.46	4.42	1.91
	Line based [28]	5.01	1.93	4.01	1.49
	Proposed	2.84	0.95	3.14	0.82

4   Conclusions of the Paper

This paper presented new methods for different problems in 4D environment perception based on Light Detection and Ranging (Lidar) measurements. We have proposed a novel set of methodologies for real time Rotating Multi-beam (RMB) Lidar-based urban scene analysis from a moving platform, relying on a reference 3D background map generated from mobile laser scanning (MLS) data. First, we introduced methods for object detection and classification in RMB Lidar streams. Thereafter, we proposed a new semantic segmentation approach of dense urban point cloud data, which can contribute to the automatic transformation process of raw MLS measurements to semantic HD maps. Next, we discussed unsupervised registration and change detection methods between real time Lidar streams and background MLS point clouds. Finally, a target-less automatic Lidar-camera registration approach was introduced.

Acknowledgement. The research work was supported by the European Union within the framework of the National Laboratory for Autonomous Systems (RRF-2.3.1-21-2022-00002), by the TKP2021-NVA-01, OTKA K-120233 and K-143274 projects of the Hungarian NRDI Office and by the project EFOP-3.6.2-16-2017-00015. The author thanks his colleagues and former colleagues from the Machine Perception Research Laboratory of SZTAKI—especially Balázs Nagy, Attila Börcs, Bence Gálai and Örkény Zováthi - for their contributions to the presented results.

References

1. Andrew, A.: Another efficient algorithm for convex hulls in two dimensions. Inf. Process. Lett. **9**(5), 216–219 (1979)
2. Azim, A., Aycard, O.: Detection, classification and tracking of moving objects in a 3D environment. In: IEEE Intelligent Vehicles Symposium (IV), pp. 802–807. Alcalá de Henares, Spain (2012)
3. Bastien, F., Lamblin, P., Pascanu, R., Bergstra, J., Goodfellow, I.J., Bergeron, A., Bouchard, N., Bengio, Y.: Theano: new features and speed improvements. In: Deep Learning and Unsupervised Feature Learning Workshop at NIPS. Lake Tahoe, USA (2012)
4. Benedek, C., Jankó, Z., Horváth, C., Molnár, D., Chetverikov, D., Szirányi, T.: An integrated 4D vision and visualisation system. In: International Conference on Computer Vision Systems (ICVS). Lecture Notes in Computer Science, vol. 7963, pp. 21–30. Springer, St. Petersburg, Russia (2013)
5. Benedek, C., Szirányi, T.: Bayesian foreground and shadow detection in uncertain frame rate surveillance videos. IEEE Trans. Image Process. **17**(4), 608–621 (2008). IF: 3.315
6. Börcs, A., Józsa, O., Benedek, C.: Object extraction in urban environments from large-scale dynamic point cloud dataset. In: IEEE International Workshop on Content-Based Multimedia Indexing (CBMI), pp. 191–194. Veszprém, Hungary (2013)
7. Börcs, A., Nagy, B., Baticz, M., Benedek, C.: A model-based approach for fast vehicle detection in continuously streamed urban LIDAR point clouds. In: Workshop on Scene Understanding for Autonomous Systems at ACCV'14. Lecture Notes in Computer Science, vol. 9008, pp. 413–425. Springer, Singapore (2015)
8. Börcs, A., Nagy, B., Benedek, C.: On board 3D object perception in dynamic urban scenes. In: IEEE International Conference on Cognitive Infocommunications (CogInfoCom), pp. 515–520. Budapest, Hungary (2013)
9. Börcs, A., Nagy, B., Benedek, C.: Fast 3-D urban object detection on streaming point clouds. In: Workshop on Computer Vision for Road Scene Understanding and Autonomous Driving at ECCV'14. Lecture Notes in Computer Science, vol. 8926, pp. 628–639. Springer, Zürich, Switzerland (2015)
10. Börcs, A., Nagy, B., Benedek, C.: Dynamic environment perception and 4D reconstruction using a mobile rotating multi-beam Lidar sensor. In: Handling Uncertainty and Networked Structure in Robot Control, pp. 153–180. Studies in Systems, Decision and Control, Springer (2016)
11. Börcs, A., Nagy, B., Benedek, C.: Instant object detection in Lidar point clouds. IEEE Geosci. Remote Sens. Lett. **14**(7), 992–996 (2017). IF: 2.892
12. Boykov, Y., Kolmogorov, V.: An experimental comparison of min-cut/max-flow algorithms for energy minimization in vision. IEEE Trans. Pattern Anal. Mach. Intell. **26**(9), 1124–1137 (2004)
13. De Deuge, M., Quadros, A., Hung, C., Douillard, B.: Unsupervised feature learning for outdoor 3D scans. In: Proceedings of Australasian Conference on Robotics and Automation (2013)
14. Fleuret, F., Berclaz, J., Lengagne, R., Fua, P.: Multicamera people tracking with a probabilistic occupancy map. IEEE Trans. Pattern Anal. Mach. Intell. **30**(2), 267–282 (2008)
15. Gálai, B., Benedek, C.: Change detection in urban streets by a real time Lidar scanner and MLS reference data. In: International Conference on Image Analysis

and Recognition (ICIAR). Lecture Notes in Computer Science, vol. 10317, pp. 210–220. Springer, Montreal, Canada (2017)

16. Gálai, B., Nagy, B., Benedek, C.: Crossmodal point cloud registration in the Hough space for mobile laser scanning data. In: International Conference on Pattern Recognition (ICPR), pp. 3363–3368. IEEE, Cancun, Mexico (2016)

17. Ge, W., Collins, R.T.: Marked point processes for crowd counting. In: IEEE Conference on Computer Vision and Pattern Recognition (CVPR), pp. 2913–2920. Miami, FL, USA (2009)

18. Ge, W., Collins, R.T.: Crowd detection with a multiview sampler. In: European Conference on Computer Vision (ECCV). Lecture Notes in Computer Science, vol. 6315, pp. 324–337. Springer, Heraklion, Crete, Greece (2010)

19. Geiger, A., Lenz, P., Urtasun, R.: Are we ready for autonomous driving? the KITTI vision benchmark suite. In: Conference on Computer Vision and Pattern Recognition (CVPR), pp. 3354–3361. Providence, Rhode Island, USA (2012)

20. Himmelsbach, M., Müller, A., Luettel, T., Wuensche, H.J.: LIDAR-based 3D object perception. In: Proceedings of 1st International Workshop on Cognition for Technical Systems. Munich (2008)

21. Huang, J., You, S.: Point cloud labeling using 3D convolutional neural network. In: International Conference on Pattern Recognition (ICPR), pp. 2670–2675. Cancun, Mexico (2016)

22. Józsa, O., Börcs, A., Benedek, C.: Towards 4D virtual city reconstruction from Lidar point cloud sequences. In: ISPRS Workshop on 3D Virtual City Modeling, ISPRS Annals Photogram. Remote Sensing and Spatial Information Sciences, vol. II-3/W1, pp. 15–20. ISPRS, Regina, Canada (2013)

23. Kaestner, R., Engelhard, N., Triebel, R., R.Siegwart: A Bayesian approach to learning 3D representations of dynamic environments. In: International Symposium on Experimental Robotics (ISER). Springer, Berlin, Germany (2010)

24. Lai, K., Fox, D.: Object recognition in 3D point clouds using web data and domain adaptation. Int. J. Rob. Res. **29**(8), 1019–1037 (2010)

25. Liu, K., Boehm, J., Alis, C.: Change detection of mobile LIDAR data using cloud computing. In: ISPRS International Archives of the Photogrammetry, Remote Sensing and Spatial Information Sciences, vol. XLI-B3, pp. 309–313 (2016)

26. Magnusson, M.: The three-dimensional normal-distributions transform—an efficient representation for registration, surface analysis, and loop detection. Ph.D. thesis, Örebro University (2009)

27. Mikic, I., Cosman, P., Kogut, G., Trivedi, M.M.: Moving shadow and object detection in traffic scenes. In: International Conference on Pattern Recognition (ICPR), vol. 1, pp. 321–324. Barcelona, Spain (2000)

28. Moghadam, P., Bosse, M., Zlot, R.: Line-based extrinsic calibration of range and image sensors. In: IEEE International Conference on Robotics and Automation (ICRA), pp. 3685–3691 (2013)

29. Nagy, B., Benedek, C.: 3D CNN based phantom object removing from mobile laser scanning data. In: International Joint Conference on Neural Networks (IJCNN), pp. 4429–4435. Anchorage, Alaska, USA (2017)

30. Nagy, B., Benedek, C.: 3D CNN-based semantic labeling approach for mobile laser scanning data. IEEE Sens. J. **19**(21), 10034–10045 (2019). https://doi.org/10.1109/JSEN.2019.2927269

31. Nagy, B., Benedek, C.: Real-time point cloud alignment for vehicle localization in a high resolution 3D map. In: Workshop on Computer Vision for Road Scene Understanding and Autonomous Driving at ECCV'18. Lecture Notes in Computer Science, vol. 11129, pp. 226–239. Springer, Munich, Germany (2019)

32. Nagy, B., Benedek, C.: On-the-fly camera and Lidar calibration. Remote Sens. **12**(7), 1137 (2020). https://doi.org/10.3390/rs12071137
33. Pusztai, Z., Eichhardt, I., Hajder, L.: Accurate calibration of multi-lidar-multi-camera systems. Sensors **18**(7), 119–152 (2018)
34. Ratha, N.K., Karu, K., Chen, S., Jain, A.K.: A real-time matching system for large fingerprint databases. IEEE Trans. Pattern Anal. Mach. Intell. **18**(8), 799–813 (1996). https://doi.org/10.1109/34.531800
35. Rusu, R., Cousins, S.: 3D is here: Point Cloud Library (PCL). In: IEEE International Conference on Robotics and Automation (ICRA). Shanghai, China (2011)
36. Scaramuzza, D., Harati, A., Siegwart, R.: Extrinsic self calibration of a camera and a 3D laser range finder from natural scenes. In: IEEE/RSJ International Conference on Intelligent Robots and Systems, pp. 4164–4169 (2007)
37. Schiller, I., Koch, R.: Improved video segmentation by adaptive combination of depth keying and Mixture-of-Gaussians. In: Scandinavian Conference on Image Analysis, Lecture Notes in Computer Science, vol. 6688, pp. 59–68. Springer, Berlin (2011)
38. Wang, Y., Loe, K.F., Wu, J.K.: A dynamic conditional random field model for foreground and shadow segmentation. IEEE Trans. Pattern Anal. Mach. Intell. **28**(2), 279–289 (2006)
39. Wu, B., Yu, B., Yue, W., Shu, S., Tan, W., Hu, C., Huang, Y., Wu, J., Liu, H.: A voxel-based method for automated identification and morphological parameters estimation of individual street trees from mobile laser scanning data. Remote Sens. **5**(2), 584 (2013)
40. Yilmaz, A., Javed, O., Shah, M.: Object tracking: a survey. ACM Comput. Surv. **38**(4) (2006)
41. Yu, Y., Li, J., Guan, H., Wang, C.: Automated detection of three-dimensional cars in mobile laser scanning point clouds using DBM-Hough-Forests. IEEE Trans. Geosci. Remote Sens. **54**(7), 4130–4142 (2016)
42. Yu, Y., Li, J., Yu, J., Guan, H., Wang, C.: Pairwise three-dimensional shape context for partial object matching and retrieval on mobile laser scanning data. IEEE Geosci. Remote Sens. Lett. **11**(5), 1019–1023 (2014). https://doi.org/10.1109/LGRS.2013.2285237
43. Zhang, Z.: Iterative point matching for registration of free-form curves and surfaces. Int. J. Comput. Vis. **13**(2), 119–152 (1994)
44. Zheng, H., Wang, R., Xu, S.: Recognizing street lighting poles from mobile LiDAR data. IEEE Trans. Geosci. Remote Sens. **55**(1), 407–420 (2017)
45. Zováthi, Ö., Nagy, B., Benedek, C.: Exploitation of dense MLS city maps for 3D object detection. In: International Conference on Image Analysis and Recognition (ICIAR). Lecture Notes in Computer Science, vol. 12131, pp. 393–403. Springer, Póvoa de Varzim, Portugal (2020)

An Extended Visual Intelligence Scheme for Disassembly in Automated Recycling Routines

Erenus Yildiz[1]([📧])[ID], Erwan Renaudo[2][ID], Jakob Hollenstein[2][ID], Justus Piater[2][ID], and Florentin Wörgötter[1][ID]

[1] III. Physics Institute, Georg-August University of Göttingen, Göttingen, Germany
{eyildiz,worgott}@gwdg.de
[2] Department of Computer Science, University of Innsbruck, Innsbruck, Austria
{erwan.renaudo,jakob.hollenstein,justus.piater}@uibk.ac.at

Abstract. The state-of-the-art of deep learning models is becoming useful in real-world tasks such as disassembly of electronic devices by robotic manipulation. We have previously proposed a visual intelligence scheme to automate the robotic disassembly of computer hard drives. This extended paper addresses the remaining problems during the scene analysis, such as encountering various screw types and wires. We propose an extension to our previously published visual scheme for disassembly of devices by robotic manipulation and implement additional supervised learning modules that utilize state-of-the-art deep learning models to solve the remaining significant problems. We evaluate these models individually and also evaluate the extended scheme's capabilities on a completely unseen device (a graphical processing unit), to evaluate the schemes generalization capability. To our knowledge, this is the first scheme to address the entire disassembly process of the chosen device including various screw types and wires.

Keywords: Wire detection · Screw classification · Automation · e-Waste · Recycling

1 Introduction

Due to the latest developments in information technology, the volume of obsolete electronic devices (e-waste) is growing. The composition of these products raise two main issues: firstly, electronic products (such as mobile phones, computers and televisions) contain heavy metals such as Mercury or Beryllium. The exposure of humans to these elements (e.g., destructive disassembly routines) have the potential to cause cancer [45] or pollute the environment. Secondly, electronic products contain precious materials in higher proportion than natural ore deposits (e.g. 100 times more gold in a tonne of discarded mobile phones than in a tonne of gold ore [40]). The destructive recycling process causes both health and economical dangers and thus there are both health and economical reasons to improve automation of the disassembly and recycling processes.

E-waste disassembly represents an interesting application for autonomous robotics: it is desirable to automate it due to the tedious repetitive actions required from the

© Springer Nature Switzerland AG 2022
P. Galambos et al. (Eds.): ROBOVIS 2020/ROBOVIS 2021, CCIS 1667, pp. 25–50, 2022.
https://doi.org/10.1007/978-3-031-19650-8_2

operator; but there is a high variability of devices or shapes within a category of devices. The latter should be addressed by using a visual scheme in such a system. This means recognizing visually slightly different devices of the same category (e.g. mobile phones) as well as generalizing the learned knowledge to unknown devices, provided similar physical features are present. In [46] we proposed a visual scheme to analyse computer hard drives (HDD) and produce a representation that can be used to disassemble them. However, it has some limitations: wires can not be detected; only the type of screws used in HDDs is detected (e.g., Torx). In this work, we address two problems: *extending the detection capabilities* of the system and assessing its *ability to generalize* to other devices (e.g., graphics processing units, GPUs). For the first problem, we introduce two modules (wire detection & screw classification) as well as a bookkeeping mechanism to better track the disassembly status and confirm removed, moved or introduced parts. For the second problem, we evaluate the performance of the system given various levels of retraining on new data. This paper is organized as follows: Sect. 2 gives a review of the literature on visual intelligence schemes, Sect. 3 presents our extended approach in detail, Sect. 5 presents the evaluation of the schemes capabilities on the unknown device. Finally, Sect. 6 discusses the impact of these results and concludes.

2   Related Work

Computer vision methods have already been used to automate certain processes in industrial applications in the past decades [2, 29]. There is, however, a lack of vision-guided automated recycling. To use robotic manipulation in this scenario certain entities of the device (e.g., wire, screw, part) need to be identified with high accuracy. Early works show that the uncertainty problem at the operational level can be solved by an integrated sensory approach. Gil et al. [12] implemented a multi-sensorial system that combines information from a tactile sensor and a vision system in order to perform visual-servoing of the robot. The conceptual test was conducted by removing a bolt from a straight slot. They also worked on detecting partial occlusions of components using vision to simplify the disassembly task [13]. The conceptual test for this system was the detection of circuit boards.

In a 2006 survey [42], Weigl-Seitz et al. list a number of limitations found in the literature: the lack of datasets for the required tasks, the inability of existing schemes to account for more than certain number of devices and that algorithms employed were mostly inspired by classical computer vision methods with no online learning paradigm involved.

In the last decade, however, there have been plenty of works [1, 2, 39] focusing on detecting certain types of parts, such as screws and bolts. Most of these works either achieved only prohibitively low accuracy or they were only usable for a very narrow set of entities (e.g., only one type/size of screw). There have also been model-based methods [9, 30, 37–39, 43] that were solving the problem for a specific model of screws or bolts found in/over a specific device model such as an electric motor. However, as stated in our previous work [46], assuming models of the parts to detect are available limits strongly the adaptability of the visual scheme as the variety of brands and models per device increase exponential the number of different models required. Finally, a visual scheme specifically trained for a device or a part type is also limited as the recycling disassembly process includes various type of devices. The most notable effort came in 2018 where Jahanian et al. [20] showed the disassembly of mobile phones using state-of-the-art segmentation networks. The prototype, however, was limited to work with a very limited set of mobile phones from a limited set of manufacturers. Our previous work [46] also partially suffer from this limitation as it is trained only on HDD data. This reduces the general application of these works in real recycling plants.

In addition, the original pipeline we proposed had three structural limitations: first, its inability to classify the type of detected screws causes problems on devices that contain more than one type of screw. Second, the pipeline has no means of handling wires, which is major issue as parts connected via wire can not be taken out of the device individually. Finally, the original pipeline has no awareness of its disassembly state. Thus when a part grabbed by the robot's gripper is dropped back into the scene due to a manipulation problem, the system does not know if it is the same part or not, preventing the rest of the system to evaluate the effect of the manipulation. The system needs to know on the next analysis step, that a part was moved, removed or re-introduced back into the scene.

Thus, current methods lack generalization capabilities, device and environment-independence, fault-tolerance to be used in robotic disassembly processes which involve a great degree of variance in parts. We showed that Deep Convolutional Neural Networks (DCNN) offer a powerful solution to analyze the inner structure of devices in the context of disassembly [46,47]. We further extend the capabilities of the scheme by adding two new DCNN-powered modules. Moreover, we make the extended pipeline fault-tolerant against manipulation errors to some degree. Last but not least, the proposed methods are CAD model-free, making the scheme independent of specific devices and parts. Instead, DCNNs learn to extract relevant features of the device entities (e.g., screws, wires), abstracting from manufacturing details specific to the device. End-of-Life (EOL) devices that belong to a family usually include similar entities (e.g., parts, wires, screws). Focusing on features common to these entities by employing the deep learning paradigm leads to reproducible and generalizable outputs that can be used for other devices as well.

Thus, the problem of extending the original visual intelligence scheme can be formulated as a problem where machine learning paradigms (e.g., segmentation, classification) are used in order to detect and classify the present entities of the target device, such as wires and screws, respectively. In contrast to the original scheme, the extended scheme satisfies the following requirements:

- Classification should be able to handle great variety screws types/sizes.
- Segmentation should not be affected by the great variety of physical features (e.g., color, shape) among wires.
- Moving, removing or introducing a detected part in the scene must be registered by comparing the consecutive analyses.

As we also mentioned in our original publication, many recent works [5, 8,11,23,24,27] have addressed the semantic segmentation problem or pixel-wise classification problem in various domains ranging from autonomous driving to biomedical imagery.

Aforementioned work in 2018 [20] and our original visual intelligence scheme [46] are amongst the first works to utilize state-of-the-art deep learning methods, in particular convolutional networks [22] in the context automated recycling of E-Waste. Previously mentioned works preferred to use the family of R-CNN networks [14,15,31] that have been evolving recently. One of the latest R-CNN models by the time the works were published, is *Mask-RCNN* [16] which is based on the Feature Pyramid Network (FPN) [25].

Although Mask-RCNN and its ensembled models were the state of the art for instance segmentation for a while, they were outperformed by recently developed *EfficientNets* [36] models. These networks achieve much better accuracy and efficiency than previous convolutional neural networks. In particular, the EfficientNetB7, which forms the basis of our wire detection module, achieves state-of-the-art 84.3% top-1 accuracy on ImageNet. According to the authors, the networks are 8.4x smaller and inference is 6.1x faster than the best existing convolutional neural networks. It has also been shown that they transfer well and achieve state-of-the-art accuracy on CIFAR-100 (91.7%), Flowers (98.8%), and 3 other transfer learning datasets. We therefore base our modules on this family.

3   Methods

On request the extended visual scheme provides an analysis of the scene with the predictions of 4 modules: a part detection module, a screw classification module, a gap detection module and a wire detection module. The screw detection module of the original pipeline has been extended to a screw classification module that classifies the detected screws according to their type and size information. The wire detection module is employed to recognize any kind of visible wires and cables that can be found inside or around the device. Finally, a bookkeeping mechanism is in place to register every change between to consecutive frames. This is required to keep track of the disassembly sequence, as well as to gain a certain degree of fault recovery. The pseudo code for the extended pipeline is given in Algorithm 1.

As mentioned earlier, the analysis of wires is a semantic segmentation problem. However, detecting the screw type and size a typical classification problem: image based classification of type and size with a deep convolutional neural network. Both problems are challenging. Wires can be any color and can occur in many shapes, including tangled wires. On top of that, there is no fixed background for wires to be used. They can be found inside or at the backside of the devices, over varying surfaces. Screws, on the other hand, are another challenge due to the high similarity between same type screws varying only in size (e.g., Torx6 and Torx7, Philips1 and Philips2). The proposed modules account for aforementioned difficulties, and execute their tasks with high accuracy.

3.1   Datasets

Datasets are at the core of any machine learning endeavour, as supervised or unsupervised machine learning algorithms heavily depend on the data available. This fact

Algorithm 1. Extended Perception Pipeline.

1: $c_p, b_p, m_p := []$	▷ part centers, boundaries, masks
2: $c_s, b_s, m_s := []$	▷ screw type/size, centers, boundaries, masks
3: $c_g, b_g, v_g := []$	▷ gap centers, boundaries, volumes
4: $c_w, b_w, v_w := []$	▷ **wire centers, boundaries, masks**
5: $I, P := NULL$	▷ I: Input Monocular Image, P: Input Pointcloud
6: $C_m, C_s := NULL$	▷ C_m: Monocular Calibration Info, C_s: Stereo Calibration Info
7: predicates$= []$	

8: **procedure** COLLECT PREDICATES
9:     **if** hddTable.State()$= 0$ **then**
10:         hddTable.changeState(angle=θ_{Stereo})
11:         $P \leftarrow$ getPointcloud(P)
12:         **if** $P \neq NULL$ **then**
13:             $c_g, b_g, v_g \leftarrow$ detectGaps(P)
14:         hddTable.changeState(angle=$\theta_{\text{Monocular}}$)
15:         $I \leftarrow$ getRGBImage(I)
16:         **if** $I \neq$ NULL & hddTable.State() $= 0$ **then**
17:             $c_p, b_p, m_p \leftarrow$ segmentParts(I)
18:             $c_w, b_w, m_w \leftarrow$ **segmentWires(I)**
19:             $c_s, b_s, m_s \leftarrow$ **detectAndClassifyScrews(I)**
20:     $C_m, C_s \leftarrow getCalibrationInfo()$
21:     predicates $\leftarrow$ mergeAllInfo($I, P, C_m, C_s, c_p,$
22:         $b_p, m_p, t_s, c_s, b_s, m_s, c_g, b_g, v_g, c_w, b_w, m_w$)
23:     **bookkeep(I, predicates)**
24:     **return** predicates

aside, even without any machine learning involved, ground truth data is required for future evaluation of any employed algorithm. In order to train the new modules of our extended pipeline, we collect and create datasets for screws and wires.

Screws are common assembling entities in electronics EOL device. Their removal is paramount to disassemble devices and access inner areas and hidden parts. A non-detected screw may hinder the entire disassembly sequence as it creates constraints between parts. Not only should screws be correctly detected, but their type must be classified so that the correct tool is selected to interacted with them.

Since we base our screw classification module on a published work [48], we use the same dataset. It was observed that most of the EOL devices considered have a certain set of screws. 12 types of screws are therefore considered: Torx 6, 7, 8, 9, Allen 2.5, 2.75, 4, Slotted 4, 6.5, 10 and Phillips 1, 2. Note that the length of the thread is irrelevant for the perception block, as they are always occluded. Therefore, any vision routine only considers the head part of the screws. Figure 1 illustrates samples from every type and size considered. In order to address detection and classification purposes, we found that 20000 positive images of screw heads are sufficient.

Note that the screw classification dataset does not require any negative samples, since the original pipeline already has a screw detection module, which operates to separate artefacts from screws. Therefore, it was sufficient to include the positive samples

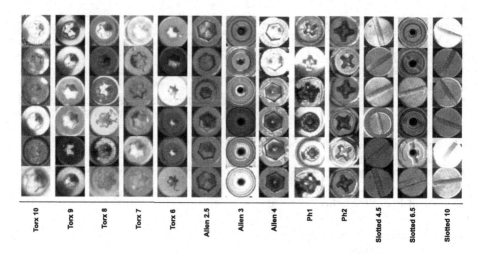

Torx 10 Torx 9 Torx 8 Torx 7 Torx 6 Allen 2.5 Allen 3 Allen 4 Ph1 Ph2 Slotted 4.5 Slotted 6.5 Slotted 10

Fig. 1. Various screw types encountered during the disassembly of EOL devices, Yildiz et al. [48].

to the screw detection dataset. It must be kept in mind that in order to classify any screw, detection of that screw has to be done first. Therefore, every positive sample in the screw classification dataset, exists in the screw detection dataset as well.

All of the illustrated images were collected using the setup presented in the original paper. However, in order to account for the great variance in the dataset, the images were collected under slightly different light conditions. They were collected by the screw classification module's offline mode that was introduced in the original paper.

Wires unlike screws, do not have specific shapes (e.g., circular), making them only suitable for pixel-wise segmentation schemes. They might only appear as discontinuous segments due to occlusion in EOL devices and can be of any color. It is safe to assume that wires are the most varying entity in this domain. This makes it very difficult or even impossible to find a dedicated dataset for specific visual tasks to detect wires. Hence, one is forced to deal with limited number of annotated training samples.

3.2 Wire Segmentation

Wire detection is not a commonly studied problem in the literature. There are few notable works: The work by Madaan et al. [28] grabbed our attention, and was built on the work presented by Kasturi et al. [21], aiming to find wires in aerial navigation. This work is interesting because it is the first work to use convolutional neural networks in order to address the wire detection problem. The authors render synthetic wires using a ray tracing engine, and overlay them on 67K images from flight videos available on the internet. This synthetic dataset is used for pre-training the models before fine-tuning on real data. The work achieved 73% of precision, however, it suffers from the fact that the dataset generation requires expert knowledge in ray tracing engines. Many times these programs are not straightforward to use, making methods based on them less desirable. Additionally, the dependency on specific software, might render the data generation impossible as the required software may become unavailable in the future. The work nevertheless investigates available network architectures that could be used to detect wires, hence, it plays an important role in this research field. The authors report that dilated convolutional layers [49] were chosen since they provide a simple and effective way to gather context without reducing feature map size.

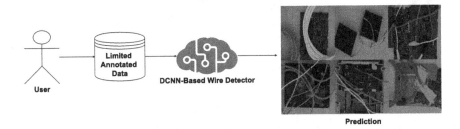

Prediction

Fig. 2. We present a DCNN-Based wire detector scheme that requires limited number of annotated data from the user and delivers accurate predictions for robotic manipulation tasks.

After considering the literature, we decided to tackle the wire detection problem with DCNNs to detect, recognize and localize the wire pixels, using a paradigm called semantic segmentation. Due to the high number of available state-of-the-art networks, we train and evaluate a set of selected methods on this semantic segmentation problem: EfficientNetB7 [36], InceptionV3 [34], InceptionResnetV2 [33], Densenet201 [19]. These networks achieve over 93% top-5 accuracy [44] on the well-known Imagenet dataset [6]. There is one more criterion that we took into account, that is the number of hyperparameters. Clearly, we do not want to pick a good performing model that requires enormous amount of hyperparameters such as SENet [18]. Hence, we only evaluate the aforementioned models.

It must be mentioned that the required training data for any DCNN should not exceed a certain amount of images, and the model should be able to generalise for all kinds of wires found in the e-waste disassembly domain. As the original visual intelligence already requires a certain amount of training data for its other modules (e.g., screw detection & classification, part segmentation), it is our intention to keep the requirement for annotated training data as low as possible. Therefore, it was decided to train any model with only 130 raw images where 100 of them would be reserved for training, 10 for validation and 20 for testing. The basic idea of our approach is shown in Fig. 2.

We propose a module for the existing setup where the monocular camera faces the device's surface perpendicularly. The proposed module has the main blocks: data generation or *Datagen*, and model, as illustrated in Fig. 3. The Datagen block aims to greatly augment the limited number of user-annotated raw images and generate massive amounts of augmented images along with their annotations for the training the deep neural network model. The Model block, on the other hand, aims to detect the learned features and build a segmentation map out of the input RGB image received by the monocular camera.

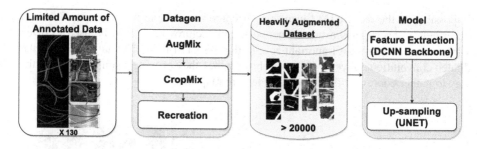

Fig. 3. Wire detection module is composed of data generation block which generates a large number of augmented images using a limited number of annotated images. An EfficientB7 [36] model trains on the massive number of generated augmented images.

Data Generation. It is usually very difficult or even impossible to find a dedicated dataset for specific visual tasks such as wire detection. This inevitably forces us to deal with limited number of annotated training data. In order to succeed under this condition, one has to enrich the amount of limited annotated images. To this end, we decided to use heavy augmentation routines and generate massive amounts of annotated training data, from our existing dataset which contains only 130 annotated wire images.

For our data augmentation block, we have chosen a 3-step routine. Below, we share the augmentation library used and the operations applied. The exact parameters of the augmentation functions can be found in the published source code.

We start off by *Augmix* [17], a popular augmentation library with many options. We, however, in this step only apply shift scale rotation, blur, elastic transform, and optical distortion. In the second step, we continue with *CropMix* [35] which allows manually cropped augmentations rather than automated ones to ensure variety and mask precision based on regions. Here we go by 4-segment crop (per image), rotation, flipping along with generation ratio as 0.001 and dataset occupancy ratio (training) as 0.488. In the final step we apply our own augmentation routine. We create a new image using 4 images applying rotation, mirroring and flipping along with dataset occupancy ratio (training) as 0.416 and clustering as sample based. At the end the datagen block creates approximately 20000 images for the training data.

Model. In order to conduct our investigation, we picked a use case of wire detection in digital entertainment devices such as DVD players, gaming consoles, etc. To this end, we collected 100 top-down images of open DVD players from online search engines and annotated the visible wires by hand. We then generated approximately 20000 augmented, annotated images, which served as training data for the models we investigated.

Throughout our study, we considered only two metrics to evaluate our scheme with. The standard metrics for pixel to pixel segmentation are mainly the COCO [26] average precision (AP) metrics: AP is average precision of multiple IoU's (Intersection of prediction and ground truth over Union of prediction and ground truth) values seen. The definition of IoU between a known segmentation of n pixels, Y, and a similar set of

Table 1. Evaluation of the state-of-the-art models. EfficientNetB7 is proven to be the most suitable model with a high SSIM and IoU score.

| Model | Metric | | | | | |
| | SSIM | | | IoU/F1 | | |
	Max.	Mean	Min.	Max.	Mean	Min.
EfficientNetB7	**0.956**	**0.877**	**0.761**	**0.988**	**0.952**	**0.897**
InceptionV3	0.944	0.863	0.758	0.977	0.947	0.894
InceptionResNetV2	0.941	0.859	0.743	0.983	0.943	0.886
DenseNet201	0.940	0.862	0.747	0.978	0.945	0.891

predicted segmentation, Y' (in the binary case, i.e. where $Y_i, Y'_i \in \{0,1\}, \forall i \in [1, n]$ is as follows in Eq. 1:

$$IoU(Y, Y') = \frac{Y \cap Y'}{Y \cup Y'} = \frac{\sum_{i=1}^n \min(Y_i, Y'_i)}{\sum_{i=1}^n \max(Y_i, Y'_i)} \tag{1}$$

However, we decided to not to only consider IoU alone, but also the SSIM (Structural Similarity Index) [41] metric, known for measuring the objective image quality. It is based on the computation of three terms, namely the luminance term (l), the contrast term (c) and the structural term (s). The overall index is a multiplicative combination of the three terms as it is seen in Eq. 2 as follows:

$$SSIM(x, y) = [l(x, y)]^\alpha \cdot [c(x, y)]^\beta \cdot [s(x, y)]^\gamma \tag{2}$$

where

$$l(x, y) = \frac{(2\mu_x\mu_y + C1)}{(\mu_x^2 + \mu_y^2 + C1)} \tag{3}$$

$$c(x, y) = \frac{(2\sigma_x\sigma_y + C2)}{(\sigma_x^2 + \sigma_y^2 + C2)} \tag{4}$$

$$s(x, y) = \frac{\sigma_{xy} + C3}{\sigma_x\sigma_y + C3} \tag{5}$$

where μ_x, μ_y, σ_x, σ_y, and σ_{xy} are the local means, standard deviations, and cross-covariance for images x, y. If $\alpha = \beta = \gamma = 1$, and $C3 = C2/2$ (default selection of $C3$) the index simplifies to Eq. 6 seen below.

$$SSIM(x, y) = \frac{(2\mu_x\mu_y + C1)(2\sigma_{xy} + C2)}{(\mu_x^2 + \mu_y^2 + C1)(\sigma_x^2 + \sigma_y^2 + C2)} \tag{6}$$

All of our experiments conducted were evaluated based one these two metrics.

Table 1 shows the evaluation of the state-of-the-art models based on the aforementioned metrics. One can clearly notice that the model EfficientNetB7 [36] scores slightly better in both metrics. The results clearly indicate that EfficientNetB7 is doing a better job at feature extraction from the given images (even with low resolution, low-feature conditions).

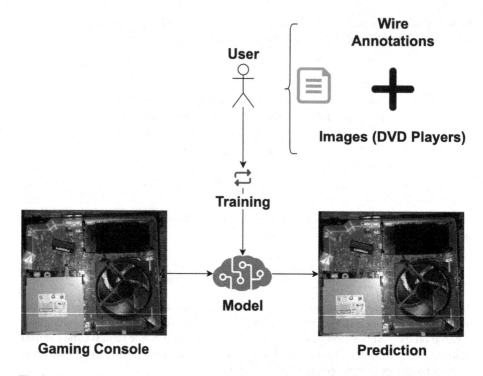

Fig. 4. We investigated the state-of-the-art models' capabilities with limited amount of data. After training the models wires of DVD players, we infer on XBox One gaming console wires. Both devices belong to the same family of devices, despite of having different inner layouts.

Having noticed the slightly better accuracy provided by the EfficientNetB7, we made inferences on the images of a different device, such as the XBox One gaming console. The model, although trained on DVD player wires, was able to make good predictions on the gaming console wires, marking their locations for a possible robotic manipulation action. Figure 4 illustrates this use case. We used the state-of-the-art UNET [32] model as our up-sampling backbone for all our feature extractor models.

3.3 Screw Classification

We base this module on the pipeline we inherit from a previous work [48]. As stated in that work, the module enables the user to collect training data by cropping circular candidates from the scene. The cropped circular candidates are then to be divided into their respective classes (e.g., artifact, Torx8, Ph2, Slotted6.5, Allen2.75, etc.) by a human.

First, the screw detector model is trained to classify screws from artefacts (circular non-screws structures), as explained in the work [47]. As the original paper for classification [48] instructed, the new screw data consisting of 12 different types of screws is included. This corresponds over 20000 samples, which are split into training and validation sets with the ratio of 2:1, as instructed in the original paper we base our approach on [48]. We refer the reader to his publication for the details of the training process.

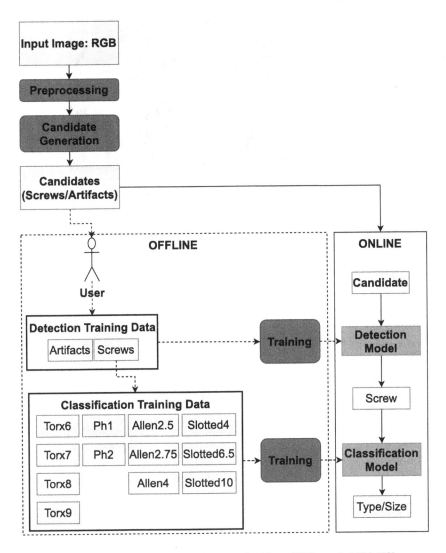

Fig. 5. Screw classification pipeline inherited from Yildiz et al. 2020 [48].

The screw classification module employed marks and returns the type/size information and locations of the screws seen in the image, as illustrated in Fig. 6.

The classifier accuracy reported in Table 2 is directly taken from the work [48] published. The table summarizes the experimental results with regards to accuracy of each classifier against the validation set, clearly showing that EfficientNet-B2 re-trained on the Noisy-Student dataset with the given parameters is proven to be the best choice.

Moreover, we underline the fact that augmentation strategy plays a pivotal role in the classifier accuracy. In case of circular objects, rotation operation guarantees that the training data accounts for screws that are rotated for each angle, as reported in the original publication [48]. The Albumentations [4] library was used to apply a rotation of 360°, horizontal and vertical flips, as well as brightness and contrast changes.

Fig. 6. Classified screw heads by the screw classification method taken from Yildiz et al. 2020 [48].

Table 2. Accuracy of the state-of-the-art models with huge variation of hyperparameters. Highlighted one is the top performing one [48].

Model	Grayscale	Size	Loss	Acc.	Min. Acc.	F1	Transfer learning
EfficientNetB2A	**No**	**256**	**0.1187**	**0.968**	**0.79**	**0.97**	**Noisy student**
EfficientNetB2A	No	64	0.2144	0.936	0.78	0.93	ImageNet
EfficientNetB2A	No	128	0.1871	0.951	0.85	0.95	ImageNet
EfficientNetB2A	Yes	128	0.2199	0.948	0.67	0.94	ImageNet
EfficientNetB3A	Yes	64	0.2072	0.937	0.75	0.93	ImageNet
EfficientNetB3A	No	64	0.2051	0.939	0.74	0.94	ImageNet
DenseNet121	No	128	0.1415	0.961	0.81	0.96	ImageNet
DenseNet121	Yes	128	0.1489	0.957	0.74	0.95	ImageNet
DenseNet121	No	64	0.1896	0.937	0.72	0.93	ImageNet
DenseNet121	No	64	0.2306	0.934	0.71	0.93	ImageNet
DenseNet201	No	256	0.1170	0.966	0.79	0.96	ImageNet
ResNet34	No	128	0.1538	0.955	0.80	0.95	ImageNet
ResNet34	Yes	128	0.2026	0.951	0.69	0.95	ImageNet
ResNet50v2	No	256	0.1732	0.942	0.73	0.94	ImageNet

4   Bookkeeping

In the context of disassembly, a bookkeeping mechanism aims to register the status of every recognized part in the scene. This is carried out by analysing the predicted pixel-level changes between part boundaries found by the part segmentation module exists in the original scheme. The mechanism accounts for multiple situations that are explained below. It also allows user to specify the sensitivity of the change it should consider before registering. This is a required feature since, every change is detected by conducting pixel-wise comparison of part boundaries and regions in consecutive frames, meaning that a larger device (and components) may require a less sensitive analysis of changes, as a few pixels of change in large part's boundaries may not exactly mean a misplacement or failed action. If the EOL device is large, then a little touch on its part is not worth registration. On the other hand, if the EOL device is a small one (as in the case of hard drives), then a few pixels may mean more, given some parts such as a *spindle hub* are relatively small, meaning that every pixel should count towards the change threshold.

- **Difference in List of Parts**: When the lists of parts are different between consecutive frames, introduction or removal of those parts are registered.
- **Difference in Locations of Parts**: When the parts appear to be in different locations (if their center points moved more than the user-specified margin) between consecutive frames, this change is registered.

The bookkeeping mechanism has a timer, additionally allowing the system to not consider a frame that is acquired beyond the user-specified time interval. This is a needed feature as well, since the registration should not occur between a frame from a previous system run. This user-specified parameter is set to 5 min by default, considering a frame as consecutive if and only if the frame is acquired within this time. If not, it registers the frame as the primary frame, and starts the timer for another 5 min, as explained in algorithm above.

By employing the described mechanism, the extended scheme gains a certain degree of fault-tolerance and guarantees the continuation of disassembly process despite of manipulation errors.

5   Experimental Evaluation

As the original visual scheme requires two inputs (a top-down RGB image and a top-down point-cloud), we use the same setup from the original paper with a Basler acA4600-7gc monocular camera which provides images with 4608×3288 resolution and 3.5 FPS and a Nerian Karmin2 stereo camera with a depth error of 0.06 cm from the minimum range of 35 cm.

We then let the extended visual scheme prove its capabilities given scenes of computer hard drives (HDDs) with wires and screws. We quantify these results and additionally conduct a study to assess the generalization ability of the extended scheme.

5.1   Evaluation Method

There are two new modules in the extended scheme and each of these modules has to be evaluated differently, as the paradigms running behind are different.

Wire Detection. Since we have investigated the state-of-the-art models and found out that EfficientNetB7 performing the best, we decided to use a dedicated wire dataset and train the model from the scratch. To this end, approximately 130 images of wires were collected manually, using the same setup introduced in the original paper. The strategy was to use any type of wires (including connectors) and manually create occlusions with arbitrary EOL components. As backgrounds, mostly PCBs were used, as wires are mostly found on PCBs in EOL devices. Figure 7 shows a few samples from the wire dataset acquired. Wires were later annotated with the VIA tool [7].

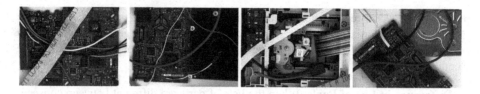

Fig. 7. Sample raw images from the wire dataset.

Table 3. Evaluation of our trained EfficientNetB7 model on the test data, using SSMI and IoU metrics.

Model	Metric	Min.	Max.	Mean
EfficientNetB7	SSIM	0.80	0.98	0.91
EfficientNetB7	IoU/F1	0.89	0.99	0.97

After choosing the model, we collected a new dataset of high (4K) resolution top-down images of wires that could be found in disassembly environments. Those are various wires taken out of devices as well as wires that connect devices to data or power supplies. As background, we chose the most commonly encountered ones such as PCBs, device lids and bays, as well as the work station surface. Having collected 130 various wires images, we split 100 of them for training, 10 for validation and 20 for testing. Below we also provide the details of the experimental evaluation and present our final model.

We use the Google provided TPU v2 for training our model via Colaboratory [3] environment which has 64 GB High Bandwidth Memory (HBM) and provides 180 TFlops computing power. The validation set was taken to be 1/10 of training dataset and training was done with early stopping enabled callbacks so that the model does not overfit. We trained our model with 4 generations of data each time taking one forth of the total data. (i.e- the augmentations are tuned in a way every time about 50% of training data is completely new). No transfer learning was used and the model was trained from scratch. For the final model, however, the best of these 4 weights were taken to train on the whole training dataset. As the MSE loss graph shows in Fig. 8, the model reaches stable losses very quickly and converges to a final point where a plateau stage can be encountered before stopping. We summarize the experimental results with regards to performance of each classifier against the testing set in Table 1.

From the collected results in Table 3, we conclude that EfficientNetB7 outperforms any other state of the art models that are capable of semantic segmentation on this task. The model outputs show high similarity and reach a good IoU score as well.

We noticed that the resolution of the images inferred must also be of the same resolution of training data, because lowering the resolution creates completely different feature maps compared to what the model was trained on. Figure 9 illustrates some of the detections on the test set by our detector. Our scheme can handle delicate cases such as wires with tangles, and partial occlusions, which are frequently encountered cases during the disassembly of an electronic device. Our model proves to be robust, handling such delicate situations with maintaining high accuracy. We report minimum SSIM and IoU of 0.80 and 0.89, respectively.

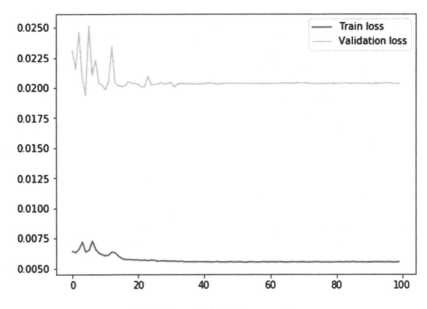

Fig. 8. Loss in MSE of our model.

Last but not least, we tested our trained model on devices that the network has never seen before, such as thermostats. Figure 9 illustrates the found wires in these devices. The results prove that our model can be used in disassembly environments where the target device was not seen before, which is usually the case.

Fig. 9. Our model has a clear generalization ability since it is able to detect wires found in devices that it has not seen before. We tested it on the back side of heat allocators as well as both sides of hard drives with arbitrarily added wires on them.

Screw Classification. Although the classifier accuracy is quite high, due to the fact that Hough circle finder method misses out finding the circles in the first place, our final average precision was found to be 80%. As the classifier expects images that are directly suggested by the Hough circle finder, any circle that is missed, is also not considered by the classifier. In other words, the classifier's ability is limited by the Hough circle finder. Therefore, the AP remains at 80%. We refer the reader to the Fig. 1 to illustrate a few detection samples during the HDD disassembly sequences.

As the pipeline is composed of two main blocks, namely the Hough circle detector and our classifier, EfficientNetB2, it is required to assess the detection as well as the classification abilities of it. To this end, the following strategy was pursued: First, the test images were annotated, each having only one hard drive with top-down view. These images contain drives with or without screws, by which the Hough circle finder could be assessed. These scene images were annotated by marking screws with squares, which would form the ground truth for assessing the Hough circle finder's accuracy. The standard VOC evaluation [10] was preferred and it was found out that the Hough circle detector actually works with 0.783 mean IoU (Intersection over Union) with the optimal parameters found for the IMAGINE setup. IoU here refers to what amount of screw region is correctly detected by the Hough circle finder. If the detected region for a screw is below 70%, it is bound to result in bad prediction for both detection and classification. It must be also noted that the pipeline is limited by the accuracy of Hough Transform and the screw detection previously introduced. Although the accuracy of Hough circle detection can vary depending on the parameters of the function such as min/max radius, min/max threshold, final accuracy of the pipeline is found 0.75, and calculated as follows:

$$Acc\_P = Acc\_CD * Acc\_SD * Acc\_SC$$

where Acc_P stands for the accuracy of pipeline, Acc_{CD} stands for the accuracy of the circle detector, Acc_{SD} stands for the accuracy of the screw detector, and Acc_{SC} stands for the accuracy of the screw classifier.

5.2   Generalization

Ideally, the scheme should also be evaluated on a second EOL product, so that its capabilities are proven to be robust and generalizing enough for an industrial use. For this purpose, another computer piece—GPU—was chosen. In total, 8 GPUs from various brands and models were collected. We evaluate the performance of the detection and classification of the system both on HDDs (which the visual intelligence is trained for) and GPUs (which the visual intelligence has never seen). In order to understand how fast the system can adapt, we define three experiments (E1–E3) with incremental retraining on the new device. This retraining is done with a limited training dataset of user-annotated GPUs data (see Table 4).

Experiment E1 corresponds to the evaluation of the system trained on HDD data and without retraining on the GPU data (no annotated training data e.g., GPU screws, GPU components, GPU wires). Between the two classes of device, the most common

Table 4. Existing data consists of RGB images of HDD images, whereas collected data consists of RGB images of GPU images. Since the modules were already trained optimally with the existing data, the collected data used was intentionally kept limited.

Module\data	RGB images existing data (E.D.)	RGB images collected data (C.D.)
Component segmentation	600	100
Screw detection	20000	2000
Screw classification	20000	2000
Wire detection	130	100

Table 5. Evaluation scheme to be used through the experiments.

Experiment	Data	Re-training	Test device
E1	E.D.	No	HDD, GPU
E2	E.D. + 50% C.D.	Yes	HDD, GPU
E3	E.D. + 100% C.D.	Yes	HDD, GPU

component is the PCB (which is also the biggest entity on the GPU). Components such as bay, fan, sockets, screws and optionally wires exist in various colors and types. For instance, PCBs found in GPUs vary in colors of black, blue and green, whereas for HDDs they are green by a very large margin. Nevertheless, by conducting E1 we expect to evaluate how our approach is able to generalize to other electronic devices, i.e. whether the initial training on HDD is representative enough of commonly found parts in E-waste in general (wires, screws, PCB, etc.). Experiment E2 and E3 on the other hand, evaluate the scheme's capabilities after retraining it with 50% and 100% training data, respectively. By conducting E2 and E3, the question of "How does retraining with limited data affect the performance of the scheme on the second device?" is answered. Note that the gap detector was not evaluated on GPUs in any experiment, since there are no gaps significant to the disassembly of the device.

Table 4 shows the experimental data in numbers. For every module, the data was split into training, validation and test sets in ratios of 70%, 20% and 10%, respectively. Evaluation scheme is illustrated in Table 5. None of the training strategies is subject to change (e.g., early stopping). Weights were reset between E1, E2 and E3 experiments to prevent learning of repetitive features and introducing bias.

Table 6. Accuracy of each module through experiments E1, E2, and E3.

Experiment	S.D.A.	S.C.A.	C.S.A.	W.D.A.
E1 (no retraining)	0.91	0.94	0.71	(0.89, 0.88)
E2 (retraining with 50% GPU data)	0.99	1.0	0.78	(0.91, 0.93)
E3 (retraining with 100% GPU data)	0.99	1.0	0.84	(0.92, 0.93)

—S.D.A.: Screw detection accuracy

—S.C.A.: Screw classification accuracy

—C.S.A.: Component segmentation accuracy

—W.D.A.: Wire detection accuracy

Experiment E1. Experiment E1 is conducted on each module, testing each one's capabilities on performing visual tasks on raw HDD and GPU images without re-training. For screws, the description of the entity is largely the same (e.g., circular shape, feature in the center) therefore there is no drastic significant drop in accuracy of screw detection network, scoring 0.91. There is an insignificant drop from the original accuracy 0.99 [47] due to the fact that GPUs have black and dark gray screws which the network misses from time to time.

As for the screw classifier, the weighted average was found to be 0.94. Here as well, an insignificant drop was observed due to the aforementioned reason. Nevertheless, it was able to find what it was trained on when the learned color was present. Figure 10 illustrates such an example. The image above contains screws that have the ordinary silver-metallic color. Note that the screws in/on HDDs were of this color. Thus, the network has the learned features from the images of these HDDs. On the image below, however, it is noticeable that the detection network misses more. Since all the screws found on that particular GPU were of dark gray or black color, the accuracy is naturally lower. However, even in this case, the classifier nevertheless correctly identified the found screws as "ph1" and "torx6" as illustrated. It must be remembered that the classifier only classifies once the detector detects an instance. If there were only two classifications, it is due to the fact that there were only two screws detected.

Fig. 10. Correctly detected and classified screws when the learned color is present (left), missed and incorrectly classified screws when the learned color is different (right).

Component segmentation requires specific user annotation and identification of the components of the device, which was only done for HDDs so far. E1 evaluated the segmentation module therefore, on an unseen device of GPU, and found out that the segmentation module reports 0.71 Mean-F score, which a bit lower than 0.78 (the Mean-F score calculated for the original network). Figure 11 illustrates a case where metallic bay partially occludes the PCB, thus the network is misidentifying PCB as bay as well. This is due to fact that the PCBs that were in the HDD image dataset had nothing on

Fig. 11. Predicted mask by the component segmentation performed on a GPU. Left image depicts an incorrectly identified component, whereas the right image depicts a correctly identified one. Portion of PCB pixels play a pivotal role in segmentation of the PCB.

them, contrary to the GPU, where it is very likely to be a metallic bay and/or cooling unit over the PCB, and making PCB features less dominant. Similarly, in the same figure, the lower image shows a correctly identified and segmented PCB. Since most of the PCB was visible. The network was able to associate it with the learned PCB features.

The wire detection network was found to be the critical one here. Although it performs remarkably well on the GPU wires (see Table 6, line 1), features that resemble wires are also detected as wires. Since the context information is not there, the wire detector considers non-wire pixels as wires, as illustrated in Fig. 12, where cooling pipes of the GPU are considered as wires.

Fig. 12. Predicted mask by the wire detection, incorrectly marking wire-like objects as wires. Metallic pipes are one example of such objects.

Experiment E2. Experiment E2 aims to assess the capabilities of each module by performing visual tasks on raw HDD and GPU images with re-training involved. The training data used is set to 50% of the entire GPU training data (in addition to the existing HDD data). Table 6, line 2 reports the accuracy per module.

For screws, 50 new cropped images of screw heads belonging to GPUs were included in the dataset. The screw detector and screw classifier scores peaked, ensuring an accurate detection and classification. Therefore, it is concluded that 50 new images for screw detection and screw classification networks are sufficient for the GPU. There is a different case for the component segmentation network. This one started to predict meaningful masks for the PCB, as it was trained with extra 50 images of annotated GPU components (bay, PCB). Figure 13a shows a sample output where correctly identified PCB borders are following the correct edges of the PCB component. Note that the network is trying to avoid predicting on the irrelevant or unexpected pixels that correspond to the white plastic attachment found on the PCB. The module reports 0.78 Mean-F score, which is equal to the original 0.78 but higher than the E1 score of it, 0.71. Note that the original network was trained on 600 HDD images. Therefore, newly introduced 50 GPU images do make a difference in terms of generalizing.

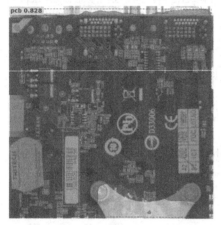

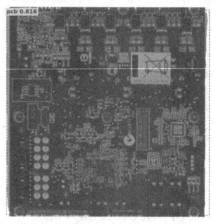

(a) Predicted mask by the component segmentation performed on a GPU. The model has been trained with 50% of GPU training data.

(b) Predicted mask by the component segmentation performed on a GPU. The model has been trained with 100% of GPU training data.

Fig. 13. Results of the component segmentation in E3: the model is evaluated on GPU images with partial or complete retraining on the GPU data.

Additionally, it was observed that the wire detection network accuracy changes positively on insignificant levels.

Experiment E3. Experiment E3 differs from the previous experiment (E2) on the amount of new data for re-training. The training data used is set to 100% of the entire training data (in addition to the existing HDD data): 100 new annotated GPU images, plus 1000 screw images (cropped from these GPU images). Table 6, line 3 reports the accuracy per module. After re-training the networks, it was noted that there is a substantial improvement for the component segmentation module, where the network was observably learning the features encountered in GPUs and showing the ability to generalize. Figure 13b depicts an example where the entire PCB was correctly identified (with a prediction score of 0.846) and segmented accordingly.

Similarly to E2, highly accurate screw detection and classification abilities were observed. Features that were learnt enough for the network to capture the screws. It must be remembered that the mentioned data augmentation functions in the screw classification module generates synthetic data out of limited images and fills in the gaps in data. Therefore, it is observed that re-training the screw detection and classification networks with a small number of images is quite possible.

Wire detection network accuracy was almost the same with the previous experiment's, no change observed in behaviors either. This is due to the fact that not all GPU models had wires and thus, the newly introduced GPU images had either no wires, or wires that were very easy to detect as illustrated in Fig. 14.

After conducting series of experiments to assess the generalization capability of the scheme, it can be concluded that the scheme generalises the learnt knowledge to an unseen device by acceptable margins. It was found out that visual commonalities (similar features) play a big role in generalization. Experiment E1 proved that PCB components in both GPU and HDD were mostly identified and segmented correctly, and drew the aforementioned conclusion. Some of the incorrect identifications and segments were there due to the fact that the PCBs were occluded by bays. Experiment E2 proved that introducing training data by 50% (on top of the existing data) definitely increases the accuracy of segmentation on PCBs, as illustrated in Fig. 13a. Screw related capabilities were remarkably improved even in E2, with less data. Experiment E3 showed that the component segmentation is the module that reacts to the training data most. This was associated with the fact that other modules have plenty of training images, whereas the original image dataset for the component segmentation consisted of around 600 annotated images. Therefore, introducing 100 new images does make a difference for the retraining. The fine prediction of the edge features were noted as shown in Fig. 13b, as well as more correct identification of components.

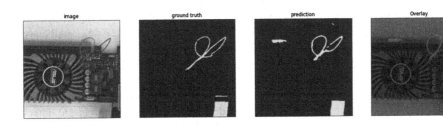

Fig. 14. Wire Detection output during the experiment E3. All wires were correctly identified.

It is acknowledged that the improvement could only be observed for each module as shown in Table 6. Wire detection proved itself to be extremely robust, scoring high in E1, and obviously in E2 and E3. Gap detection had to be skipped for the experiments involving GPUs as there is no gap entity in this EOL device. It must be also noted that not all collected images were able to contain the entire view of the GPU, since the camera lens and the setup height were initially chosen for operating with HDDs. Therefore, the acquired results are the reported predictions on images that partially contain GPUs in their view, as illustrated in the referred figures. While this is not an issue, the optimal scheme would have to operate with a view that contains the chosen EOL device from a reasonable height, proportional to the dimensions of the device.

6 Discussion and Conclusion

In this paper, we presented an extended visual intelligence scheme to analyze a disassembly scene and extract the composition of parts inside a device. We proposed new wire detection and inherited a screw classification method published [48], and, additionally a bookkeeping mechanism that compares the analysis results of consecutive scenes to find out the abnormalities that may be caused by manipulation errors (e.g., end-effector dropping the grasped PCB back into the scene).

We pointed out that the wire detection problem itself is a challenging one, since wires have variable physical properties such as geometry, color, thickness and not every electronic device has the same type of wires. We mentioned that these were the challenging features because of which the previously developed methods were not useful as a general solution to this problem. We proposed a model, which is based on the heavy augmentation and deep convolutional neural networks. The proposed model easily lets the user use the system for any device of his/her choice, as long as the user manages to collect a limited number of hand-annotated images, which we found out to be approximately 130 for accurate detection. We conducted an investigation with the-state-of-the-art models and picked EfficientNetB7 based on the results of a use case we selected for the evaluation of these models. After picking the model, we collected a limited amount of dedicated data using real wire backgrounds that can be found in disassembly environments. We generated a massive amount of data via our datagen block and trained the model from the scratch (e.g., no transfer learning), we could demonstrate that the model achieves high accuracy on scenes with random wires on the GPUs which were not seen by the network before. Our evaluation was quantified with testing images of disassembly scenes, containing different models and sizes of wires. Additionally, we pointed out that wire-looking parts such as pipes are also detected by the wire detector we propose, which we note as a limitation. Increasing the amount of annotated training data with scenes including pipes could potentially help the model.

The screw classification inherited has the default shortcomings mentioned in its original paper [48]. Replacing the initial circle detection method (Hough circle detector) with a more robust circle detector would help. Although using another DCNN is an option for circle detection, increasing the amount of required training data is not always preferable. Therefore, replacing the Hough circle detector with another method based on classical computer vision is advised. Additionally, through our experiment we discovered that color plays a pivotal role in screw classification.

The part recognition is found to be the least directly generalizing component and requires collection, annotation and retraining for other class of devices. This is a foreseeable result as it is the component that learns about the specific components in a device. However, the HDD use case offers a wide range of parts that can also be found in other devices (e.g., PCB, lid, bay), even if they have different appearances. We evaluated the performance of each module of the extended visual scheme on a second device

-GPU- and quantified the results, proving that the extended scheme indeed generalizes even without any new training data. We showed the impact of the additional training data and quantified the results by conducting experiments, accordingly. The dataset as well as the implementation are going to be published to facilitate further research.

In conclusion, the extended scheme is designed to complete the required objectives. To our knowledge, it is the first visual intelligence scheme that has the demonstrated capabilities for automated disassembly. Therefore, the novel contribution of this work is promising for recycling plants that are likely to use robotic systems. As of this writing, there is a prototype developed and demonstrated[1] as one of the milestones of the IMAGINE project[2,3].

Acknowledgment. The research leading to these results has received funding from the European Union's Horizon 2020 research and innovation programme under grant agreement no. 731761, IMAGINE. We would like to also express our gratitude to Maik Bergamos and Electrocycling GmbH for the data and hardware used in this work as well as their expertise on the recycling domain.

References

1. Bailey-Van Kuren, M.: Automated demanufacturing studies in detecting and destroying, threaded connections for processing electronic waste. In: Conference Record 2002 IEEE International Symposium on Electronics and the Environment (Cat. No.02CH37273), pp. 295–298 (2002). https://doi.org/10.1109/ISEE.2002.1003283

2. Bdiwi, M., Rashid, A., Putz, M.: Autonomous disassembly of electric vehicle motors based on robot cognition. In: Proceedings—IEEE International Conference on Robotics and Automation 2016-June(July), 2500–2505 (2016). https://doi.org/10.1109/ICRA.2016.7487404

3. Bisong, E.: Google colaboratory. In: Building Machine Learning and Deep Learning Models on Google Cloud Platform, pp. 59–64. Springer, Berlin (2019)

4. Buslaev, A., Iglovikov, V.I., Khvedchenya, E., Parinov, A., Druzhinin, M., Kalinin, A.A.: Albumentations: fast and flexible image augmentations. Information **11**(2), 125 (2020)

5. Dai, J., He, K., Sun, J.: Instance-aware semantic segmentation via multi-task network cascades. In: Proceedings of the IEEE Conference on Computer Vision and Pattern Recognition, pp. 3150–3158 (2016)

6. Deng, J., Dong, W., Socher, R., Li, L.J., Li, K., Fei-Fei, L.: Imagenet: a large-scale hierarchical image database. In: 2009 IEEE conference on computer vision and pattern recognition, pp. 248–255. IEEE (2009)

7. Dutta, A., Zisserman, A.: The VIA annotation software for images, audio and video. In: Proceedings of the 27th ACM International Conference on Multimedia. MM '19, ACM, New York, NY, USA (2019). https://doi.org/10.1145/3343031.3350535

8. Dvornik, N., Shmelkov, K., Mairal, J., Schmid, C.: Blitznet: A real-time deep network for scene understanding. In: Proceedings of the IEEE International Conference on Computer Vision, pp. 4154–4162 (2017)

---

[1] https://www.youtube.com/watch?v=m8aEZnSdiCA.

[2] By the time this demonsration took place, the extended modules were not included yet. However, the final prototype does include wire detection and screw classification modules.

[3] http://www.electrocycling.de.

9. ElSayed, A., Kongar, E., Gupta, S.M., Sobh, T.: A robotic-driven disassembly sequence generator for end-of-life electronic products. J. Intell. Robot. Syst. **68**(1), 43–52 (2012)

10. Everingham, M., Van Gool, L., Williams, C.K.I., Winn, J., Zisserman, A.: The pascal visual object classes (VOC) challenge. Int. J. Comput. Vision **88**(2), 303–338 (2010). https://doi.org/10.1007/s11263-009-0275-4

11. Fu, C.Y., Shvets, M., Berg, A.C.: Retinamask: learning to predict masks improves state-of-the-art single-shot detection for free (2019). arXiv:1901.03353

12. Gil, P., Pomares, J., Diaz, S.V.P.C., Candelas, F., Torres, F.: Flexible multi-sensorial system for automatic disassembly using cooperative robots. Int. J. Comput. Integr. Manuf. **20**(8), 757–772 (2007)

13. Gil, P., Torres, F., Ortiz, F., Reinoso, O.: Detection of partial occlusions of assembled components to simplify the disassembly tasks. Int. J. Adv. Manuf. Technol. **30**(5–6), 530–539 (2006)

14. Girshick, R.: Fast R-CNN. In: Proceedings of the IEEE International Conference on Computer Vision, pp. 1440–1448 (2015)

15. Girshick, R., Donahue, J., Darrell, T., Malik, J.: Rich feature hierarchies for accurate object detection and semantic segmentation. In: Proceedings of the IEEE Conference on Computer Vision and Pattern Recognition, pp. 580–587 (2014)

16. He, K., Gkioxari, G., Dollár, P., Girshick, R.: Mask R-CNN. In: Proceedings of the IEEE International Conference on Computer Vision, pp. 2961–2969 (2017)

17. Hendrycks, D., Mu, N., Cubuk, E.D., Zoph, B., Gilmer, J., Lakshminarayanan, B.: Augmix: a simple data processing method to improve robustness and uncertainty (2019). arXiv:1912.02781

18. Hu, J., Shen, L., Sun, G.: Squeeze-and-excitation networks. In: Proceedings of the IEEE Conference on Computer Vision and Pattern Recognition, pp. 7132–7141 (2018)

19. Huang, G., Liu, Z., van der Maaten, L., Weinberger, K.Q.: Densely connected convolutional networks (2016)

20. Jahanian, A., Le, Q.H., Youcef-Toumi, K., Tsetserukou, D.: See the e-waste! training visual intelligence to see dense circuit boards for recycling. In: Proceedings of the IEEE Conference on Computer Vision and Pattern Recognition Workshops (2019)

21. Kasturi, R., Camps, O., Huang, Y., Narasimhamurthy, A., Pande, N.: Wire detection algorithms for navigation. NASA Technical report (2002)

22. Krizhevsky, A., Sutskever, I., Hinton, G.E.: Imagenet classification with deep convolutional neural networks. In: Advances in Neural Information Processing Systems, pp. 1097–1105 (2012)

23. Li, Y., Qi, H., Dai, J., Ji, X., Wei, Y.: Fully convolutional instance-aware semantic segmentation. In: Proceedings of the IEEE Conference on Computer Vision and Pattern Recognition, pp. 2359–2367 (2017)

24. Lin, D., et al.: ZigzagNet: fusing top-down and bottom-up context for object segmentation. In: Proceedings of the IEEE Conference on Computer Vision and Pattern Recognition, pp. 7490–7499 (2019)

25. Lin, T.Y., Dollár, P., Girshick, R., He, K., Hariharan, B., Belongie, S.: Feature pyramid networks for object detection. In: Proceedings of the IEEE Conference on Computer Vision and Pattern Recognition, pp. 2117–2125 (2017)

26. Lin, T.-Y., et al.: Microsoft COCO: common objects in context. In: Fleet, D., Pajdla, T., Schiele, B., Tuytelaars, T. (eds.) ECCV 2014. LNCS, vol. 8693, pp. 740–755. Springer, Cham (2014). https://doi.org/10.1007/978-3-319-10602-1_48

27. Liu, S., Qi, L., Qin, H., Shi, J., Jia, J.: Path aggregation network for instance segmentation. In: Proceedings of the IEEE Conference on Computer Vision and Pattern Recognition, pp. 8759–8768 (2018)
28. Madaan, R., Maturana, D., Scherer, S.: Wire detection using synthetic data and dilated convolutional networks for unmanned aerial vehicles. In: International Conference on Intelligent Robots and Systems (2017)
29. Malamas, E.N., Petrakis, E.G., Zervakis, M., Petit, L., Legat, J.D.: A survey on industrial vision systems, applications and tools. Image Vis. Comput. **21**(2), 171–188 (2003)
30. Pomares, J., Puente, S., Torres, F., Candelas, F., Gil, P.: Virtual disassembly of products based on geometric models. Comput. Ind. **55**(1), 1–14 (2004)
31. Ren, S., He, K., Girshick, R., Sun, J.: Faster R-CNN: Towards real-time object detection with region proposal networks. In: Advances in Neural Information Processing Systems, pp. 91–99 (2015)
32. Ronneberger, O., Fischer, P., Brox, T.: U-net: convolutional networks for biomedical image segmentation (2015)
33. Szegedy, C., Ioffe, S., Vanhoucke, V., Alemi, A.: Inception-v4, inception-resnet and the impact of residual connections on learning (2016)
34. Szegedy, C., Vanhoucke, V., Ioffe, S., Shlens, J., Wojna, Z.: Rethinking the inception architecture for computer vision (2015)
35. Takahashi, R., Matsubara, T., Uehara, K.: Data augmentation using random image cropping and patching for deep CNNs. IEEE Trans. Circuits Syst. Video Technol. **30**(9), 2917–2931 (2019)
36. Tan, M., Le, Q.V.: Efficientnet: rethinking model scaling for convolutional neural networks (2019)
37. Tonko, M., Nagel, H.H.: Model-based stereo-tracking of non-polyhedral objects for automatic disassembly experiments. Int. J. Comput. Vis. **37**(1), 99–118 (2000)
38. Torres, F., Puente, S., Aracil, R.: Disassembly planning based on precedence relations among assemblies. Int. J. Adv. Manuf. Technol. **21**(5), 317–327 (2003). https://doi.org/10.1007/s001700300037
39. Ukida, H.: Visual defect inspection of rotating screw heads. In: SICE Annual Conference 2007, pp. 1478–1483. IEEE (2007)
40. United Nations Envrionment Programme, P., ITU, I., UNIDO, U.N.U.: A new circular vision for electronics time for a global reboot (2019)
41. Wang, Z., Bovik, A.C., Sheikh, H.R., Simoncelli, E.P.: Image quality assessment: from error visibility to structural similarity. IEEE Trans. Image Process. **13**(4), 600–612 (2004)
42. Weigl-Seitz, A., Hohm, K., Seitz, M., Tolle, H.: On strategies and solutions for automated disassembly of electronic devices. Int. J. Adv. Manuf. Technol. **30**(5–6), 561–573 (2006). https://doi.org/10.1007/s00170-005-0043-8
43. Xie, S.Q., Cheng, D., Wong, S., Haemmerle, E.: Three-dimensional object recognition system for enhancing the intelligence of a KUKA robot. Int. J. Adv. Manuf. Technol. **38**(7–8), 822–839 (2008). https://doi.org/10.1007/s00170-007-1112-y
44. Yakubovskiy, P.: Segmentation models (2019). github.com/qubvel/segmentation models
45. Yang, J., et al.: Arsenic burden in e-waste recycling workers-a cross-sectional study at the agbogbloshie e-waste recycling site Ghana. Chemosphere **261**, 127712 (2020)
46. Yildiz, E., et al.: A visual intelligence scheme for hard drive disassembly in automated recycling routines. In: Proceedings of the International Conference on Robotics, Computer Vision and Intelligent Systems - Volume 1: ROBOVIS, pp. 17–27. INSTICC, SciTePress (2020). https://doi.org/10.5220/0010016000170027

47. Yildiz, E., Wörgötter, F.: DCNN-based screw detection for automated disassembly processes. In: 2019 15th International Conference on Signal-Image Technology & Internet-Based Systems (SITIS), pp. 187–192. IEEE (2019)

48. Yildiz., E., Wörgötter., F.: DCNN-based screw classification in automated disassembly processes. In: Proceedings of the International Conference on Robotics, Computer Vision and Intelligent Systems - Volume 1: ROBOVIS, pp. 61–68. INSTICC, SciTePress (2020). https://doi.org/10.5220/0009979900610068

49. Yu, F., Koltun, V.: Multi-scale context aggregation by dilated convolutions (2015). arXiv:1511.07122

Multi-agent Path Finding and Acting with Small Reflex-Based Mobile Robots

Ján Chudý, Nestor Popov, and Pavel Surynek[✉]

Faculty of Information Technology, Czech Technical University in Prague,
Thákurova 9, 160 00 Praha 6, Czechia
{chudyja1,popovnes,pavel.surynek}@fit.cvut.cz

Abstract. Multi-agent pathfinding (MAPF) represents a core problem in robotics. In its abstract form, the task is to navigate agents in an undirected graph to individual goal vertices so that conflicts between agents do not occur. Many algorithms for finding feasible or optimal solutions have been devised. We focus on the execution of MAPF solutions with a swarm of simple physical robots. Such execution is important for understanding how abstract plans can be transferred into reality and vital for educational demonstrations. We show how to use a swarm of reflex-based Ozobot Evo robots for MAPF execution. We emulate centralized control of the robots using their reflex-based behavior by putting them on a screen's surface, where control curves are drawn in real-time during the execution. In this way, we bridge the gap between simple discrete planning phase and continuous acting phase. We identify critical challenges and ways to address them to execute plans successfully with the swarm. The MAPF execution was evaluated experimentally on various benchmarks. We also compare our new reflex-based execution with compilation-based approach.

Keywords: Multi-agent pathfinding (MAPF) · Centralized control · Swarm of robots · Reflex-based control · Automated planning · Acting

1 Introduction

Multi-agent pathfinding problem (MAPF) is a task of finding paths for multiple agents from their initial positions to their goal positions while ensuring that they do not collide at any point in their path execution [9,16–18,20,22,27]. The abstract form of the MAPF problem assumes an undirected graph $G = (V, E)$ that models the environment. We assume multiple distinguishable agents placed in vertices of G such that at most one agent is placed in each vertex. Agents can be moved between vertices across edges, while problem-specific rules must not be violated. MAPF usually assumes that agents are moved to unoccupied neighbors only. The task of MAPF is to reach a given goal configuration of agents from a given starting configuration using valid movements.

Due to its real-world applications, MAPF has been a deeply researched topic over recent years. New variations of this problem and approaches to solving them, emerged, and new solving algorithms have been designed. Many practical problems from robotics

© Springer Nature Switzerland AG 2022
P. Galambos et al. (Eds.): ROBOVIS 2020/ROBOVIS 2021, CCIS 1667, pp. 51–75, 2022.
https://doi.org/10.1007/978-3-031-19650-8_3

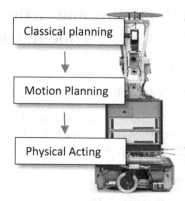

Fig. 1. Shakey the robot: the first notable implementation of planning and acting.

can be interpreted as MAPF. Applications can be found in discrete multi-robot navigation and coordination, automated warehousing [30], transport [13], or coordination and maneuvering of aerial vehicles [31].

However, most of the solutions are tested in the virtual environment. Although this type of simulation is suitable for theoretical research and agile solver benchmarking, it is not sufficient to understand how abstract plans can be transferred into reality. It might also not be the most exciting for students or someone interested in understanding this topic. Moreover, using physical robots usually requires a fundamentally different approach to solving MAPF problems.

The major challenge faced during the execution of abstract plans on real robotic hardware is that most of the contemporary MAPF solvers produce discrete plans, while physical robots act continuously in a continuous environment. The viability of discrete MAPF solvers is that existing solvers for the continuous multi-robot motion planning do not scale for a large number of robots [19], and finding the optimal robot trajectories is often unattainable.

Planning and acting has been first notably introduced in now legendary Shakey the robot [10] (see Fig. 1). The notable difference in our research is that instead of single robot we are implementing the planning-acting chain for a swarm of robots.

1.1 Contribution

This paper describes a novel approach to simulating the existing MAPF algorithms using a swarm of small mobile robots–Ozobot Evo. This robot is equipped with simple reflex-based control and relatively limited programming capabilities. Precisely, Ozobot can follow a curve drawn on a surface and has its reflex-based behavior modified using a small set of instructions. We used these capabilities to emulate centralized control by placing the swarm on a screen's surface, where control curves are displayed to navigate the robots in real-time. The novel approach aims to:

– Verify if discrete plans can be successfully executed on a swarm of physical robots that move continuously.

– Create a scalable solution for a large number of robotic agents that can utilize contemporary MAPF solvers.
– Provide researchers and educators with an affordable solution for testing and demonstrating their findings in the physical world.

This paper extends the conference version [3]. We extend the conference paper with more detailed description of the development of control curves and their animation to navigate the robots. In addition to this we add a completely new evaluation of compilation-based approach in which discrete plans are compiled into sequences of primitive commands that are directly uploaded to robots.

The paper is organized as follows. In Sects. 2 and 3, we introduce MAPF formally and recall major solving algorithms. Then Ozobot Evo, a robot we use for execution, is described in Sect. 4. In Sects. 5 and 6, we introduce the execution of MAPF solution on a swarm of Ozobot Evo robots through reflex-based control. Experimental evaluation of swarm executions on various MAPF benchmarks is presented in Sect. 7. In this section the compilation-based approach is evaluated too.

2 Overview of MAPF

Almost all of the previous MAPF research and proposed solvers were built on top of several assumptions about time and agents:

– Time is not continuous, but rather *discretized* into time steps.
– Agents can move to any direction and their actions take the same amount of time to execute, precisely one time step.
– Agents are of the same size and shape and occupy a single point in the environment representation.

2.1 Classical Discrete MAPF

The classical MAPF problem [16,20] is modeled on an undirected graph $G = (V, E)$ with a set of agents $A = \{a_1, a_2, ..., a_k\}$ such that $|A| < |V|$. Each agent is placed in a vertex so that at most one agent occupies each vertex. The configuration of agents is denoted $\alpha : A \rightarrow V$. Next, we are given a starting configuration of agents α_0 and a goal configuration α_+.

An agent can either *move* to an adjacent vertex or *wait* in its current vertex at each time step. The task is to find a sequence of move/wait actions for each agent a_i that moves the agent from $\alpha_0(a_i)$ to $\alpha_+(a_i)$ such that agents do not *collide*[1]. So an agent can move into a vertex only if it is unoccupied, and no other agent enters it at the same time. Different constraints might be applied in various MAPF problems as well. An example of a MAPF problem instance is shown in Fig. 2.

Below, we define a classical *move-to-unoccupied* variant of MAPF.

Definition 1 (Move-to-unoccupied MAPF). *Configuration α' results from α if and only if the following conditions hold:*

---

[1] We understand a *collision* when at least two agents occupy the same vertex simultaneously.

Fig. 2. A MAPF problem instance with three agents a_1, a_2, and a_3 [3].

(i) $\alpha(a) = \alpha'(a)$ or $\{\alpha(a), \alpha'(a)\} \in E$ *for all* $a \in A$ *(agents move along the edges or wait in the current vertex);*

(ii) *for all* $a \in A$ *it holds that if* $\alpha(a) \neq \alpha'(a) \Rightarrow \alpha'(a) \neq \alpha(a')$ *for all* $a' \in A$ *(target vertex must be unoccupied);*

(iii) *and for all* $a, a' \in A$ *it holds that if* $a \neq a' \Rightarrow \alpha'(a) \neq \alpha'(a')$ *(no two agents enter the same vertex).*

Solving the MAPF instance is to find a sequence of configurations $[\alpha_0, \alpha_1, ..., \alpha_\mu]$ such that α_{i+1} results from α_i for $i = 1, 2, ..., \mu - 1$ using only valid actions, and $\alpha_\mu = \alpha_+$. A *feasible solution* of a solvable MAPF instance can be found in polynomial time [9,29]. Precisely the worst-case time complexity of most practical algorithms for finding feasible solutions is $\mathcal{O}(|V|^3)$ (asymptotic size of the solution is also $\mathcal{O}(|V|^3)$) [12].

2.2 Cumulative Objectives in MAPF

Various objectives are used to evaluate the quality of a solution. The most common objectives are *makespan* and *sum-of-costs*. With the *makespan* [24], we need to minimize μ in the solution sequence mentioned after Definition 1. Below, we define the *sum-of-costs* objective [4,17,18]:

Definition 2 (Sum-of-costs Objective). *The sum-of-costs objective is the summation, over all agents, of the number of time steps required to reach the goal vertex. Denoted* ξ, *where* $\xi = \sum_{i=1}^{k} \xi(path(a_i))$, *where* $\xi(path(a_i))$ *is an individual path cost of agent* a_i *connecting* $\alpha_0(a_i)$ *calculated as the number of edge traversals and wait actions.*[2]

Finding an optimal solution with respect to the sum-of-costs objective is NP-hard [14].

2.3 Real-World Complications

Besides the already mentioned assumptions, the environment is usually modeled as an undirected graph or a tiled grid. Even though this can often be sufficient even for a real-world scenario, the reality is not generally that easy to model. Also, physical agents have

---

[2] The notation $path(a_i)$ refers to a path in the form of a sequence of vertices and edges connecting $\alpha_0(a_i)$ and $\alpha_+(a_i)$, while ξ assigns the cost to a given path.

their specific form, and they can collide in many different ways–they are geometrical. Different agent representation and collision detection are therefore needed if pursuing a more realistic model. Geometry-aware collision detection for agents of different shapes, speeds, and continuous movements is studied in [1]. Also, a study [11] solely around this concept of geometrical agents was done. In that work, authors refer to such agents as *large agents*, and they formalize and study a *MAPF for large agents*, then propose a new algorithm for this problem.

Actions of physical agents do not usually take the same time, and they do not merely snap between positions in the environment instantaneously, as in the discrete approach. The agents require continuous movement to reposition. Continuous MAPF can adequately accommodate this problem, but also other approaches might sufficiently simulate the fluid transfer of agents.

In the classical MAPF, the agents can move in any direction for every time step of the plan. Even though this might be true for some agents like drones, this is not true for most mobile agents moving on the ground. When an agent wants to change the direction of movement, it must rotate what takes some time and adds to the plan desynchronization. These rotation movements can also be incorporated in the MAPF abstraction, as proposed in [2]. The authors suggest splitting *position vertices* into *directional vertices*, which represent the direction the agent is facing. Edges between these new vertices represent rotation actions and original edges movements between the original vertices. This change also requires a modification in the solver, namely in conflict detection. The study's primary purpose was to test the behavior of several defined MAPF models when executed on physical robots. The experiments concluded that classical MAPF plans are not suitable for such use, and some of the other proposed models yielded better results than the classical one.

3   Optimal MAPF Solvers

We use optimal solutions with respect to the sum-of-costs objective in our prototype of the novel approach. There are several solvers used for fining od optimal MAPF solutions based on different paradigms. There are currently two major streams of optimal solvers for MAPF: **(i) search-based** solvers and **(ii) compilation-based** solvers.

Search-based solvers are often variants of A* search [21], but also other than common search spaces derived from actions are used. The notable examples are ICTS [18] or textsc [17]. These algorithms implement a two-level search. In the ICTS, distributions of the cost to individual agents are searched at the high-level search. The low-level search of the algorithm tries to find non-conflicting paths for individual agents that follow the cost distributions. On the other hand, the ICTS algorithm performs a search across all possible conflicts between agents at the high-level, and at the low-level paths that avoid the conflicts are assigned to individual agents.

Compilation-based solvers reduce the MAPF problem instance to an instance in a different paradigm for which an efficient solver exists. Such target paradigms include Boolean satisfiability (SAT) [23], constraint satisfaction problem (CSP) [7,15], or answer set programming (ASP) [8]. The major challenge in using compilation-based methods is designing the encoding of MAPF in the target formalism.

3.1   SAT Based Solver

The *SAT-based solver* [26] transforms an instance of a MAPF problem into a *propositional formula* that is satisfiable only if the MAPF problem is solvable. This formula can be consulted with an already existing state-of-the-art SAT solver. When the *satisfying assignment* is found, the solution of the MAPF problem can be reconstructed from this assignment. Therefore, the main challenge is the encoding of the MAPF problem into a propositional formula.

The primary concept, allowing the encoding of a MAPF problem into a propositional formula, is a *time expansion graph* (TEG) of the original graph from the problem instance. The TEG is created by duplicating all vertices from the original graph for all time steps from 0 to a given bound μ. This can be imagined as a layered graph where each layer of vertices represents an individual time step. Then all possible actions are represented by directed edges between consecutive layers. An edge between corresponding vertices in two layers represent a *wait action*, while an edge between neighboring vertices in the layers represent a *move action*. This TEG is created for each agent. In the encoding, a *propositional variable* is introduced for each of the vertices of these new graphs. The variable is *true* if the agent occupies the vertex at the time step that the variable represents. Similarly, each directed edge is encoded, and other constraints are added so that the found satisfying assignments correspond to a valid MAPF solution. However, because of the bound μ of the TEG, the encoded formula can only be satisfied if a solution that takes up to μ time steps exists. Note that this corresponds to the makespan of the solution.

The optimal solver repeatedly asks the SAT solver, if a solution of a certain makespan, which is incremented in a loop, exists. When it finally finds a solution, this solution has the lowest possible makespan and therefore is optimal. First, a lower bound makespan of the MAPF solution is determined by finding the optimal single-agent pathfinding solutions for each agent, which can be done very efficiently. The makespan of the MAPF solution cannot be lower than the longest path of these agents. For each increment of μ, the problem is encoded into a propositional formula $\mathcal{F}(\mu)$, and consulted with the SAT solver. If the formula could not be satisfied, μ incremented, and a new formula is created. If a satisfying assignment has been found, the MAPF solution is extracted from this assignment and returned.

The framework, how it is described, is not complete because if a solution to a given MAPF instance does not exist, the solver would never stop. The existence of a solution is usually checked with another algorithm, for example, Push-and-Rotate [28].

4   Physical Robot: Ozobot Evo

Ozobot Evo [5] is a small, reflex-based robot without an internal state. Compared to other robots used in research like *e-puck* or *Khepera*, Ozobot is simple and limited, but also affordable. An image of the Ozobot Evo can be found in Fig. 3, and its sensor layout is visualized in Fig. 4.

The primary capability of Ozobot is to follow lines. Its reflex-based behavior can also be altered, and it can be done in two different ways–*Color Codes* and *OzoBlockly*. Color Codes are instruction markers on lines that can be read by the robot, and

Fig. 3. Ozobot Evo (photo from [5]).

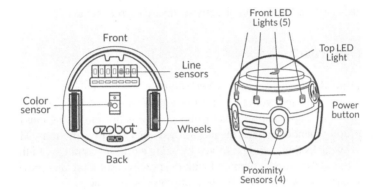

Fig. 4. Sensor layout of Ozobot Evo (photo from [6]).

OzoBlockly is a visual coding editor providing a set of movement and sensory instructions.

Two main factors were considered when choosing this particular robot for the task:

- We want to test the limits of our proposed approach, and if it is possible to deploy discrete MAPF solutions on such primitive hardware.
- Building large swarms of Ozobot Evo robots is more affordable.

4.1 Important Hardware

The *motor and wheels* provide the robot with mobility. Ozobot turns by moving the wheels separately at different speeds.

Under the base of the robot are several *line sensors* and an optical *color sensor*. The purpose of these sensors is to detect lines, intersections, and surface color. The color sensor can distinguish eight different colors. Ozobot is highly dependent on this sensor because it allows the robot to read *Color Codes*, and it is also used to load *OzoBlockly* programs into the robot. Four *infrared proximity sensors* can be used to detect an object as far as 10 cm from the robot.

4.2 Movement and Line Following

The essential reflex functionality of Ozobot we used in our approach is following lines drawn on the surface of the physical environment. By default, Ozobot follows lines at a default speed of 30 mm/s. When the line is lost, it stops its movement. At each line intersection, Ozobot chooses one of the possible directions at random, with all the possibilities having the same probability of being chosen. It is important to know that Ozobot does not register a 90-degree turn as an intersection. While following lines, Ozobot will also read and execute *Color Codes* if found.

The accuracy of the optical sensors is limited, and sensors need to be calibrated to ensure better functionality. This is especially true when there is a change in the display brightness or the surrounding light conditions. Line parameters, like line thickness or angle of turns, also need to be set correctly to ensure correct behavior.

5   Novel Approach

Previous solution deploying discrete MAPF solutions on physical robots based on compilation from is simple and works fine for the comparison of MAPF models. However, because of how that approach utilizes Ozobots, there is not much that can be done to enhance the deployment or expand the usability to other MAPF variations. Moreover, it has several drawbacks that could be solved by using a different strategy. In this section, a novel approach is proposed, compared with the previous solution, and previous drawbacks are explained as well as how the new approach solves them.

5.1   ESO-NAV: Reflex-Based Navigation

The main idea of this novel MAPF deployment approach is to have robots with *fixed reflex behavior* and an *environment that can output information* for the robots, affecting their behavior and controlling them in effect. The environment is a physical representation of a given MAPF problem instance that can navigate the agents in itself by showing them the planned paths and additional information. The plans are obtained from a *centralized MAPF solver* and then processed for the execution in the environment. Since the less constrained MAPF solvers are more efficient than the sophisticated multi-robot motion planning solvers, we hope to make the planning part of the deployment more efficient and scalable for large number of robots. The computational complexity of the system is, therefore, shifted towards solution postprocessing and execution. We call our approach *Navigation by Environment Surface Outputs* (ESO-NAV).

In our prototype, the environment is represented by the surface of a screen capable of providing outputs for Ozobots. A grid map of a MAPF problem instance is displayed on the screen, and the planned paths are animated for the robots. The behavior of the agents can be determined with a simple *OzoBlockly program* loaded into each robot. This approach provides freedom of creating a more sophisticated and highly customizable MAPF simulation.

5.2 Improvements from Previous Work

There are two significant improvements compared to the previous approach [2].

(i) **Synchronization of Simulation Start.** In the previous solution, the map of the problem instance was constructed from the following lines, which leads Ozobots into movement. The execution had to be initiated manually, so scalability for multiple robots is limited. Since robots in ESO-NAV are regarded as entirely reflex, the previous issues with synchronization of the execution start can be easily solved. Before the start, the environment does not output any paths, and robots can *initiate waiting* in that situation. Additionally, ESO-NAV provides more *flexibility* in environment representation and map design since the planned paths are only a piece of extra information. The novel approach could be used for environments that are not grid-based, and the paths could be continuous curves instead of straight lines between positions.

(ii) **No Need to Memorize the Plan in Advance.** Another factor we consider to be an improvement from the previous approach is that robots entirely modular for all problem instances. In the ESO-NAV approach, the robots can be quickly used on different maps without changing their programming. The paths can even be replanned during the execution without the agents noticing. This allows simulation of sub-optimal MAPF solutions optimized during the agent execution, or replanning can be performed if agents fail to follow their paths. Moreover, different behaviors of agents can be tested and compared with this approach.

5.3 Expected Problems

Some of the *real-world complications* are still concerning this novel approach, but the complications can be mitigated by correct path processing and outputting. The robot *collisions* can still be an issue, even if a MAPF solver finds a valid solution. The environment needs to be designed so that agents can move around each other without any contact. Incorrect path processing and outputting can also introduce conflicts that are unanticipated and would interrupt the execution. The biggest challenge remains the fact that different robot movements take different time durations, creating *desynchronization* in the plan execution. However, the ESO-NAV approach with the use of Ozobots provides various ways of solving this desynchronization issue without modifying the MAPF solver nor the problem abstraction.

6 From Discrete Planning to Physical Acting

In this section, a working prototype of the ESO-NAV approach to MAPF simulation that utilizes Ozobots is presented. The prototype can take a MAPF problem instance in the form of a map and execute the solution on the robots. The prototype in fact implements the planning-acting chain as known from the times of Shakey on homogeneous multi-robot system consisting Ozobots. The prototype implementation is the first step towards making research in balancing the complexity of planning and acting phase in MAPF problem.

6.1   Overview

The prototype application could be divided into several modules that interact with each other during the execution. Most of these modules should be easy to modify or extend to simulate different MAPF models or situations. The program takes a map file that contains the MAPF problem instance to be executed. The problem is passed to the SAT-based MAPF solver which computes a discrete solution. This solution contains paths for individual agents that should be animated in the environment. The main simulation module then takes the discrete solution and transforms it to continuous animation which is outputted in the environment. The animated outputs should make the robots execute their planned paths in the reflex-based style without any manual interference.

6.2   Environment

During the simulation, the *abstract discrete* representations of environment and plans need to be transformed into the *physical map and continuous animation*. This is done by displaying the map on the screen on which the Ozobots can move. For this prototype, *grid-based maps* were chosen to be used and can be displayed as tiles. If there is not an edge between two neighboring vertices in the original graph, a *wall* is displayed on the map between the corresponding tiles. If a particular tile is a *start* or *goal* position of any agent, the tile is colored green or red. If there is a start and also a goal position on a single tile, the tile is filled with both colors using a checker pattern. Note that the colors need to have very *low opacity*, so as the Ozobots do not register them as following lines.

Before the simulation, Ozobots are placed on all green tiles, as shown in Fig. 5, and at the end of the simulation, they should stand on the red tiles. When all bots are in place, the *following lines* are displayed on the map as well by the simulation module.

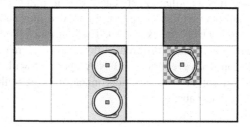

Fig. 5. The map example with Ozobots ready to execute paths.

6.3   MAPF Solver

The prototype uses an already existing MAPF solver that implements the SMT-CBS algorithm [25], which combines the SAT-based solving principle and the CBS algorithm via lazy encoding of the MAPF problem. The solver produces *sum-of-costs* optimal solutions. The solver represents the planning phase. It is important to note that resulting plans are discrete sequences of actions for individual robots.

6.4   Acting via Path Animation

The main and most sophisticated module of the application is the *simulator*. The simulator bridges the conceptual gap from discrete planning to acting in the physical environment. It takes the loaded map of the problem and an obtained solution from the solver module and is responsible for animating the paths for Ozobots. Ozobots themselves can be regarded as reflex-based agents with no advanced reasoning. The only task done by the Ozobot is to follow the line drawn on the surface. Hence the simulator is responsible for transforming the discrete solution obtained from the solver module into continuous animated curves for Ozobots, and displaying them on the surface of physical environment.

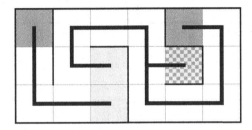

Fig. 6. Full agent paths displayed in the map.

The multi-robot system capable of planning and acting for MAPF problem not only consists of Ozobots but the display in which the animation takes place is the integral part of the system.

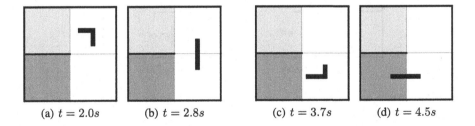

(a) $t = 2.0s$ (b) $t = 2.8s$ (c) $t = 3.7s$ (d) $t = 4.5s$

Fig. 7. Basic path segments displayed in the map after t seconds from the start of the execution.

For pedagogical reasons we describe the evolution of path animation from the simplest one and mention problems that we encountered and how did we address them.

The simplest solution for the path outputting would be to display the whole plan at once, as shown in Fig. 6. With this outputting method, the robots cannot perform some of their essential actions like wait or turn around at a specific position. They even choose a random direction at each intersection. Such approach is not sufficient to carry

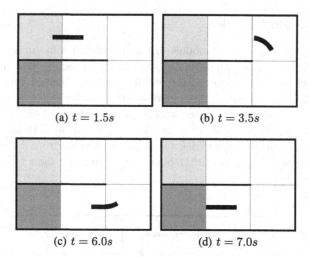

(a) $t = 1.5s$ (b) $t = 3.5s$

(c) $t = 6.0s$ (d) $t = 7.0s$

Fig. 8. Curved path segments displayed in the map after t seconds from the start of the execution.

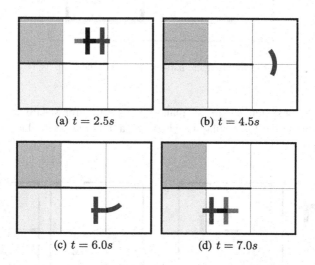

(a) $t = 2.5s$ (b) $t = 4.5s$

(c) $t = 6.0s$ (d) $t = 7.0s$

Fig. 9. Colored path segments displayed in the map after t seconds from the start of the execution [3].

out the acting phase for MAPF correctly as wait actions and the choice of direction are essential in MAPF plans.

The improvement of displaying path at once is to animate them, the process of animation is shown in Fig. 7. This straightforward improvement eliminated the problem of choosing wrong direction. However does not allow robots to wait and moreover at the robots are differential driven, sharp turns cause significant delays as the robot needs to turn in play which may cause de-synchronization in plan execution.

The potential delay in plan execution caused by sharp turn can be eliminated by making smooth turns instead as shown in Fig. 8. This improvement eliminated the need to turn in place however still this style of animation robots may lose especially in long plans. This is causes by small disturbances and different than assumed speed of robots that accumulates throughout time.

Finally all problems have been addressed through colored animated paths, as shown in Fig. 9. The colors are used to utilize another reflex-based behavior of the robots, namely the interpretation of color where red means to accelerate while blue means to slow down which altogether can keep the robot more precisely at a correct position in time.

The screen outputs animated path segments around the map, on which the Ozobots are moving. The segments are divided into three colored parts, so the robot can reflex-ively change its movement speed based on the line color. This dynamic speed adapta-tion provides an active correction of execution desynchronization. However, to make an Ozobot read the line color and change its movement speed, *artificial intersections* had to be displayed on the paths.

If the agent has to wait at a specific position, the path segment stops its animation at the position. When the robot has to stop on a curved turn, a guiding line is displayed to bring the Ozobot into a correct orientation. This ensures that the bot can continue on its path when the path segment reappears under it. In some scenarios, the robot is required to make a U-turn. For this functionality, a special color code supported by the Ozobot is displayed on the screen. The robot can read the code and perform the turn.

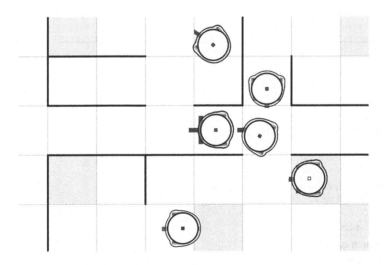

Fig. 10. Illustration of Ozobots following colored path segments on a map [3].

An illustration of Ozobots navigating on the path segments is shown in Fig. 10.

6.5 Modifying Ozobot Behavior

Ozobots need to follow the lines outputted by the environment and change their movement speed according to the color of the lines. This modified behavior can be written as an OzoBlockly editor and loaded to all robots.

The OzoBlockly program can be found in Algorithm 1. The main loop runs until the program is manually terminated. As can be seen on line 7 of the code, the robot moves on the path segments between the artificial intersections or until it loses the following line. When an intersection or a line end is encountered, the line-following speed is updated on line 2. Because the Ozobot naturally wants to choose a random direction at any intersection, line 4 makes it always go straight. However, if the movement was interrupted and there is no line under the robot, line 6 stops it from moving.

The function getSpeedFromLineColor from line 2 is shown in Algorithm 2. First, the function reads the surface color from the optical color sensor on line 2. On lines 3–10, the speed is chosen according to the color, and on line 11, it is returned. The speeds on each of the segments were chosen based on the path segment animation speed.

Algorithm 1. Ozobot behavior program [3].

```
1  while true do
2  |   set line-following speed: getSpeedFromLineColor() mm/s;
3  |   if there is way straight then
4  |   |   pick direction: straight;
5  |   else
6  |   |   stop motors;
7  |   follow line to next intersection or line end;
```

Algorithm 2. Function reading line color and returning speed [3].

```
1  Function getSpeedFromLineColor()
2  |   color ← get surface color;
3  |   if color = surface color red then
4  |   |   speed ← 37;
5  |   else if color = surface color black then
6  |   |   speed ← 30;
7  |   else if color = surface color blue then
8  |   |   speed ← 23;
9  |   else
10 |   |   speed ← 21;
11 |   return speed
```

---

7 Experimental Evaluation

We tested the prototype with various scenarios where the focus was on success of execution and problematic maneuvers. Each of the problem instances, represented by a map,

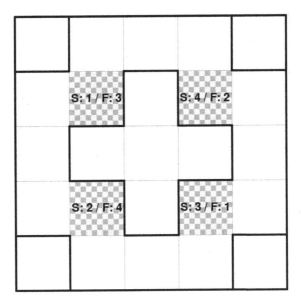

Fig. 11. Experiment map: the rotation [3].

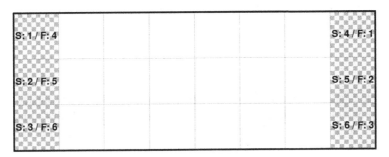

Fig. 12. Experiment map: the swap [3].

was solved with both the move-to-unoccupied variant (denoted *m2u*) and the *standard* MAPF solver[3]. For some maps, both variants yield the same plan[4].

7.1 Maps

For the experiments, six maps were used. Some of the maps aim to test a specific feature or a critical maneuver of the system, others provide a balanced scenario for the execution. All of the maps are listed in Table 1. For each map, its width, height, and number of agents are provided in the table.

---

[3] Which allows an agent to moved to an occupied position if the occupant will leave the position at the same time step.

[4] For example, the map *rotation* from our experiments.

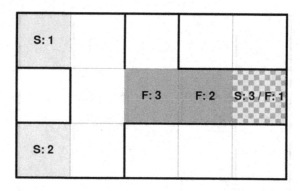

Fig. 13. Experiment map: the ordering [3].

Table 1. Maps created for experiments [3].

Map name	Width	Height	Agents	Image of the map
Snake	10	2	6	–
Rotation	5	5	4	In Fig. 11
Swap	8	3	6	In Fig. 12
Ordering	5	3	3	In Fig. 13
Evacuation	10	5	6	In Fig. 14
Roundabout	9	5	6	In Fig. 15

In Table 2, all plans for these maps are listed. For each plan, some maneuvers that could be problematic for the robots are counted. Namely, the number of turns without waiting, the number of *Color Codes* displayed (CC), and the number of *wait on a turn* positions (WoT).

7.2 Results

Every plan was executed 32 times with the implemented prototype. The execution is marked as *successful* if all Ozobots reach their goal positions. If at least one loses the following line and does not reach the goal, the execution is marked as a *failure*. The results of the experiments are summarized in Table 3. During the testing, five different reasons for execution failure were recorded. The occurrence of these failures was counted and is presented in the table of results.

Sometimes during the execution, a *severe collision* (SC) can occur, where the robots push against each other or lift their wheels from the surface. This collision results in an execution failure because the robots lose their following lines and are unable to continue. This problem does not occur very often and is non-existent in the move-to-unoccupied plans, , which are generally safer for physical execution.

Table 2. Plans executed with the prototype [3].

Plan name	Map	Turns	CC	WoT
snake	Snake	12	0	0
snake_m2u	Snake	12	0	0
rotation	Rotation	20	0	0
swap	Swap	10	0	1
swap_m2u	Swap	9	0	3
ordering	Ordering	5	1	0
ordering_m2u	Ordering	3	1	2
evacuation	Evacuation	26	0	1
evacuation_m2u	Evacuation	25	0	1
roundabout	Roundabout	33	0	0
roundabout_m2u	Roundabout	30	0	1

On the other hand, more frequent was the failure due to *missed intersection* (MI). Sometimes, an Ozobot failed to update its speed at an intersection because it was not detected by its sensors. This almost always resulted in an execution failure if the agent did not slow down before a turn. The first experiments showed that the success rate of an Ozobot to detect an intersection correctly fluctuates with changing light conditions and performing calibrations. However, results from the plan executions on the *roundabout* map suggest that the complexity of the paths might also affect the frequency of these mistakes.

The maneuvers as *CC* and *WoT* also caused a few execution failures. To fail to execute the *U-turn*, the robot can either arrive at the tile too soon or too late. If it

Table 3. Results of the experiments [3].

Plan name	Success	Fail	SC	MI	CC	WoT	EC
snake	32	0	0	0	0	0	0
snake_m2u	32	0	0	0	0	0	0
rotation	29	3	0	3	0	0	0
swap	30	2	0	1	0	1	0
swap_m2u	30	2	1	0	1	0	0
ordering	30	2	1	0	1	0	0
ordering_m2u	24	8	0	0	4	3	1
evacuation	28	4	2	0	0	2	0
evacuation_m2u	30	2	0	2	0	0	0
roundabout	23	9	0	9	0	0	0
roundabout_m2u	19	13	0	8	0	3	2

arrives too soon, it fails to read the whole code and does not rotate at all. If it arrives too late, it reads the code twice and makes two rotations ending up in the original orientation. Both of these scenarios ensure the failure of plan execution. Performing the *WoT* maneuver, the robot sometimes makes a U-turn at the end of the following guiding line. This behavior is most likely triggered when Ozobot loses the following line without detecting a line end.

The last problem noticed during the experiments was Ozobot failing to *exit a curve* (EC). Even though this was a rare occurrence, sometimes, when the bot passed through a curved turn, it was unable to detect the following line correctly and lost the path.

7.3 Compilation-Based Approach

To give more complete comparison we implemented compilation-based approach to control the Ozobots. In this approach, the plan is first found offline and then the

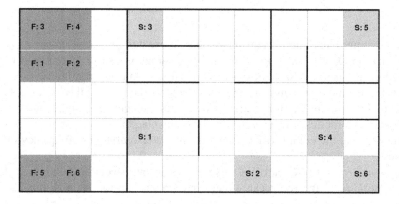

Fig. 14. Experiment map: The evacuation [3].

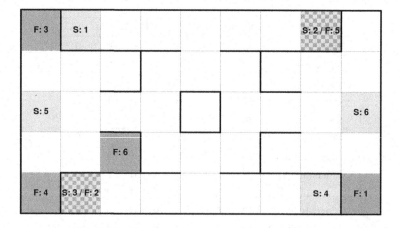

Fig. 15. Experiment map: The roundabout [3].

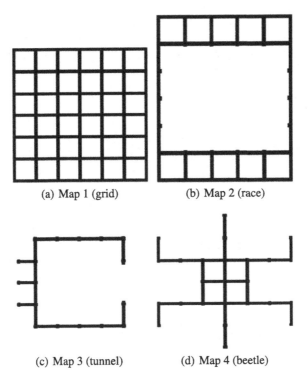

(a) Map 1 (grid)   (b) Map 2 (race)

(c) Map 3 (tunnel)   (d) Map 4 (beetle)

Fig. 16. Testing environments used in experiments for compilation-based approach.

sequence of move/wait actions for each robot is compiled into their the sequence of their primitive commands. The sequence of primitive commands is then uploaded to each individual Ozobot. Ozobots are in this way pre-programmed and their reflex-based behavior becomes limited in comparison with our major approach.

Experimental setup for compilation-based approach is also different in terms of the environment. The environment is no longer represented by the surface of a display but instead a printed map scaled so to correspond to robots' sizes is used as the environment. We used environments shown in Fig. 16 in our experiments. In each map a characteristic initial and goal configuration of robots is used.

In map 1 (a grid) the initial and goal configuration of robots is selected randomly, 6 Ozobots were used. The task for robots in map 2 (race) is to go from the upper part of the map to the lower part while their ordering should be preserved, 6 Ozobots were used. The idea behind map 3 (a tunnel) is to represent a tunnel while two robots from both ends of the tunnel should exchange their positions via avoiding each other in the middle section. There is third robot in the middle section that should behave as a gate. Finally, in map 4 (a beetle) there are 6 robots, one robot per leg of the beetle. The task for robots from opposite legs is to exchange their positions, intensive avoidance is made in the body of the beetle.

For each map we divided the plan into multiple steps, these steps correspond to occurrence of a robot at reference positions, corresponding to points where edges of the underlying grid crosses. For each reference position we calculated theoretical time

Table 4. Experiment on map 1—grid: the difference of expected time of occurrence and the actual time (two measurements are shown).

Test 1	Ozobot 1	Ozobot 2	Ozobot 3	Ovozot 4	Ozobot 5	Ozobot 6
0	0 / 0	0,03 / 0,03	0,03 / 0,07	0 / 0,03	0 / 0,03	0,03 / 0,03
1	0,05 / 0,05	0,02 / 0,02	0,05 / 0,12	0,02 / 0,15	0,02 / 0,09	0,12 / −0,02
2	0,07 / 0,03	0,03 / 0,03	0,07 / 0,1	0,07 / 0,17	0,03 / 0,07	0,03 / −0,04
3	0,02 / 0,05	0,05 / 0,05	−0,05 / −0,05	0,09 / 0,22	−0,09 / −0,05	0,05 / −0,02
4	0 / 0,03	0,03 / 0,03	−0,04 / −0,04	0,07 / 0,27	−0,07 / -0,04	0,03 / −0,07
5		0,02 / 0,05	0,02 / −0,02	0,05 / 0,22	−0,05 / 0,02	0,02 / −0,05
6		−0,04 / 0,03	0 / −0,04	0,03 / 0,2	−0,07 / 0,03	0,1 / −0,04
7		−0,05 / 0,08	0,02 / −0,02		−0,09 / 0,02	0,12 / −0,05
8		−0,07 / 0,1	0 / -0,03		−0,1 / 0,03	0,1 / −0,03
9			−0,02 / −0,05		−0,09 / 0,05	0,05 /−0,05
10			0 / −0,04			0,07 / −0,04
11			0,02 / −0,05			
12			0,07 / 0			

Table 5. Experiment on map 2—race: the difference of expected time of occurrence and the actual time (two measurements are shown).

Test 1	Ozobot 1	Ozobot 2	Ozobot 3	Ovozot 4	Ozobot 5	Ozobot 6
0	0 / 0	0 / 0	0,07 / 0	0 / 0	0 / 0	0,03 / 0
1	−0,02 / −0,05	−0,02 / −0,09	0,02 / −0,02	0,02 / −0,05	0,02 / 0,02	0,02 / 0,09
2	−0,03 / −0,07	−0,03 / −0,07	0,03 / 0	−0,07 / 0	0,03 / 0,03	−0,03 / 0,1
3	−0,12 / −0,22	0,02 / −0,05	0,02 / −0,02	−0,19 / −0,12	0,05 / 0,09	−0,19 / −0,02
4	−0,14 / −0,21	0 / −0,07	0,03 / 0	−0,21 / −0,1	0,03 / 0,1	−0,17 / −0,03
5	−0,12 / −0,19	−0,02 / −0,09	0,05 / 0,02	−0,22 / −0,12	−0,02 / 0,05	−0,12 / −0,02
6	−0,14 / −0,2	−0,03 / −0,07	0,07 / 0,03	−0,14 / −0,07	−0,03 / 0,07	−0,14 / 0
7	−0,12 / −0,09	0,02 / −0,05	0,09 / 0,02	−0,12 / −0,09	−0,02 / 0,05	−0,09 / 0,05
8	−0,1 / −0,1	0 / −0,07	0,07 / 0,03	−0,14 / −0,1	0 / 0,07	−0,1 / 0
9		0,02 / 0,02	0,09 / 0,05	−0,12 / −0,05	0,02 / 0,09	
10		−0,04 / 0	0,1 / 0,03	−0,14 / −0,07	0,03 / 0,17	
11		−−0,02 / 0,02	0,08 / 0,02	−0,05 / −0,02	−0,05 / 0,09	
12		0 / 0,03	0,1 / 0,03	−0,04 / 0,03	0 / 0,1	
13		0,05 / 0,02	0,12 / 0,02	−0,12 / −0,05	−0,02 / 0,05	
14			0,17 / 0,1	−0,1 / −0,04		
15			0,19 / 0,05	−0,09 / −0,02		
16			0,13 / 0	−0,14 / −0,07		

when a robot should visit the reference position. This time can be calculated using the known constant linear and rotation speed of the robot and the discrete plan.

The experiment with real robots was focused on how the actual occurrence time of a robot at a reference point deviates from the calculated theoretical value. We hypothesize using the fact that Ozobots are quite inaccurate, that the error, that is the difference between the actual and the theoretical time, will grow as the acting phase proceeds.

The results showing the difference of expected theoretical time of occurrence of robots at selected positions and the actual time for difference maps is shown in Tables 4, 5, 6, and 7. The results partially confirms the hypothesis that the plan finishes with non-zero difference from the expected finish. There is also some observable evidence that the difference grow as the execution proceeds but this does not hold universally.

Due to significant difference from expected occurrence times the compilation-based method is unsuitable for large scenarios with complex plans. The experience from

Table 6. Experiment on map 3—tunnel: the difference of expected time of occurrence and the actual time (one measurement is shown).

Test 1	Ozobot 1	Ozobot 2	Ozobot 3
0	0,03 / 0,03	0 / 0,03	0,03 / 0
1	0,19 / 0,15	−0,02 / 0,02	−0,02 / 0,05
2	0,21 / 0,17	−0,1 / −0,03	−0,07 / 0,07
3	0,19 / 0,15	−0,26 / −0,19	−0,09 / 0,05
4	0,2 / 0,17	−0,21 / −0,27	−0,07 / 0
5	0,22 / 0,25	−0,22 / −0,22	−0,05 / −0,02
6	0,17 / 0,34	−0,21 / −0,21	−0,04 / −0,04
7	0,19 / 0,29	−0,22 / −0,22	−0,05 / −0,05
8	0,24 / 0,31	−0,21 / −0,27	−0,04 / −0,03
9	0,22 / 0,29	−0,15 / −0,22	−0,05 / −0,05
10	0,24 / 0,31	−0,17 / −0,21	−0,1 / −0,07
11	0,22 / 0,25	−0,12 / −0,16	−0,09 / −0,05
12	0,17 / 0,2	−0,14 / −0,22	−0,1 / −0,04
13	0,15 / 0,25	−0,19 / −0,22	−0,09 / −0,05
14	0,17 / 0,27	−0,21 / −0,21	−0,1 / −0,04
15	0,21 / 0,25	−0,16 / −0,19	−0,16 / −0,09
16	0,24 / 0,31	−0,14 / −0,21	
17	0,25 / 0,29	−0,16 / −0,19	
18	0,24 / 0,27	−0,14 / −0,17	
19	0,25 / 0,25		
20	0,24 / 0,24		
21	0,22 / 0,36		
22	0,2 / 0,31		

Table 7. Experiment on map 4—beetle: the difference of expected time of occurrence and the actual time (one measurement is shown).

Test 1	Ozobot 1	Ozobot 2	Ozobot 3	Ovozot 4	Ozobot 5	Ozobot 6
0						
1	0,0101	0,0136	−0,0309	0,1091	0,1942	0,1363
2	−0,0239	−0,0278	−0,0205	−0,007	−0,0139	−0,0034
3	−0,0547	−0,1122	−0,0552	0,0067	−0,0204	−0,0412
4	−0,0089	0,0169	0,0072	−0,0171	0,0014	0,017
5	−0,0016	−0,0035	0,0136	0,0169	0,002	−0,0173
6	0,0171	−0,0146	0,0238	−0,0069	0,0109	0,0033
7	0,0067	0,0177	−0,0068	0,0169	0,0026	−0,0171
8	0,0169	−0,0002	−0,0276	−0,0137	0,0066	0,0034
9	−0,041	−0,0103		0,034	0,0138	−0,0103
10	0,0169	0,0101		−0,0102	−0,0347	0,0236
11	−0,0038	0,0102		0,0271	−0,0034	3,55E-16
12	−0,017	0,0033		0,0032	−0,0376	−0,0206
13		0,0203				0,0109
14		0,0137				−0,0111
15		0,0272				−0,0206
16		0,0467				0,0375
17		0,0213				
18		0,0273				

testing also indicates that the compilation-based approach is prone to failure in execution. Moreover, as can be seen from experiments with two measurements, the repeatability of acting in compilation-based approach is relatively poor.

Altogether we can conclude that the approach based on path animations is much more reliable and versatile as the error accumulation is successfully mitigated during the execution phase. Moreover there is no need to pre-program the robots which is relatively work intensive task.

8   Conclusion

This work has introduced a novel approach to bridge discrete multi-agent path finding and acting on a swarm of physical robots called ESO-NAV. The approach uses environment outputs and reflex-based robotic agents to emulate centralized control and shifts the computational complexity of the system from planning towards execution. That is the planning phase is kept simple due to its discrete character while discrete plans are transformed before execution. This makes the system more scalable for a large number of robots. A swarm of Ozobot Evo robots has been used for the prototype.

Despite the limitation of these robots, the tests showed that the ESO-NAV approach can deploy various MAPF scenarios on physical agents using existing MAPF algorithms that use classical discrete models. We also identified various problems that need to be overcome to carry out the execution successfully. Most of them are dependent on the capabilities of robots being used. Unlike previous works dealing with robotic agents deployment, we did not need to augment the classical MAPF model in any sense, and an off-the-shelf MAPF solver based on SAT was used. Using reflex control of robots through path animation on the surface of the screen makes our approach more flexible and easy to use.

To provide more complete picture, we also tested compilation-based approach to execute discrete plan. In this approach, plans are translated into sequence of primitive actions that are uploaded to individual robots. Our experiments confirmed that the reflex-based approach using path animation is much more flexible and provides higher precision of execution.

The secondary contribution of our simulation approach is the prototype that can be used for demonstration in research or academics, as well as in testing of real-world applications. We believe the novel approach could be used in applications like intelligent evacuation systems or indoor transporter navigation.

Acknowledgement. This work has been supported by GAČR - the Czech Science Foundation, grant registration number 22-31346S.

References

1. Andreychuk, A., Yakovlev, K.S., Atzmon, D., Stern, R.: Multi-agent pathfinding with continuous time. In: Proceedings of 28th International Joint Conference on Artificial Intelligence (IJCAI), 2019, pp. 39–45 (2019). https://doi.org/10.24963/ijcai.2019/6
2. Barták, R., Svancara, J., Skopková, V., Nohejl, D.: Multi-agent path finding on real robots: First experience with ozobots. In: Advances in Artificial Intelligence - IBERAMIA 2018– 16th Ibero-American Conference on AI, Trujillo, Peru, November 13–16, 2018, Proceedings Lecture Notes in Computer Science, vol. 11238, pp. 290–301 (2018). https://doi.org/10.1007/978-3-030-03928-8_24
3. Chudý, J., Popov, N., Surynek, P.: Deployment of multi-agent pathfinding on a swarm of physical robots centralized control via reflex-based behavior. In: Galambos, P., Madani, K. (eds.) Proceedings of the International Conference on Robotics, Computer Vision and Intelligent Systems, ROBOVIS 2020, Budapest, Hungary, November 4–6, 2020. pp. 28–38. SCITEPRESS (2020)
4. Dresner, K.M., Stone, P.: A multiagent approach to autonomous intersection management. J. Artif. Intell. Res. (JAIR) **31**, 591–656 (2008). https://doi.org/10.1613/jair.2502
5. Evollve, I.: Ozobot (2020), https://ozobot.com/
6. Evollve, I.: Ozobot sensor layout images (2020). https://files.ozobot.com/classroom/2019-Educator-Guide.pdf
7. Gange, G., Harabor, D., Stuckey, P.J.: Lazy CBS: implicit conflict-based search using lazy clause generation. In: Proceedings of 29th International Conference on Automated Planning and Scheduling (ICAPS), pp. 155–162 (2019)
8. Izmirlioglu, Y., Pehlivan, B.A., Turp, M., Erdem, E.: A general formal framework for multi-agent meeting problems. In: 2017 IEEE International Conference on Robotics and Automation (ICRA), pp. 1299–1306 (2017). https://doi.org/10.1109/ICRA.2017.7989153

9. Kornhauser, D., Miller, G.L., Spirakis, P.G.: Coordinating pebble motion on graphs, the diameter of permutation groups, and applications. In: Proceedings of 25th Annual Symposium Foundations of Computer Science (FOCS), pp. 241–250 (1984). https://doi.org/10.1109/SFCS.1984.715921

10. Kuipers, B., Feigenbaum, E.A., Hart, P.E., Nilsson, N.J.: Shakey: from conception to history. AI Mag. **38**(1), 88–103 (2017)

11. Li, J., Surynek, P., Felner, A., Ma, H., Kumar, T.K.S., Koenig, S.: Multi-agent path finding for large agents. In: 33rd AAAI Conference on Artificial Intelligence, 31st Innovative Applications of Artificial Intelligence Conference, 9th AAAI Symposium on Educational Advances in Artificial Intelligence, Honolulu, Hawaii, USA, Jan./Feb., 2019, pp. 7627–7634 (2019). https://doi.org/10.1609/aaai.v33i01.33017627

12. Luna, R., Bekris, K.E.: Push and swap: fast cooperative path-finding with completeness guarantees. In: Proceedings of 22nd International Joint Conference on Artificial Intelligence (IJCAI), 2011, pp. 294–300 (2011). https://doi.org/10.5591/978-1-57735-516-8/IJCAI11-059

13. Morris, R., Pasareanu, C.S., Luckow, K.S., Malik, W., Ma, H., Kumar, T.K.S., Koenig, S.: Planning, scheduling and monitoring for airport surface operations. In: Planning for Hybrid Systems, Papers from the 2016 AAAI Workshop, Phoenix, Arizona, USA, February 13, 2016. AAAI Workshops, vol. WS-16-12 (2016)

14. Ratner, D., Warmuth, M.K.: Finding a shortest solution for the N × N extension of the 15-puzzle is intractable. In: Proceedings of 5th National Conference on Artificial Intelligence, Volume 1: Science, pp. 168–172 (1986)

15. Ryan, M.: Constraint-based multi-robot path planning. In: IEEE International Conference on Robotics and Automation (ICRA), pp. 922–928 (2010). https://doi.org/10.1109/ROBOT.2010.5509582

16. Ryan, M.R.K.: Exploiting subgraph structure in multi-robot path planning. J. Artif. Intell. Res. (JAIR) **31**, 497–542 (2008). https://doi.org/10.1613/jair.2408

17. Sharon, G., Stern, R., Felner, A., Sturtevant, N.R.: Conflict-based search for optimal multi-agent pathfinding. Artif. Intell. (AIJ) **219**, 40–66 (2015). https://doi.org/10.1016/j.artint.2014.11.006

18. Sharon, G., Stern, R., Goldenberg, M., Felner, A.: The increasing cost tree search for optimal multi-agent pathfinding. Artif. Intell. (AIJ) **195**, 470–495 (2013). https://doi.org/10.1016/j.artint.2012.11.006

19. Shome, R., Solovey, K., Dobson, A., Halperin, D., Bekris, K..E.: dRRT*: scalable and informed asymptotically-optimal multi-robot motion planning. Auton. Robots **44**(3), 443–467 (2019). https://doi.org/10.1007/s10514-019-09832-9

20. Silver, D.: Cooperative pathfinding. In: Proceedings of 1st Artificial Intelligence and Interactive Digital Entertainment Conference (AIIDE), pp. 117–122 (2005)

21. Standley, T.S.: Finding optimal solutions to cooperative pathfinding problems. In: Proceedings of 24th AAAI Conference on Artificial Intelligence (2010)

22. Surynek, P.: A novel approach to path planning for multiple robots in bi-connected graphs. In: 2009 IEEE International Conference on Robotics and Automation (ICRA), pp. 3613–3619 (2009). https://doi.org/10.1109/ROBOT.2009.5152326

23. Surynek, P.: Towards optimal cooperative path planning in hard setups through satisfiability solving. In: Proceedings of 12th Pacific Rim International Conference on Artificial Intelligence 2012. Lecture Notes in Computer Science, vol. 7458, pp. 564–576 (2012). https://doi.org/10.1007/978-3-642-32695-0_50

24. Surynek, P.: Time-expanded graph-based propositional encodings for makespan-optimal solving of cooperative path finding problems. Ann. Math. Artif. Intell. **81**(3), 329–375 (2017). https://doi.org/10.1007/s10472-017-9560-z

25. Surynek, P.: Unifying search-based and compilation-based approaches to multi-agent path finding through satisfiability modulo theories. In: Proceedings of 28th International Joint Conference on Artificial Intelligence (IJCAI), Macao, China, August 10–16, pp. 1177–1183 (2019). https://doi.org/10.24963/ijcai.2019/164

26. Surynek, P., Felner, A., Stern, R., Boyarski, E.: Efficient SAT approach to multi-agent path finding under the sum of costs objective. In: 22nd European Conference on Artificial Intelligence (ECAI). Frontiers in Artificial Intelligence and Applications, vol. 285, pp. 810–818 (2016). https://doi.org/10.3233/978-1-61499-672-9-810

27. Wang, K.C., Botea, A.: MAPP: a scalable multi-agent path planning algorithm with tractability and completeness guarantees. J. Artif. Intell. Res. (JAIR) 42, 55–90 (2011). https://doi.org/10.1613/jair.3370

28. de Wilde, B., ter Mors, A., Witteveen, C.: Push and rotate: a complete multi-agent pathfinding algorithm. J. Artif. Intell. Res. (JAIR) 51, 443–492 (2014). https://doi.org/10.1613/jair.4447

29. Wilson, R.M.: Graph puzzles, homotopy, and the alternating group. J. Comb. Theory, Ser. B 16(1), 86–96 (1974)

30. Wurman, P.R., D'Andrea, R., Mountz, M.: Coordinating hundreds of cooperative, autonomous vehicles in warehouses. AI Mag. 29(1), 9–20 (2008). https://doi.org/10.1609/aimag.v29i1.2082

31. Zhou, D., Schwager, M.: Virtual rigid bodies for coordinated agile maneuvering of teams of micro aerial vehicles. In: IEEE International Conference on Robotics and Automation (ICRA) 2015, Seattle, WA, USA, 26–30 May, pp. 1737–1742 (2015). https://doi.org/10.1109/ICRA.2015.7139422

Design and Experimental Analysis
of an Adaptive Cruise Control

Khaled Alomari$^{(\boxtimes)}$, Stephan Sundermann, Daniel Goehring, and Raúl Rojas

Dahlem Center for Machine Learning and Robotics, Freie Universität Berlin, Arnimallee 7,
14195 Berlin, Germany
khaled.alomari@fu-berlin.de
https://www.mi.fu-berlin.de/inf/groups/ag-ki

Abstract. Nowadays, cars are equipped with quite a few Advanced Driver Assistant Systems(ADAS) to increase comfortability and safety while driving. Adaptive Cruise Control (ACC) is one of these ADAS systems that keeps a certain distance to a heading vehicle in front by smoothly adapting the vehicle's speed. Usually, this is implemented using a separate PID controller for the velocity and distance or a MIMO system. This paper proposes a novel Fuzzy Logic approach for an autonomous model car called Autominy. The AutoMiny platform was developed at Dahlem Center for Machine Learning and Robotics at Freie Universität Berlin. It is equipped with a software stack for fully autonomous driving with custom modules for localization, control, and navigation. AutoMiny navigates using a pre-build vector force field approach. The proposed Fuzzy Logic controller can handle two states with different profiles. We extend the evaluating between our approach against a standard PID controller approach.

Keywords: Advanced Driver Assistance Systems · Adaptive Cruise Control · Fuzzy logic · Vector force field

1 Introduction

Advanced Driver Assistance Systems (ADAS) focuses on building up a context-aware system utilizing sensing, computing, and communicating technologies to perform reassured and efficient driving [10]. ADAS should sense, analyze, anticipate and react to the road environment, which are the critical features of context-awareness. The sole intention of ADASs is to support the drivers rather than to substitute them [11]. It could replace some human driver decisions and actions with explicit machine tasks [10], making it possible to eliminate many human errors potentially induced by distraction, poor judgment, or absence of situation perception [6]. Vehicles equipped with components like Smart rear-view camera, 360-degree cameras park assistance technology, Radar systems, Etc.) employed in several ADAS, such as automatic parking system, Blind Spot Monitor, and Collision Avoidance System, begun to appear in the market from various manufacturers [12]. These systems help the driver perform more settled and steady vehicle control with expanded capacity and associated energy and environmental benefits [10].

© Springer Nature Switzerland AG 2022
P. Galambos et al. (Eds.): ROBOVIS 2020/ROBOVIS 2021, CCIS 1667, pp. 76–97, 2022.
https://doi.org/10.1007/978-3-031-19650-8_4

Adaptive Cruise Control (ACC) is a commercially available vehicle longitudinal control system [1] that was initially introduced on Japan's market in 1995, then later in Europe and North America [6]. It couples cruise control with a distance control system to prevent rear-end crashes [15]. ACC is recognized as a vital ADAS of any future generations of Intelligent Cars [10]. Thus, developing it went through many steps and took a long time of research and experiments [14, 16, 17]. Xiao et al., summarises the development and achievements of the ACC systems [6].

Vehicles provided with ACC are considered level 1 autonomous cars defined in SAE J3016 standard [18]. It aims at substituting a driver from adjusting speed manually to achieve safe cruise driving. ACC uses onboard sensors such as laser scanners, radars, or cameras to distinguish if the vehicle is approaching a vehicle ahead and adopt its longitudinal speed, within limited ranges [14], to the preceding one in keeping with a safe gap to prevent a collision. Consequently, both throttle and brake action is done automatically [1]. In free traffic, the system holds a preset speed, like a standard cruise control system. While following another vehicle, the system automatically maintains a coveted gap from the preceding vehicle [10]. The spacing policy's selection and arrangement are essential in inventing an ACC system where the spacing policy refers to the desired steady-state distance between two successive vehicles [6]. The established ACCs are based on three spacing policy Constant Space-Headway (CSH), Constant Time-Headway (CTH), and Variable Time-Headway (VTH) [3, 4].

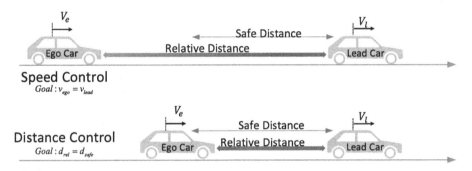

Fig. 1. Conception of the Adaptive Cruise Control system. It is used to control both velocity and distance at the same time. When the vehicle is approaching a vehicle ahead, it adjusts its speed, maintaining a safe distance to the car ahead to prevent a collision; otherwise, it drives at a preset speed.

Obtaining reliable ACC performance demands steadily, receiving the preceding vehicle's kinematics information under various conditions, e.g., weather, including relative distance and relative speed concerning the host vehicle. Furthermore, the driver should be able to take over the control whenever needed [10]. Shang et al. investigated the consequences on highway traffic capacity of human-piloted vehicles, theoretical ACC vehicles, and commercially available ACC vehicles. Moreover, they studied the intended correlation between string stability and highway throughput [2].

Xiao et al., categorizes the controversial critical issues related to an ACC system's design manner into three types: human issues, traffic issues, and social issues. Moreover, it explains the need for more real traffic data collection and real traffic operational tests to complement and validate the recent results. Furthermore, it defined individual stability, string stability, and traffic flow stability as the performance specifications that any ACC controller design should meet [6,7].

Existing ACC methods are categorized into optimization-based, artificial intelligence technique-based, and rule-based ACCs [3]. Optimization-based techniques produce reliable results but with high computational and design costs [13]. The Literature [3] theoretically discusses the stabilization effect of rule-based adaptive cruise control on traffic flow. The proposed ACC aims to improve the stability and behavior of the Intelligent Driver Model and estimate its performance by comparing it with existing models.

Indeed not all implied problems with the ACC have been solved; still, some criteria make market launching beneficial, even inevitable. Consequently, the system's development never stopped by combining new features such as Start & Stop function [8–10]. Moreover, car2car communication promotes the development of a new cruise control technique called Cooperative Adaptive Cruise Control (CACC), in which the system comprises data provided from the head vehicle [5,11].

This paper is an extended version of our paper [12] which proposes and analyzes a fuzzy logic-based Adaptive Cruise Controller. In this version, a selection of the most related work is comprised, and the experimental setup is described in more detail. Furthermore, The Evaluation section is enriched with more experimental data.

2   Adaptive Cruise Control

There are diverse methods to implement conventional feedback control systems like Adaptive Cruise Control. Typical mathematical control-based techniques defined using the system differential equations or employing their state-space representation [8] produce reliable results but with high computational and design costs [13]. Moreover, the analytical model of the control plants, especially nonlinear systems, may not be easy to obtain. Therefore, artificial intelligence approaches (such as fuzzy logic control) are a way to reach a human-like speed control. The strength of empirical rules-based control is that it allows relative human thinking and an intuitive control edifice. Even though Fuzzy logic is somehow argumentative, it is a sturdy technique. It allows control without comprehensive knowledge of the controlled system state. Moreover, since the characterizations of the unobservable vehicle dynamics are not required, it represents in a very productive way the rational argumentation means [12]. This allows the controller applicable to other vehicles with different dynamics [8].

2.1   Fuzzy Logic Approach

Figure 2 shows a typical fuzzy logic control block diagram. The Fuzzy control itself involves four essential steps: fuzzification, a fuzzy rule base, an inference engine, and a defuzzification. However, a preprocessing step of the input data and postprocessing step of the controller output values are usually involved in the system.

In the preprocessing step, the data acquired from the sensors are averaged, filtered from noise, scaled onto a particular standard range so that it is ready to be passed into the fuzzy controller [20]. A fuzzy controller deals only with linguistic terms, also known as

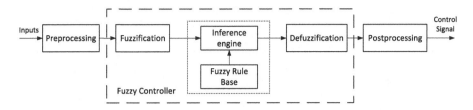

Fig. 2. Fuzzy controller block diagram [21].

a fuzzy set, rather than crisp variables. The fuzzification block converts each obtained input data to degrees of membership by a lookup in all related membership functions of the fuzzy set to use it in the Fuzzy controller rules [20]. The fuzzy rule base reserves the empirical observation of the performance of the process of the domain experts [8]. Fuzzy control rules have an if-then format. The relational format essentially assumes a logical connective between the inputs. It should be emphasized that it has to be the same operation for all rules and not a mixture of connectives [22]. Logical **AND**, and logical **OR** are the most prominent ones; they are always defined in pairs [20].

$$\textbf{a and b} = \textbf{min(a,b)}$$

$$\textbf{a or b} = \textbf{max(a,b)}$$

Fuzzy rules are determined based on designer expertise and demands. An example of one fuzzy rule in the case of multi-input-multi-output systems (MIMO) is:
If Relative Distance is *Small* and Relative Velocity is *Slow*
then *Decelerate*
The inference engine is the core of the fuzzy controller. It can simulate human decision-making by performing comparative argumentation to achieve a coveted control policy [8]. i.e., It looks up the membership grades in the condition for each rule. The defuzzification step remodeled the resulting fuzzy set into a number that needs to be sent for processing as a control signal. There are numerous techniques for defuzzification, such as Center of Gravity, Bisector of Area, and Mean of Maxima. Fuzzy controller output scaling is also essential. In most cases, the output value needs to be scaled to physical units. The postprocessing block often contains an output gain that can be tuned, and sometimes also an integrator.

2.2 Fuzzy Logic-Based ACC

This subsection presents in detail the proposed adaptive cruise controller. For this work, we use the Mamdani fuzzy inference method. The controller's inputs are the relative distance and relative speed between the two successive vehicles, and the output is the acceleration [9]. The input information, including both cars' positions and speeds, is provided to the controller 30 Hz frequency. Fuzzy logic gives the designer the flexibility to define the error based on the implementation needs. Here we choose the controller error as the difference between the desired value and the actual value. The relative speed is calculated from the speed difference between the two successive vehicles.

$$\Delta v = V_p - V_h \tag{1}$$

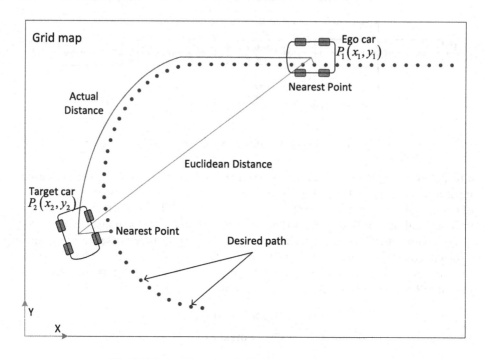

Fig. 3. Relative distance calculation. Adapted from [12].

Table 1. Input–Output variables intervals.

Variable	Desired range	Actual range	Final range
$\Delta d\ [cm]$	$[+200, +300]$	$[+200, +500]$	$[-300, +100]$
$\Delta v\ [cm/s]$	$[+10, +100]$	$[+5, +105]$	$[-95, +95]$

where v_p and v_h represents the speed of the front car and the speed of the host car, respectively. However, calculating the Euclidean distance between the cars is not always correct. An example scenario is presented in Fig. 3. In this case, if we calculate the Euclidean distance between the two vehicles, it will be much smaller than the actual distance between them on the path they both follow as they navigate the desired path. i.e., the distance between the ego- and the target car is the distance between them along the path. There are many different ways to calculate it. Though we choose the most common way as follows: Once we obtain the position's data of both cars, we suspect a slight deviation from the path point, so we use a KD-Tree to find the closest point on the path for each car from the known path points array then we calculate the distance between them. The path points array is constructed with a 1 cm resolution, so we consider the distance between the path array points is 1 cm (even for the curve points for simplicity).

Distance and velocity values lay within known operational intervals. Thus, input-output data should cover these intervals. Table Table 1 shows the desired and the actual intervals for each input variable of the controller.

The actual intervals are determined based on different perspectives, including safety distance and sensors' accuracy. However, sensor performance investigation is beyond the work presented in this paper. The desired intervals are determined based on the tolerance of the design. The final intervals (the controller inputs) are calculated as follows:

$$\Delta d_{min} = 200 - 500 = -300 \quad [cm]$$
$$\Delta d_{max} = 300 - 200 = +100 \quad [cm]$$
$$\Delta v_{min} = 10 - 105 = -95 \quad [cm/s]$$
$$\Delta v_{max} = 100 - 5 = +95 \quad [cm/s]$$

Each input and output interval requires its own set of linguistic terms. This is after the Input-Output range values have been concluded. In addition, for each linguistic variable, a membership function must be chosen.

Given the importance of a quick response from the ACC, a triangular membership function was chosen based on the results from [23]. This type of membership function makes it convenient for the defuzzification process because it simplifies the computational efforts compared with other membership functions. Moreover, it turned out that triangular or trapezoidal membership functions consumed fewer computing resources than the Gaussian approach. Although Gaussian membership requires more computing time to process the information, the result is more accurate. Nevertheless, in our system, the controller is designed to operate on a model car in a lab environment. Thus, the rejoinder is weighted more than the accuracy of the output value [19].

Figure 4 visualizes fuzzy set partitioning and membership functions of input and output intervals, and Tables 2 and 3 display the list and arrangement of the ACC input and output quantities with its fuzzy set.

Table 2. List of input variables for the fuzzy controller.

Input	Value range	Linguistic variable	Linguistic terms
Δd [cm]	$[-300, +100]$	Relative distance	Small, normal, high
Δv [cm/s]	$[-95, +95]$	Relative speed	Fast, normal, slow

Table 3. List of output variables for the fuzzy controller.

Output	Value range	Linguistic variable	Linguistic terms
Δa [cm/s^2]	$[-0.5, +0.5]$	Acceleration	Decelerate, Zero, Accelerate

The fuzzy control rules are created based on the expertise of human drivers. Safety, power consumption, and ride comfort were all taken into consideration when determining the rules. Table 4 shows the fuzzy rules base for our proposed ACC. These fuzzy driving rules are easily understood. For example, if the relative distance is close and the relative speed is Fast, then the control signal is Decelerate. This rule states that if the host car is approaching the ego car quickly and the two cars are close to each other, the host car's speed should be reduced dramatically to prevent a collision. Furthermore, the diagonal entries of the rule matrix are symmetric.

We proceeded with the Center of Gravity as a defuzzification method. The output value X can be calculated using the formula:

$$X = \frac{\sum_i \mu(x_i)\, x_i}{\sum_i \mu(x_i)} \tag{2}$$

where $\mu(x_i)$ is the membership value of the membership function and $\mu(x_i)$ is a running point in the discrete universe. In most cases, as discussed in Sect. 2.1, the output value must be scaled to physical units. The controller output value in our case is a change in acceleration. Since we cannot pass an acceleration command to the speed motor, we will use a low-level controller to transform the controller output into a value sent to the motor (based on motor calibration and desired response time) [12].

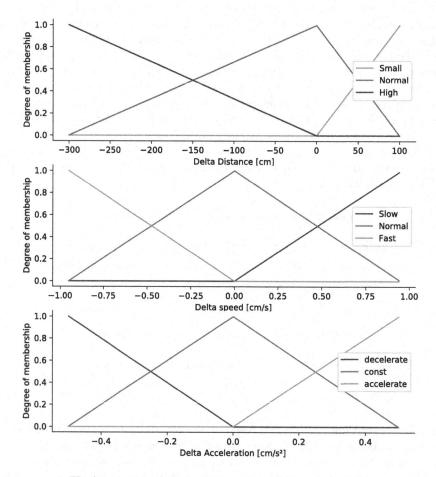

Fig. 4. Definition of membership functions and Fuzzy sets [12].

Table 4. Fuzzy rule base.

Δv	Δd		
	Small	Normal	High
Slow	Decelerate	Zero	Accelerate
Normal	Decelerate	Zero	Zero
Fast	Decelerate	Decelerate	Decelerate

2.3 Designing of Low-Level Control

Low-Level Control (LLC) is used to map the output of the ACC from acceleration to a speed command that can be fed to the motor. The equation of this control is based on both motor calibration curve and the desired response time. However, the same LLC is employed for both ACC fuzzy logic-based and PID based systems. The equation is set as follows:

$$\Delta a = a_{des} - a_{act} \tag{3}$$

$$a_{des} = a_{act} + \Delta a \tag{4}$$

$$\frac{v_{des}}{t} = \frac{v_{act}}{t} + \Delta a \tag{5}$$

$$v_{des} = v_{act} + \Delta a\, t \tag{6}$$

Now, the actual speed is measured in [m/s] while we send the desired speed to the motor in [rpm]. Thus, based on motor calibration curve we choose a constant K_1 as:

$$V_{act}[rpm] = \frac{v_{act}[m/s]}{K_1} \tag{7}$$

we also define a second constant K_2 so that:

$$t = K_2 \tag{8}$$

from all above, we get the final LLC equation as follow:

$$V_{des} = \frac{v_{act}}{K_1} + \Delta a\, K_2 + K_3 \tag{9}$$

where V_{des} is the speed command send to the motor in [rpm], v_{act} is the ego car actual speed in [m/s], K_1 is a constant coefficient based on motor calibration, K_2 is a constant represent the desired response time, and K_3 is constant positive speed value to prevent jerky maneuvers in [rpm].

3 Experimental Setup

3.1 AutoMiny

AutoMiny is a 4WD Ackermann steering model-vehicle (scale 1:10), developed at the Dahlem Center for Machine Learning and Robotics - Freie Universität Berlin, for

Fig. 5. AutoMiny; Self-driving Model-car developed at the Dahlem Center for Machine Learning and Robotics—Freie Universität Berlin. It is equipped with a software stack for fully autonomous driving with custom modules for localization, control, and navigation.

school and research purposes. It is utilized to develop and test various advanced driver-assistance systems before taking high risks in a full-scale autonomous car. It is programmed to drive in fully autonomous mode. The vehicle has the dimensions (L x W x H) 445 mm x 195 mm x 300 mm, made of a carbon fiber chassis and shock towers. It has CVD front and rear driveshafts, fully adjustable aluminum oil-pressure shock absorbers, fully adjustable suspension, and independent suspension with double wishbones, front and rear anti-roll wheels.

Sensors and electronics are fixed in one layer. The vehicle sensors include a 360° rotating laser scanner that detects obstacles and walls around the vehicle, and an IMU module provides measurements from a combined 3-axis gyroscope and 3-axis accelerometer. A Kinect-type stereoscopic system has been mounted on top of the car's body. It has an Intel D435 RealSense camera and an ArUco marker mounted on top of it. The aruco marker encodes the car ID and is used to obtain the global localization of the car. The vehicle has 2 LED stripes for simulating the head- and taillights and turning, and brake lights [12]. The central computer is a mini-PC Intel NUC running Ubuntu 18.04, and the Robotic Operating System (ROS) melodic on top [24]. The model car has been motorized with a brushless DC-servomotor with a built-in encoder and a servo motor with analog feedback for steering. All control and power supply are combined in one control board. The platform empowers integrating GPUs (Jetson Nano or Jetson Xavier) for intensive calculation power.

3.2 Lab Setup

A testing environment was prepared to test the proposed controller. It consists of A 600 * 430 [cm^2] road-map and an enclosed indoor localization system, as shown in Fig. 6.

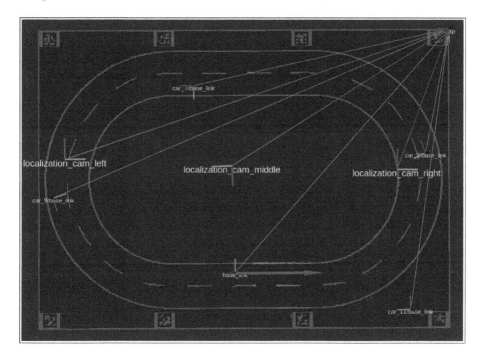

Fig. 6. Lab testing environment. It consists of A 600 * 430 [cm^2] road-map and an indoor localization system [12].

The map had two lanes, the outer one is 14.78 [m] long, and the inner one is 12.76 [m], and eight different aruco markers fixed on it. The car's navigation on the map relies on the indoor localization system. The system consisted of 3 cameras mounted on the ceiling and pointing towards the floor. Those three cameras captured a complete picture of the map, allowing the car to drive around it. Each ceiling camera could simultaneously see four aruco markers fixed on the map to determine their pose and detect the car if it was in its field of view, generally between those four markers.

3.3 Steering Control

The Vector Force Field (VFF) approach for robot navigation and path planning has been a persuasive research topic since the mid of 80th. It has been used to supervise and regulate mobile robots in the accomplishment of different duties [26,27]. The essential idea

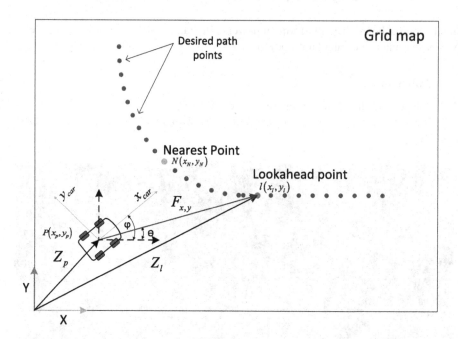

Fig. 7. Vector Force Field for a robot in the grid map.

of the VFF is to control the robot by establishing attractive and repulsive forces representing goals and obstacles, respectively, which allow a robot to gather with nonexclusive paths defined in up to 6-dimensional spaces. This method has been used in [28,29]. Since AutoMiny is moving on a defined map inside the lab, we use a VFF approach as a navigation algorithm to let both ego and lead cars following a defined path with minimum error. Only attractive forces will be considered. Our goal is accomplished by pushing the vehicle to steer at the proper angle and converge to the desired path. The attractive force vector pulls the car toward the lookahead point on the lane, making the car follow the path. A PID controller is being implemented to adjust the steering angle of the motor.

The idea of the vector force field is to identify for each point $P(x, y)$ of the map a vector $F_i(x, y)$ that influences from this point to the coveted position on the path. Figure 7 shows a simulation of the scenario. Point $P(x_p, y_p)$ is a random point on the map where the car might be, point $N(x_N, y_N)$ is the closest path point and the point $l(x_l, y_l)$ is called lookahead point. The lookahead point is used to achieve consistent couple to the lane. Normally the offset is different between the straight path and a curved one [30]. From the figure, we can also define Z_p as the vector from map origin to the point P, Z_l is the vector from map origin to point l, and $F_{x,y}$ the force vector for point P. $|Z_p|$ and $|Z_l|$ are calculated as follows:

$$|Z_p| = \sqrt{X_p^2 + Y_p^2} \tag{10}$$

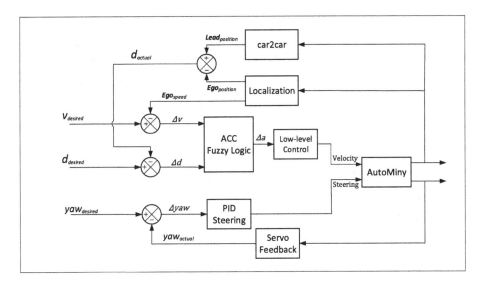

Fig. 8. AutoMiny control block diagram with Fuzzy ACC [12].

$$|Z_l| = \sqrt{X_l^2 + Y_l^2} \tag{11}$$

$$F = Z_l - Z_p \tag{12}$$

$$\theta = \arctan \frac{F_y}{F_x} \tag{13}$$

At the end, we compare the force vector angle θ with the robot's yaw from the robot's orientation data. A PID controller is implemented to minimize the difference between yaw, and θ so that the robot joins the lane.

Figure 8 shows the block diagram for implementing ACC utilizing a fuzzy logic approach and steering with a PID controller on AutoMiny. When using the ACC, the desired speed is taken from the leading vehicle, while the desired distance is manually set.

4   Evaluation

This section will rich the evaluation, presented in [12], of the performance of the proposed controller for our self-driving model car quantitatively and qualitatively. The goal is to distinguish how stable the controller is, compared to a standard PID controller. The ACC has two inputs, delta distance, and delta speed, and operates in velocity control mode and distance control mode [31]. Since the PID controller can control one input variable only, we need to compare each operation mode of the fuzzy controller with a different PID controller.

The tests involved an adequately rich set of behaviors (straight-line motion, on curve motion). All experiments were performed inside the lab using two model cars, the leading one used as a dynamic target and the ego car following it with the proposed controllers. Since the experiment was in a lab, the input and output variables of the ACC intervals were set to limit the car's speed and the desired distance range [25].

4.1 Steering Control

The Vector Force Field is dynamic because it varies according to the robot's relative locations. Therefore the PID controller keeps adjusting the motor steering, ensuring that the robot follows its path with fewer errors. Figure 9 exhibits one loop of the car following the path using the VFF navigation approach while controlling the steering and without the controller and the desired path as a reference. The controller minimizes the error significantly.

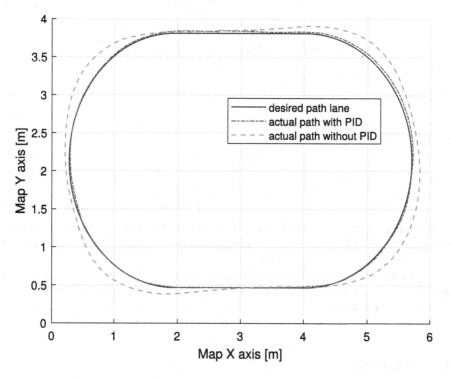

Fig. 9. AutoMiny navigates using VFF approach with and without steering control.

To make the demands of the steering control more manifest, the Root Mean Squared Error and Standard Deviation for the cross-track error, which is car deviation from the nominal to the actual trajectory, are calculated for two loops around the road map and presented in Table 5. Remarkably, the PID controller could reduce the cross-track error by a factor of up to 80%.

Table 5. RMS error and SD for the cross-track error.

	Loop 1		Loop 2	
	RMS	SD	RMS	SD
w/, PID	0.0258	0.0148	0.0194	0.0105
w/o, PID	0.1151	0.0570	0.1169	0.0580

4.2 Distance Control Mode

For this experiment, a standard PID distance control is designed. Figure 10 shows the final block diagram for AutoMiny control after implementing the distance PID controller.

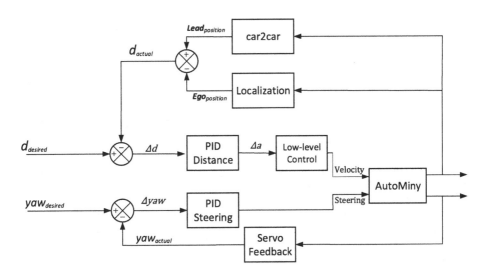

Fig. 10. AutoMiny control block diagram with PID distance control [12].

The initial parameters in this experiment were granted and set as follows:

– Leading car initial speed $= 0.75$ [m/s]
– Ego car initial speed $= 0.85$ [m/s]
– Initial desired distance $= 100$ [cm]
– ACC activates automatically when $\Delta d \leq 200$ [cm]

During the experiments, the desired distance was changing between 100 [cm] and 160 [cm] in 30 [s] steps. The head vehicle maintained driving at its initial steady speed. The goal was to observe how the distance PID controller and the fuzzy logic controller responded to desired distance changes and determine which one had a better response in the same operating condition.

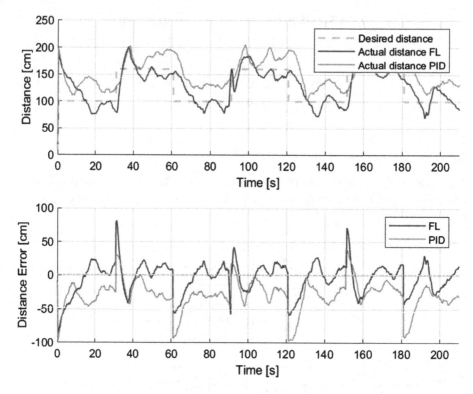

Fig. 11. Actual distance and the distance error as a consequence of changing the desired distance; the desired distance was changed between 100 [cm] and 160 [cm] in steps of 30 [s] while the heading vehicle maintained driving at an initial constant speed.

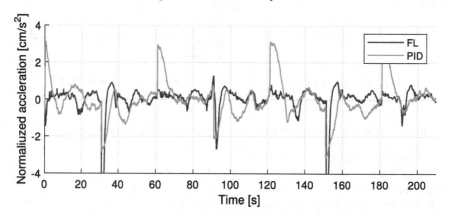

Fig. 12. Controllers output as a consequence of changing the desired distance. The desired distance was adjusted at 30 [s] steps demanding a sharp decelerate or accelerate. The fuzzy logic controller responded more gently than the PID one.

Table 6. ACC controller's Root Mean Squared Error and Standard Deviation for distance, speed, and acceleration as a result of adjusting the target distance.

	e_{dis}		e_{vel}		e_{acc}	
	RMS	SD	RMS	SD	RMS	SD
FL	23.5080	23.3105	0.0951	0.0947	0.0129	0.0117
PID	36.2654	30.5489	0.0830	0.0828	0.0363	0.0223

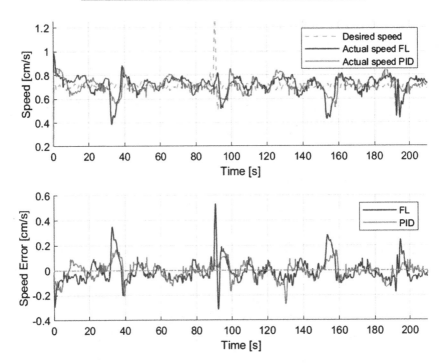

Fig. 13. Actual speed and the speed error as a consequence of changing the desired distance. The desired distance was modified at 30 [s] steps obliging sharp changes in speed.

Figure 11 shows in the first plot the actual distance behavior of the ACC controller while changing the desired distance. The second plot shows the error in the distance. We can see that the ACC controller reacted to the changes in the desired distance with a minor error indicating the controller's dynamic response.

Figure 12 shows the controller normalized output. The fuzzy logic controller has a consistent response to changes in the desired distance, as can be shown.

In Fig. 13, we can see both the measured velocity and the velocity error for the proposed controller. We can see that both controllers are capable of controlling the car speed adequately. Nevertheless, distance was the primary controlled variable in this experiment, and the fuzzy logic controller demonstrated more steady behavior.

In order to summarize the explorations of Figs. 11, 12, and 13, the Root Mean Squared Error and the Standard Deviation for distance, speed, and acceleration of each controller are shown in Table 6. Here, we can distinguish that both controllers could control the distance reducing the error. Nevertheless, Fig. 12 showed that the fuzzy logic controller had a more stable response to the changes in the controlled variable. As a conclusion of this analysis, we observed that the fuzzy logic controller had a better performance adjusting the desired distance to a dynamic obstacle moving with a constant speed.

4.3   Speed Control Mode

For this experiment, a standard speed PID controller is designed for the ego car to analyze the velocity control mode between the fuzzy logic controller and the speed PID controller. Figure 14 exposes the block diagram for AutoMiny control after implementing the speed PID controller.

The initial parameters in this experiment were set as follows:

- Lead car initial speed = 0.5 [m/s]
- Ego car initial speed = 0.85 [m/s]
- Initial desired distance = 120 [cm]
- ACC activates automatically when $\Delta d \leq 200$ [cm]

During the experiment, the dynamic target velocity was changed between 0.5 [m/s] and 0.75 [m/s] at 60 [s] steps. The desired distance (the distance to the front car) remained constant. The idea is to test both the speed PID controller and the fuzzy logic controller and determine which one has a more reliable rejoinder in the same operating condition. Figure 15 shows in the first plot the actual velocity behavior for both controllers and while changing the target speed. The second plot shows the error in the velocity for both controllers. Notably, both controllers reacted almost the same way; however, the PID controller oscillated more than the fuzzy logic controller.

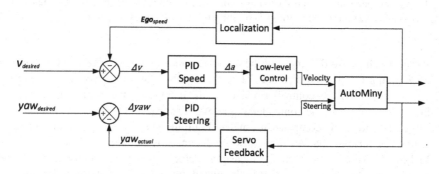

Fig. 14. AutoMiny control block diagram with PID speed control [12].

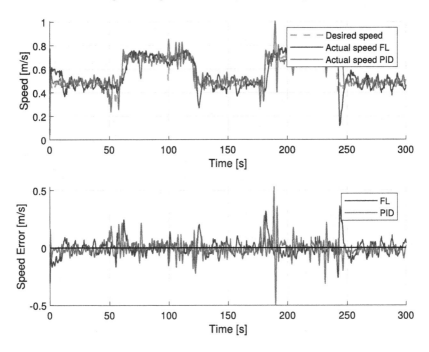

Fig. 15. Actual speed and the speed error as a consequence of changing the desired speed. The desired velocity was changed between 0.5 [m/s] to 0.75 [m/s] in 60 [s] steps while the desired distance remain constant.

Figure 16 shows both controllers' normalized output versus time. We can see that the PID controller output oscillated, indicating that such a controller would not be ideal for a real vehicle despite controlling the speed dramatically.

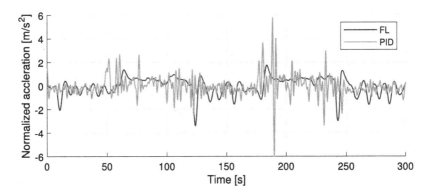

Fig. 16. Controllers output as a consequence of changing the desired velocity. The desired distance was adjusted in 60 [s] steps demanding a sharp decelerate or accelerate. Both controllers responded significantly.

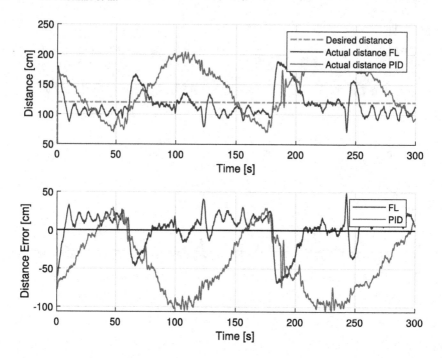

Fig. 17. Actual distance and the distance error as a consequence of changing the desired speed. The desired velocity was adjusted in steps of 60 [s]. The fuzzy controller could control the desired distance as a consequence of changing the desired speed.

In Fig. 17, we plot the actual distance and distance error in both the speed PID controller and the fuzzy logic one. The figure shows that while the fuzzy logic controller approached the desired distance, it still could not appropriately control it, while the speed PID controller was utterly incapable of controlling the distance during speed control mode.

Table 7. Root Mean Squared Error and Standard Deviation for distance, speed, and acceleration for both controllers as a consequence of changing the desired speed.

	e_{dis}		e_{vel}		e_{acc}	
	RMS	SD	RMS	SD	RMS	SD
FL	24.4127	24.3957	0.0784	0.0782	0.0087	0.0069
PID	55.6506	38.0479	0.0656	0.0654	0.0119	0.0119

Again, we summarize the information of Figs. 15, 16, and 17, the Root Mean Squared Error and the Standard Deviation for distance, speed, and acceleration of each controller in Table 7. We can observe that both controllers could control the velocity and maintain a relatively small error during transitioning. However, we acknowledge that the fuzzy controller responded to the changes in desired controlled variable smoothly while maintaining a small distance error.

5 Conclusions

This paper proposes and analyzes a fuzzy logic-based Adaptive Cruise Controller. Section 1 introduces the subject and comprises a selection of the most related work. Section 2 presents a brief overview of the Fuzzy Logic approach and describes the development of the Adaptive Cruise Controller using Fuzzy Logic and a low-level controller. Section 3 details the experimental setup used to test the proposed controllers. Finally, in Sect. 4, we evaluate the controller against a distance PID and a velocity PID using a second leading model car in a lab environment on a race track.

Analysis results exposed that the ego vehicle follows a head vehicle gently by controlling both speed and distance even when their coveted values are changed during operation. It intimates the possibility of constructing an independent desired behavior per state in the appropriate environment and condition, considering other essential driveability factors such as the comfort of acceleration rate or optimal energy consumption. Challenges with these controlling approaches rely on fuzzy controllers having many adjustable variables that must be calibrated by hand. Depending on the complexity of the aspired operation, the number of calibration variables can be more than triple the parameters on a conventional PID controller. Nevertheless, we show that the trade-off between controller simplicity and performance of the proposed fuzzy controller is advantageous for ACC systems.

References

1. He, Y., et al.: Adaptive cruise control strategies implemented on experimental vehicles: a review. IFAC-PapersOnLine **52**(5), 21–27 (2019). https://doi.org/10.1016/j.ifacol.2019.09.004
2. Shang, M., Stern, R.E.: Impacts of commercially available adaptive cruise control vehicles on highway stability and throughput. Transp. Res. Part C: Emerg. Technol. **122**, 102897 (2021). https://doi.org/10.1016/j.trc.2020.102897
3. Lu, C., Aakre, A.: A new adaptive cruise control strategy and its stabilization effect on traffic flow. Eur. Transp. Res. Rev. **10**(2), 1–11 (2018). https://doi.org/10.1186/s12544-018-0321-9
4. Ntousakis, I.A., Nikolos, I.K., Papageorgiou, M.: On microscopic modelling of adaptive cruise control systems. Transp. Res. Proc. **6**, 111–27 (2015). https://doi.org/10.1016/j.trpro.2015.03.010
5. Chang, B.-J., Tsai, Y.-L., Liang, Y.-H.: Platoon-based cooperative adaptive cruise control for achieving active safe driving through mobile vehicular cloud computing. Wirel. Person. Commun. **97**(4), 5455–5481 (2017). https://doi.org/10.1007/s11277-017-4789-8
6. Xiao, L., Gao, F.: A comprehensive review of the development of adaptive cruise control systems. Veh. Syst. Dyn. **48**(10), 1167–92 (2010). https://doi.org/10.1080/00423110903365910
7. Rajamani, R.: Vehicle Dynamics and Control, 2nd edn. Springer, Berlin (2012). https://doi.org/10.1007/978-1-4614-1433-9
8. Tsai, C.-C., Hsieh, S.-M., Chen, C.-T.: Fuzzy longitudinal controller design and experimentation for adaptive cruise control and stop & go. J. Intell. Robot. Syst. **59**(2), 167–89 (2010). https://doi.org/10.1007/s10846-010-9393-z

9. Milanes, V., Villagra, J., Godoy, J., Gonzalez, C.: Comparing fuzzy and intelligent pi controllers in stop-and-go manoeuvres. IEEE Trans. Control Syst. Technol. **20**(3), 770–778 (2012). https://doi.org/10.1109/TCST.2011.2135859

10. Piao, J., McDonald, M.: Advanced driver assistance systems from autonomous to cooperative approach. Transp. Rev. **28**(5), 659–84 (2008). https://doi.org/10.1080/01441640801987825

11. Paul, A., Chauhan, R., Srivastava, R., Baruah, M.: Advanced Driver Assistance Systems, pp. 2016–28-0223 (2016). https://doi.org/10.4271/2016-28-0223

12. Alomari, K., Mendoza, R., Sundermann, S., Goehring, D., Rojas, R.: Fuzzy logic-based adaptive cruise control for autonomous model car. In: Proceedings of the International Conference on Robotics, Computer Vision and Intelligent Systems, vol. 1: ROBOVIS, pp. 121–130 (2020). ISBN 978-989-758-479-4. https://doi.org/10.5220/0010175101210130

13. Naranjo, J., González, C., Reviejo, J., García, R., de Pedro, T.: Adaptive fuzzy control for inter-vehicle gap keeping. IEEE Trans. Intell. Transp. Syst. **4**(3), 11 (2003)

14. Marsden, G., McDonald, M., Brackstone, M.: Towards an Understanding of Adaptive Cruise Control (2001), 19

15. Basjaruddin, N.C., Kuspriyanto, K., Saefudin, D., Khrisna Nugraha, I.: Developing adaptive cruise control based on fuzzy logic using hardware simulation. Int. J. Electric. Comput. Eng. (IJECE) **4**(6), 944–951 (2014)

16. Karasudani, K.: Inter-Vehicle Distance Detecting Device, US Patent 5,369,590 (November 29, 1994)

17. Zhao, D., Wang, B.: Data-based vehicle adaptive cruise control: a review. In: Proceedings of the 32nd Chinese Control Conference, Xi'an, China, pp. 7840–7845 (2013)

18. SAE-J3016: Taxonomy and Definitions for Terms Related to Driving Automation Systems for On-Road Motor Vehicles, SAE J3016–201806 (2018). https://doi.org/10.4271/J3016-201806

19. Pananurak, W., Thanok, S., Parnichkun, M.: Adaptive cruise control for an intelligent vehicle. In: 2008 IEEE International Conference on Robotics and Biomimetics, pp. 1794–99. IEEE, Bangkok (2009). https://doi.org/10.1109/ROBIO.2009.4913274

20. Jantezn, J.: Design of Fuzzy Controllers. Technical University of Denmark, Department of Automation, vol. 326, pp. 362–367 (1998)

21. Jantzen, J.: Foundations of Fuzzy Control; a Practical Approach, 2nd edn. Wiley, Greece (2013)

22. Michels, K., Klawonn, F., Kruse, R., Nürnberger, A.: Fuzzy Control; Fundamentals, Stability and Design of Fuzzy Controllers. Springer, Berlin (2006). https://doi.org/10.1007/3-540-31766-XISBN: 978-3-540-31766-1

23. Ahmad, H., Basiran, S.N.A.: Fuzzy logic based vehicle speed control performance considering different membership types. ARPN J. Eng. Appl. Sci. **10**(21) (2015). ISSN: 1819–6608

24. Stanford Artificial Intelligence Laboratory et al. (2018) Robotic Operating System, ROS Melodic Morenia. https://www.ros.org

25. Driankov, D., Saffiotti, A.: Fuzzy Logic Techniques for Autonomous Vehicle Navigation. Springer, Berlin (2001). https://doi.org/10.1007/978-3-7908-1835-2, ISBN: 978-3-7908-1835-2

26. Rimon, E., Koditschek, D.E.: Exact robot navigation using artificial potential functions. IEEE Trans. Robot. Autom. **8**(5), 501–518 (1992). https://doi.org/10.1109/70.163777

27. Li, P.Y., Horowitz, R.: Passive velocity field control of mechanical manipulators. IEEE Trans. Robot. Autom. **15**(4), 751–763 (1999). https://doi.org/10.1109/70.782030

28. Rasekhipour, Y., Khajepour, A., Chen, S., Litkouhi, B.: A potential field-based model predictive path-planning controller for autonomous road vehicles. IEEE Trans. Intell. Transp. Syst. **18**(5), 1255–1267 (2017). https://doi.org/10.1109/TITS.2016.2604240

29. Iscold, P., Pereira, G.A.S., Torres, L.A.B.: Development of a hand-launched small UAV for ground reconnaissance. IEEE Trans. Aerosp. Electron. Syst. **46**(1), 335–348 (2010). https://doi.org/10.1109/TAES.2010.5417166

30. Goncalves, V.M., Pimenta, L.C.A., Maia, C.A., Dutra, B.C.O., Pereira, G.A.S.: Vector fields for robot navigation along time-varying curves in n-dimensions. IEEE Trans. Robot. **26**(4), 647–659 (2010). https://doi.org/10.1109/TRO.2010.2053077

31. Singh, A., Satsangi, C.S., Panse, P.: Adaptive Cruise Control using Fuzzy Logic. Int. J. Digital Appl. Contemp. Res. (IJDACR) **3**(8), 1–7 (2015). ISSN: 2319–4863. Accessed from 8 March 2015

Human-Likeness Indicator for Robot Posture Control and Balance

Vittorio Lippi[1,2]([⊠])[iD], Christoph Maurer[2][iD], and Thomas Mergner[2][iD]

[1] Institute of Digitalization in Medicine, Faculty of Medicine and Medical Center,
University of Freiburg, Freiburg, Germany
[2] Clinic of Neurology and Neurophysiology, Medical Centre-University of Freiburg,
Faculty of Medicine, University of Freiburg, Breisacher Straße 64,
79106 Freiburg im Breisgau, Germany
{vittorio.lippi,christoph.maurer,thomas.mergner}@uniklinik-freiburg.de

Abstract. Similarly to humans, humanoid robots require posture control and balance to walk and interact with the environment. In this work posture control in perturbed conditions is evaluated as a performance test for humanoid control. A specific performance indicator is proposed: the score is based on the comparison between the body sway of the tested humanoid standing on a moving surface and the sway produced by healthy subjects performing the same experiment. This approach is here oriented to the evaluation of a human-likeness. The measure is tested using a humanoid robot in order to demonstrate a typical usage of the proposed evaluation scheme and an example of how to improve robot control on the basis of such a performance indicator score.

Keywords: Humanoids · Benchmarking · Human likeness · Posture control · Balance

1 Introduction

1.1 Overview

The benchmarking of humanoid performance is gaining interest in the research community [6,9,27,28,40,46,47]. The performance of a humanoid is a complex issue that covers several aspects, e.g. sensor fusion, cognitive and motor functions, mechanics, and energy efficiency. In particular, a recent European project, EUROBENCH [42,44,45] is proposing to implement standard and repeatable experimental procedures to evaluate and compare the performance of different robots. This work describes one specific posture control performance indicator to be implemented within the project, evaluating human-likeness based on the similarity between human and robot responses to external disturbances [24,27,28].

Posture control is here particularly relevant because falling is one of the typical reasons for failures for humanoids [4,5,13]. This work focuses on posture control from the point of view of human-likeliness. A formal and unanimous definition of human-likeness is still missing, although the concept is relevant both for

P. Galambos et al. (Eds.): ROBOVIS 2020/ROBOVIS 2021, CCIS 1667, pp. 98–113, 2022.
https://doi.org/10.1007/978-3-031-19650-8_5

Fig. 1. Posture control experiment with a moving support surface, a 6-Dof Stuart Platform. On the left, a human subject with active markers visible on the back (blue triangular plates) is shown. On the right, the *Lucy* robot standing on a different platform that implements the same support surface tilt profile. (Color figure online)

robotics and neuroscience [46]. Notwithstanding the difficulty in defining human-like behavior, it is expected to be superior to the one of state-of-the-art robots [36]. Human-likeness is envisaged to be associated with some advantages such as mechanical compliance (also important for safety) and low energy consumption. Both of these features are typically associated with the low feedback loop gain typical for biological systems in face of the presence of neural delay. In robotics, the delay associated with the transport of signals is usually negligible, but the robustness in face of delays may be important in limiting the required computational resources needed to implement the real-time control [37]. Often human-likeness is defined (1) in terms of perception from the point of view of human observers [1,38,49], (2) identified with the presence of a specific feature, e.g. reproducing human trajectories [21] or exhibiting mechanical compliance [8], or defined in relation to a set of tasks, e.g. in challenges as used in the DARPA challenge [10,31]. The measure proposed here is based on body kinematics with the aim to provide an indicator of human-likeness that is repeatable and objective.

The idea of testing robots in the experimental setup used for human posture control dates was inspired by the necessity of implementing and testing human posture control models in a "real world" set-up, including factors that are not usually well accounted for by simulations such as sensor and actuation noise [14,25,32,34]. Once this approach was defined, posture control experiments provided a way to compare alternative control systems (bio-inspired or not) on the same robotic platform [2,37]. The general benchmarking issue represents a generalization and a formalization of such studies. In general, the mutual inspiration between humanoid robotics and neuroscience is well recognized and considered promising in both the robotics and neuroscience fields [7].

This article represents an extended version of [24], a conference paper where the benchmarking principle was tested with simulated experiments. In the present work, the system is tested with a real humanoid robot. In the remainder of the Introduction, we describe the proposed benchmarking approach summarizing the method previously detailed in [24]. In the Method section, the robotic platform, the control system, and the experimental testbed are described as well as the set-up used to produce the human data-set. The Results section will show the scores obtained with different settings in the control system. The implications of the proposed performance indicator and the limitations associated with human likeliness in humanoid posture control will be discussed in the conclusions.

1.2 Description of the Approach

The proposed benchmarking measure is based on a data-set of results from human experiments. The experimental data consist of the body sway of human body segments induced by an external stimulus, here specifically the tilt of the support surface in the body sagittal plane. The measured body sway is characterized as a *Frequency Response Function*, FRF, i.e. an empirical transfer function between the stimulus characterized by a Pseudo Random Ternary Sequence (PRTS) profile [39] and the response computed on specific frequency points. The data-set has been produced with healthy subjects. The comparison aims to assess the similarity in the balancing behavior between the robot and a set of average healthy subjects. Such measure does not make explicit assumptions about specific advantages of the human behavior, in contrast to the performance indexes proposed in other studies that identify some goal like minimum torque or energy consumption in robots [20], or a specific problem in human subjects [43].

Body sway profiles FRFs have been chosen as a basis for the benchmarking because such analysis has already been studied in several previous publications with human subjects. These provide a reference for comparison and tools for analysis. There are several reasons why the body sway induced by support surface tilt has been repeatedly used to study human posture control. As a repeatable stimulus, it can be used to formally characterize the behavior in terms of responses to a well-defined input. Furthermore, the tilting support surface requires the balancing mechanism to integrate vestibular input and proprioception (and vision, with eyes open), and hence it is well apt to study human sensor fusion mechanisms.

1.3 Human Data-Set

A group of 38 young healthy subjects serves as a reference for the human-likeness criterion. The subjects were presented with a stimulus consisting of a tilt of the support surface in the body sagittal plane, while the recorded output was the body sway. The typical set-up is shown in Fig. 1, the body sway tracking was performed using active markers (Optotrak 3020; Waterloo, ON, Canada), attached to subjects' hips and shoulders and the platform. A PC with custom software was used to generate the support surface tilt in the body-sagittal plane. The marker positions were recorded $100\,Hz$ using software written in LabView (National Instruments; Austin, TX, United States). The profile used for the stimulus is a pseudorandom ternary signal, PRTS [39]. The peak-to-peak amplitude was set to $1°$. The amplitude is rather small compared to what a healthy subject can withstand. Usually, in similar studies, the tilt may go up to $8°$ and more [3,39]. This was motivated by the aim to provide a data-set that could be compared safely with elderly subjects and patients and, in the specific case of robotic benchmarking, can be used to characterize the behavior of the robot without the risk of making it fall (and potentially break).

1.4   Performance Indicator

The performance indicator is here a measure of similarity with human behavior. The body sway profiles, i.e. the angular sway of the body COM with respect to the ankle joint, are used to characterize and compare the responses. The comparison is defined in terms of the norm of the difference between frequency response functions (FRFs). The PRTS power-spectrum has a profile with peaks at f_{peak} separated by ranges of frequencies with no power [19,23,39]. The response is evaluated for a specific set of frequencies where the PRTS spectrum has peaks: $\mathbf{f_{peak}}$=[0.05, 0.15, 0.25, 0.35, 0.45, 0.55, 0.65, 0.75, 0.85, 0.95, 1.05, 1.15, 1.25, 1.35, 1.45, 1.55, 1.65, 1.75, 1.85, 1.95, 2.05, 2.15, 2.25, 2.35, 2.45] Hz. Such a discrete spectrum is then transformed into a vector of 11 components by averaging the FRF over neighboring frequencies as illustrated in Fig. 2:

$$f_{x(k)} = \frac{\sum_{i \in B_k} f_{peak(i)}}{N_k} \tag{1}$$

where k and i are the indexes of the components of the frequency vectors, and B_k is a set of N_k frequencies averaged to obtain the kth sample. The B_k are shown in Fig. 2 as white and pink bands (notice that the bands are overlapping, light-pink has been used to indicate a zone belonging to two adjacent bands). Similarly the Fourier transform of the PRTS $P(f_x)$ and the Fourier transform of the responses are averaged over the bands B_k before computing the FRFs. The final representation of the FRF is a function of the 11 frequencies f_x =[0.1, 0.3, 0.6, 0.8, 1.1, 1.4, 1.8, 2.2, 2.7, 3.5, 4.4]

In a previous description of the system in [27] the frequency vector had 16 components as proposed in other works using the PRTS, e.g. [12,22,23,39]. In this work, a shorter version of the signal is used, which is considered safer and less fatiguing for human subjects, sometimes elderly patients, and convenient for robotics experimenters. Consequently, the discrete Fourier transform of the signal and the resulting FRFs have fewer components.

The choice of the frequencies in B_k and their overlapping follows the method described in [39], but here is adapted to the 11 frequencies considered. The rationale behind such a choice was to get a representation with the frequencies equally spaced on a logarithmic scale, which is often used in posturography papers to present the FRF, with the overlapping providing a smoothing effect. The FRF is computed from the 11 components of the Fourier transform of the input U, and the output Y as

$$H = \frac{G_{UY}}{G_U} \tag{2}$$

where $G_{UY} = U^* \odot Y$ and $G_U = U^* \odot U$ are empirical estimations of the cross power spectrum and the input power spectrum ("$\odot$" is the Hadamard, element-wise product). The peaks of the PRTS power-spectrum have larger values at lower frequencies [19]. This implies a better signal-to-noise ratio for the first components. A weighting vector $\mathbf{w}$ based on $P(f_x)$ is then defined in a similar way to Eq. 1, but considering the power

$$w_k = \sqrt{\sum_{i \in B_k} ||P(f_{peak(i)})||^2}. \tag{3}$$

The distance between two FRFs is defined and the norm of the difference weighted by the precision matrix, i.e. the inverse of the covariance matrix Σ, computed for the data-set of normal subjects. Before doing this, the FRF is expanded into a vector with the real and imaginary components as separated elements, i.e. 22 components. This together with the foretold weighting leads to the definition of the norm:

$$D = \sqrt{S \Delta^T \Sigma^{-1} \Delta S} \tag{4}$$

where $S = diag([\mathbf{w}, \mathbf{w}])$ is the diagonal matrix representing the re-weighting due to the power-spectrum, repeated twice to cover the 22 elements, and Δ is the difference between the two FRFs expanded to 22 components. This approach does not require model identification because it is performed on the basis of the data. The comparison can be performed between the tested robot and the average of the groups of humans (healthy or with defined deficient conditions) or between two single samples to quantify how much two robots differ from each other. The score of human-likeness is obtained comparing the sample with the mean of the human sample set μ so that

$$\Delta = H - \mu. \tag{5}$$

The parameters μ and Σ defining the score are given in Fig. 2. the score in Eq. 4 resembles a Mahalanobis distance

$$D = \sqrt{\Delta^T \Sigma^{-1} \Delta}, \tag{6}$$

but with the addition of weights. Assuming a joint normal distribution for the weighted FRFs, $\mathcal{N}(\mu, \Sigma)$, the Mahalanobis distance defines probability density, where a smaller distance associated with higher probability density.

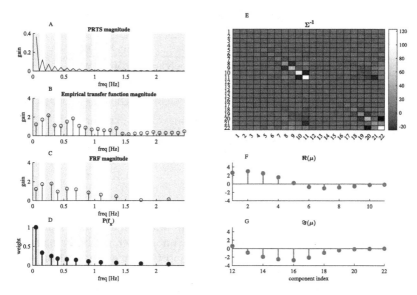

Fig. 2. Input and parameters used in the definition of the performance indicator. **A** Magnitude of the spectrum of the input PRTS, with the typical "comb" profile alternating peaks to zeros. **B** Example of the empirical transfer function from a trial. **C** 11-component FRF associated with the transfer function in B. Note that, as the FRF is averaged in the complex domain the magnitude of the average shown in the plot is not the average of the magnitudes. The bands on the background show the frequency ranges over which the spectrum is averaged: white and pink represent ranges associated with groups of frequencies. The sets of frequencies are overlapping, with light-pink bands belonging to both the two contiguous groups, and a sample on the transition between two bands belongs to both the groups. **D** Weights representing the values of $P(f_x)$ in Eq. 4. **E** Inverse of Σ from Eq. 4. Notice how the values on the diagonal corresponding to the highest frequencies are associated with high values (less variance in the dataset). This would make the metrics particularly sensitive to accidental changes in such components (e.g. due to noise). This is compensated by the weighting profiles in D, which associate almost zero weight to high-frequency components. **D** μ from Eq. 5.

2 Materials and Methods

2.1 Humanoid Robot

The test is performed with the humanoid robot *Lucy*, a custom platform designed to simulate human posture control [41]. Lucy Posturob has 14 degrees of freedom controlling posture in the frontal and the sagittal plane. The anthropometric parameters of the robot are shown in Table 1

2.2 Control System

The robot is controlled using the Disturbance Estimation and Compensation model, DEC [25,29]. The DEC model was proposed as a model of human posture

Table 1. Robot anthropometrics.

Body mass	15.30	kg
Upper body mass (including pelvis)	9.50	kg
Thighs mass	2.80	kg
Shanks mass	3.00	kg
Total height (from ankle joints)	1.52	m
Body COM height (from ankle joints)	0.68	m
Shank COM height	0.32	m
Thigh COM height	0.31	m

control in steady-state [33]. The DEC exploits human-like sensor-fusion [14–16] to reconstruct external disturbances having an impact on body posture and balance, i.e. gravity, support surface tilt, support surface acceleration, external push. The reconstructed disturbances are compensated using a servo controller implemented as a PD. The resulting control law for a joint can be expressed in Laplace domain as

$$T_{joint} = (K_p + sK_d)e^{\Delta_t s} (-\epsilon + \alpha_{grav} + \alpha_{trans} + \alpha_{push}) (K_p^{pass} + sK_d^{pass})\alpha_{joint} \tag{7}$$

where T_{joint} is the torque applied at a joint, α_{grav}, α_{trans}, and α_{push} are angle equivalent of the external disturbances, i.e. the required torque divided by the proportional gain K_p[1]. The support surface tilt is compensated by identifying the support surface tilt and using it in the definition of the controlled error ϵ. The specific definition of ϵ may change depending on which variable is controlled (e.g. joint angle or COM sway of the above segments). The model is nonlinear because it includes sensory thresholds [30] and the disturbance estimators are non-linear functions. The control loop includes a lumped delay (one for each joint). Specifically the threshold non-linearity is formulated as:

$$\hat{\alpha}_{FS} = \int_0^t f_\theta (\dot{\hat{\alpha}}_{FS}) \tag{8}$$

where $\dot{\hat{\alpha}}_{FS}$ is the support surface rotation velocity (FS = foot-in-space) reconstructed from the vestibular and the proprioceptive input $\hat{\alpha}_{FS}$ is

---

[1] In the ideal formulation proposed in [32] the controller gain $K_p \cong m \cdot g \cdot h$, where m is the body (or segment) mass, g the gravity acceleration, and h the height of the COM, is equal or slightly smaller than the one required to compensate the gravity torque (that is, with small-angle approximation, $T_g = m \cdot g \cdot h \cdot \alpha_{bs}$). Because of this, the angle equivalent of the gravity torque is the body sway α_{bs}. In general additional gains are imposed on the disturbance compensations in order to reproduce human behavior (that does not compensate disturbances perfectly) or to achieve the desired dynamic response on a robot. Notice that the compensating torque is not exactly equal to the estimated disturbance because of the derivative component of the servo loop sK_d.

the reconstructed signal used in the servo loop (Fig. 3A). The function f_θ is the dead-band threshold:

$$f_\theta(\alpha) = \begin{cases} \alpha + \theta \ if & \alpha < -\theta \\ 0 & if \ -\theta < \alpha < \theta \\ \alpha - \theta \ if & \alpha > \theta \end{cases} \tag{9}$$

The formulation of the DEC model leads to a modular control system with one control module for each degree of freedom, based on a servo loop controlled with a PD. The servo loop concept is established in neurological models [35, 48]. The modularity, in this specific case, was proposed as a generalization of the two DOF model presented in [14]. Interestingly the resulting architecture with low-level servo loops resembles state-of-the-art humanoid control systems, e.g. [17,18]. The modular control scheme is shown in Fig. 3B. The control parameters are reported in Table 2

Table 2. Control parameters for the sagittal plane from [26]. The ω_{ext} is the cutoff frequency of a Butterworth filter applied to the external contact torque (push) feedback. A gain G of 1.2 was applied to the output of the PD controller, leading to a slightly overcompensation of the external disturbances. in the here presented experiments this will be modified in order to obtain different responses.

Symbol	Quantity	Value	
ANKLE			
P	Proportional gain	119.57	Nm/rad
D	Derivative gain	11.95	Nms/rad
G_{ext}	External torque gain	0.5	
ω_{ext}	External torque filter cutoff frequency	5	rad/s
G	Loop gain (multiplies everything)	1.2	
KNEE			
P	Proportional gain	55.72	Nm/rad
D	Derivative gain	0.4458	Nms/rad
G_{ext}	External torque gain	0.5	
ω_{ext}	External torque filter cutoff frequency	5	rad/s
HIP			
P	Proportional gain	22.71	Nm/rad
D	Derivative gain	5.67	Nms/rad
G_{ext}	External torque gain	0.5	
ω_{ext}	External torque filter cutoff frequency	5	rad/s
PELVIS			
P	Proportional gain	10.59	Nm/rad
D	Derivative gain	0.07	Nms/rad
G_{ext}	External torque gain	0	
ω_{ext}	External torque filter cutoff frequency	N.A	rad/s

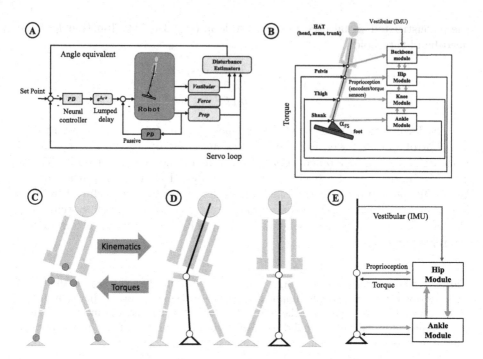

Fig. 3. The DEC control system. (A) The servo loop concept showing the compensation of external disturbances. The control scheme is presented for the single inverted pendulum (SIP) case, the generalization to more DOFs is produced with modules controlling each joint as a SIP. (B) The modular contol system in the sagittal plane. (C) The modelling in the frontal plane. With fixed feet position and neglecting knee bend, legs, pelvis and the support surface represent a four bar linkage with one DOF, an additional DOF is represented by the link between the hip and the trunk. This is mapped to a DIP model similar to the one used in the description of human balance from [11]. The torque feedback is computed on the DIP model and then mapped back to the actuators. (D) Two example positions with the associated DIP kinematics. (E) The control scheme for the frontal plane with two modules. The two degrees of freedom represented by the rotation of the legs around the vertical axis are controlled with a PD feedback (simulating a passive DOF).

2.3   Test Protocol

The robot Lucy has been tested five time with different control system configurations. Specifically the implementation of the DEC from [26] was used as base and tested, modified version consisted in one without derivative control of the ankle joints and one with twice the derivative gain. Two further trials have been performed with a version of the controller with a lower loop gain (multiplying the output of the PD controller). In one case the gain was 1 and in the other 0.8, versus the 1.2 from [26]. The body sway used to compute the human likeness measure was computed using the internal sensors of the robot. The signal were synchronized alligning the ideal PRTS samples with the profile of the foot-in-space tilt α_{FS} computed with internal sensors. The alignment was performed on the basis of maximum auto-correlation.

3   Results

The results obtained, ordered by score are:

The values in the third column give estimates of the cumulative distribution function (CDF) of the data-set at the given score. It is computed by counting the fraction of samples with a score smaller than the one produced in the specific simulation (due to the discrete nature of such measure, two results with a slightly similar score may have the same CDF). Figure 4 shows the obtained scores together with human samples for reference. The Mahalanobis distance is also plotted as function of the score.

Table 3. Scores obtained with different control configurations.

Control	Score	CDF
No D	2.9798	92.1053 %
Lower gain (1)	3.1297	92.9825 %
Lowest gain (0.8)	3.3708	95.6140 %
Standard DEC [26]	3.3823	95.6140 %
Double D	3.5646	95.6140 %

4   Discussion

The results in Table 3 show how the best score was obtained without derivative control on the ankle while the largest score was the one with twice the derivative gain. Loop gains smaller than the base model from [26] led to better scores although the lowest gain tested (0.8) led to a score that was similar to the one of the original control. Interestingly the result confirms the idea that human like behavior is in general relaxed (i.e. slightly under-compensation of disturbances). The larger Mahlanobis distance exhibited by the controller with the *lowest gain (0.8)* and with *no D* is due to oscillations produced at frequencies that are cut by the weights in Eq. 3. Such oscillations are induced by the lack of sufficient damping. One may ask, for example, if the human like behavior is advantageous in terms of energy. An indirect estimation of the energy used by the ankle actuators during the trials is shown in Fig. 5. The picture suggests

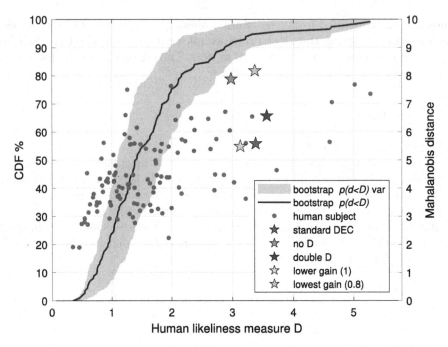

Fig. 4. Mahalanobis distance for the samples in the data-set (red dots) as a function of the metric from Eq. 4 and the bootstrap estimated cumulative distribution of the metric (blue line) and its variance (light blue bands). The human-likeness score is smaller than the Mahalanobis distance because if the coefficients in Fig. 2D that are ≤ 1, and in general there is a spread of the Mahalanobis distances of samples associated with the same D because the weighting almost removes the variation due to high-frequency components. The stars represent the results obtained with different configurations. (Color figure online)

that the most efficient is the original control system (that was carefully tuned to reduce the sway, in contrast to the other that were produced modifying D and G with the sole purpose of creating examples). The lowest gain $G = 0.8$ produces less energy consumption than $G = 1$ but more than the original $G = 1.2$. This nonlinear relationship is the result of a trade off between the smaller oscillations produced by higher gains and the smaller torques associated with smaller gains. The Example with double derivative gain is the less human like and the less efficient.

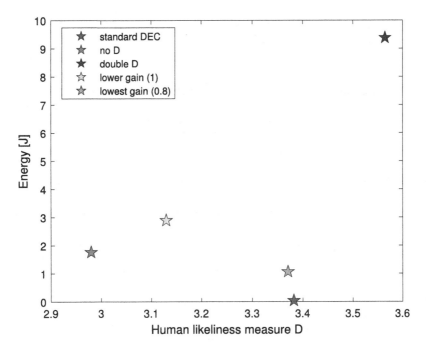

Fig. 5. Energy produced by the actuators of the ankles, computed indirectly on the basis of torque and joint angle profiles.

5   Conclusions

This work proposed a score for the evaluation of a human-likeness in humanoid posture control experiments. The experimental set up and the analysis pipeline has been described. The examples shown how different combinations of parameters lead to different scores, suggesting that low loop gain results in more human like FRF profiles. A final consideration on energy consumption by ankle actuators shown that the most human like behavior is not always the most efficient. Hence human-likeness should be associated with other measures to assess the performance of the robot completely. In general human like movements can be an advantage by themselves in human-robot interaction and for assistive devices, while in other contexts it can be sacrificed for efficiency and precision.

Testbed and Code Availability

The presented benchmarking performance indicator is par of the project EUROBENCH https://eurobench2020.eu/. The EUROBENCH framework includes several tests and performance indicators provided with the aim of testing the performance of robots at any stage of development.

The code will be updated in the docker hub:

https://hub.docker.com/repository/docker/eurobenchtest/pi_comtest.

In Linux, code can be run without being installed locally, as indicated on the *readme* page: https://github.com/eurobench/pi_comtest#docker-based-code-access

Acknowledgment. This work is supported by the project COMTEST, a sub-project of EUROBENCH (European Robotic Framework for Bipedal Locomotion Benchmarking, www.eurobench2020.eu) funded by H2020 Topic ICT 27-2017 under grant agreement number 779963.

References

1. Abel, M., et al.: Gender effects in observation of robotic and humanoid actions. Front. Psychol. **11**, 797 (2020)
2. Alexandrov, A.V., Lippi, V., Mergner, T., Frolov, A.A., Hettich, G., Husek, D.: Human-inspired eigenmovement concept provides coupling-free sensorimotor control in humanoid robot. Front. Neurorobot. **11**, 22 (2017)
3. Assländer, L., Hettich, G., Mergner, T.: Visual contribution to human standing balance during support surface tilts. Hum. Mov. Sci. **41**, 147–164 (2015)
4. Atkeson, C.G., et al.: No falls, no resets: reliable humanoid behavior in the darpa robotics challenge. In: 2015 IEEE-RAS 15th International Conference on Humanoid Robots (Humanoids), pp. 623–630. IEEE (2015)
5. Atkeson, C.G., et al.: What happened at the DARPA robotics challenge finals. In: Spenko, M., Buerger, S., Iagnemma, K. (eds.) The DARPA Robotics Challenge Finals: Humanoid Robots To The Rescue. STAR, vol. 121, pp. 667–684. Springer, Cham (2018). https://doi.org/10.1007/978-3-319-74666-1_17
6. Behnke, S.: Robot competitions-ideal benchmarks for robotics research. In: Proceedings of IROS-2006 Workshop on Benchmarks in Robotics Research. Institute of Electrical and Electronics Engineers (IEEE) (2006)
7. Cheng, G., et al.: CB: a humanoid research platform for exploring neuroscience. Adv. Rob. **21**(10), 1097–1114 (2007)
8. Colasanto, L., Van der Noot, N., Ijspeert, A.J.: Bio-inspired walking for humanoid robots using feet with human-like compliance and neuromuscular control. In: 2015 IEEE-RAS 15th International Conference on Humanoid Robots (Humanoids), pp. 26–32. IEEE (2015)
9. Conti, R., Giovacchini, F., Saccares, L., Vitiello, N., Pons, J.L., Torricelli, D.: What do people expect from benchmarking of bipedal robots? preliminary results of the EUROBENCH survey. In: Carrozza, M.C., Micera, S., Pons, J.L. (eds.) WeRob 2018. BB, vol. 22, pp. 132–136. Springer, Cham (2019). https://doi.org/10.1007/978-3-030-01887-0_26
10. DeDonato, M., et al.: Human-in-the-loop control of a humanoid robot for disaster response: a report from the darpa robotics challenge trials. J. Field Rob. **32**(2), 275–292 (2015)
11. Goodworth, A.D., Peterka, R.J.: Influence of stance width on frontal plane postural dynamics and coordination in human balance control. J. Neurophysiol. **104**(2), 1103–1118 (2010)
12. Goodworth, A.D., Peterka, R.J.: Identifying mechanisms of stance control: a single stimulus multiple output model-fit approach. J. Neurosci. Methods **296**, 44–56 (2018)

13. Guizzo, E., Ackerman, E.: The hard lessons of DARPA's robotics challenge [News]. IEEE Spect. **52**(8), 11–13 (2015)
14. Hettich, G., Assländer, L., Gollhofer, A., Mergner, T.: Human hip–ankle coordination emerging from multisensory feedback control. Hum. Mov. Sci. **37**, 123–146 (2014)
15. Hettich, G., Lippi, V., Mergner, T.: Human-like sensor fusion mechanisms in a postural control robot. In: Londral, A.E., Encarnacao, P., Pons, J.L. (eds.) Proceedings of the International Congress on Neurotechnology, Electronics and Informatics. Vilamoura, Portugal, pp. 152–160. (2013)
16. Hettich, G., Lippi, V., Mergner, T.: Human-like sensor fusion implemented in the posture control of a bipedal robot. In: Londral, A.R., Encarnação, P., Rovira, J.L.P. (eds.) Neurotechnology, Electronics, and Informatics. SSCN, vol. 13, pp. 29–45. Springer, Cham (2015). https://doi.org/10.1007/978-3-319-15997-3_3
17. Hyon, S.H., Osu, R., Otaka, Y.: Integration of multi-level postural balancing on humanoid robots. In: 2009 IEEE International Conference on Robotics and Automation, pp. 1549–1556. IEEE (2009)
18. Ishihara, K., Morimoto, J.: Computationally affordable hierarchical framework for humanoid robot control. In: 2021 IEEE/RSJ International Conference on Intelligent Robots and Systems (IROS), pp. 7349–7356. IEEE (2021)
19. Jilk, D.J., Safavynia, S.A., Ting, L.H.: Contribution of vision to postural behaviors during continuous support-surface translations. Exp. Brain Res. **232**(1), 169–180 (2014)
20. Kashiri, N., Ajoudani, A., Caldwell, D.G., Tsagarakis, N.G.: Evaluation of hip kinematics influence on the performance of a quadrupedal robot leg. In: Proceedings of the 13th International Conference on Informatics in Control, Automation and Robotics, vol. 1: ICINCO, pp. 205–212. INSTICC, SciTePress (2016). https://doi.org/10.5220/0005986502050212
21. Kim, S., Kim, C., You, B., Oh, S.: Stable whole-body motion generation for humanoid robots to imitate human motions. In: 2009 IEEE/RSJ International Conference on Intelligent Robots and Systems, pp. 2518–2524. IEEE (2009)
22. Lippi, V., Assländer, L., Akcay, E., Mergner, T.: Body sway responses to pseudo-random support surface translations of vestibular loss subjects resemble those of vestibular able subjects. Neurosci. Lett. **736**, 135271 (2020)
23. Lippi, V., Brands, K.G., Seel, T.: Real-time implementation and evaluation of magneto meterless tracking system for human and humanoid posture control benchmarking based on inertial sensors. In: Proceedings of the 17th International Conference on Informatics in Control, Automation and Robotics, vol. 1: ICINCO, pp. 675–680. INSTICC, SciTePress (2020). https://doi.org/10.5220/0009869106750680
24. Lippi, V., Maurer, C., Mergner, T.: Evaluating robot posture control and balance by comparison to human subjects using human likeness measures. In: Proceedings of the 2nd International Conference on Robotics, Computer Vision and Intelligent Systems - ROBOVIS, pp. 77–85. INSTICC, SciTePress (2021). https://doi.org/10.5220/0010646900003061
25. Lippi, V., Mergner, T.: Human-derived disturbance estimation and compensation (DEC) method lends itself to a modular sensorimotor control in a humanoid robot. Front. Neurorobot. **11**, 49 (2017)
26. Lippi, V., Mergner, T.: A challenge: Support of standing balance in assistive robotic devices. Appl. Sci. **10**(15), 5240 (2020)
27. Lippi, V., Mergner, T., Maurer, C., Seel, T.: Performance indicators of humanoid posture control and balance inspired by human experiments. In: 2020 International Symposium on Wearable Robotics and Rehabilitation (WeRob) (2020)

28. Lippi, V., Mergner, T., Seel, T., Maurer, C.: COMTEST project: a complete modular test stand for human and humanoid posture control and balance. In: 2019 IEEE-RAS 19th International Conference on Humanoid Robots (Humanoids) Toronto, Canada, 15–17 October 2019 (2019)

29. Lippi, V., Mergner, T., Szumowski, M., Zurawska, M.S., Zielińska, T.: Human-inspired humanoid balancing and posture control in frontal plane. In: Parenti-Castelli, V., Schiehlen, W. (eds.) ROMANSY 21 - Robot Design, Dynamics and Control. CICMS, vol. 569, pp. 285–292. Springer, Cham (2016). https://doi.org/10.1007/978-3-319-33714-2_32

30. Lippi, V., Molinari, F.: Lyapunov stability of a nonlinear bio-inspired system for the control of humanoid balance. In: Proceedings of the 17th International Conference on Informatics in Control, Automation and Robotics - ICINCO, pp. 726–733. INSTICC, SciTePress (2020). https://doi.org/10.5220/0009970307260733

31. Luo, J., et al.: Robust ladder-climbing with a humanoid robot with application to the darpa robotics challenge. In: 2014 IEEE International Conference on Robotics and Automation (ICRA), pp. 2792–2798. IEEE (2014)

32. Mergner, T.: A neurological view on reactive human stance control. Ann. Rev. Control **34**(2), 77–198 (2010)

33. Mergner, T., Maurer, C., Peterka, R.J.: A multisensory posture control model of human upright stance. Progr. Brain Res. **142**, 189–201 (2003)

34. Mergner, T., Schweigart, G., Fennell, L.: Vestibular humanoid postural control. J. Physiol. - Paris **103**, 178–194 (2009)

35. Merton, P.: Speculations on the servo-control of movement. In: Ciba Foundation Symposium-The Spinal Cord, pp. 247–260. Wiley Online Library (1953)

36. Nori, F., Peters, J., Padois, V., Babic, J., Mistry, M., Ivaldi, S.: Whole-body motion in humans and humanoids. In: Workshop on New Research Frontiers for Intelligent Autonomous Systems (2014)

37. Ott, C.: Good posture, good balance: comparison of bioinspired and model-based approaches for posture control of humanoid robots. IEEE Rob. Autom. Mag. **23**(1), 22–33 (2016)

38. Oztop, E., Franklin, D.W., Chaminade, T., Cheng, G.: Human-humanoid interaction: is a humanoid robot perceived as a human? Int. J. Hum. Rob. **2**(04), 537–559 (2005)

39. Peterka, R.: Sensorimotor integration in human postural control. J. Neurophysiol. **88**(3), 1097–1118 (2002)

40. del Pobil, A.P., Madhavan, R., Messina, E.: Benchmarks in robotics research. In: Proceedings of IROS-2006 Workshop on Benchmarks in Robotics Research. Citeseer (2006)

41. Posture Control Laboratory, Uniklinik Freiburg - Neurozentrum.: Lucy posturob. https://www.uniklinik-freiburg.de/neurologie/forschung/neurologische-arbeitsgruppen/postural-control.html

42. Remazeilles, A., Dominguez, A., Barralon, P., Torricelli, D.: Towards a unified terminology for benchmarking bipedal systems. In: Moreno, J.C., Masood, J., Schneider, U., Maufroy, C., Pons, J.L. (eds.) WeRob 2020. BB, vol. 27, pp. 609–613. Springer, Cham (2022). https://doi.org/10.1007/978-3-030-69547-7_98

43. Singh, N.K.: Detection of hesitant dynamic postural control. In: 2016 IEEE 12th International Colloquium on Signal Processing & its Applications (CSPA), pp. 36–40. IEEE (2016)

44. The EUROBENCH consortium: Eurobench Github Repository (2022). https://github.com/eurobench

45. The EUROBENCH consortium: Eurobench Software documentation (2022). https://eurobench.github.io/sofware_documentation/latest/index.html
46. Torricelli, D., et al.: Benchmarking human-like posture and locomotion of humanoid robots: a preliminary scheme. In: Duff, A., Lepora, N.F., Mura, A., Prescott, T.J., Verschure, P.F.M.J. (eds.) Living Machines 2014. LNCS (LNAI), vol. 8608, pp. 320–331. Springer, Cham (2014). https://doi.org/10.1007/978-3-319-09435-9_28
47. Torricelli, D., et al.: Benchmarking human likeness of bipedal robot locomotion: state of the art and future trends. In: Bonsignorio, F., Messina, E., del Pobil, A.P., Hallam, J. (eds.) Metrics of Sensory Motor Coordination and Integration in Robots and Animals. CSM, vol. 36, pp. 147–166. Springer, Cham (2020). https://doi.org/10.1007/978-3-030-14126-4_8
48. Wiener, N.: Cybernetics or Control and Communication in the Animal and the Machine. Technology Press, Beijing (1948)
49. von Zitzewitz, J., Boesch, P.M., Wolf, P., Riener, R.: Quantifying the human likeness of a humanoid robot. Int. J. Soc. Robot. 5(2), 263–276 (2013)

Visual Guidance of an On-Orbit Free-Floating Manipulator Using a Mobile Camera

José L. Ramón[1] ⓘ, Jorge Pomares[1](✉) ⓘ, and Leonard Felicetti[2] ⓘ

[1] University of Alicante, 03690 Alicante, Spain
{jl.ramon,jpomares}@ua.es
[2] Cranfield University, Cranfield MK43 0AL, UK
Leonard.Felicetti@cranfield.ac.uk

Abstract. A direct visual-servoing algorithm for control a space-based manipulator is proposed. A two-arm manipulator is assumed as a baseline scenario for this investigation, with one of the arms performing the manipulation and the second arm dedicated to the observation of the target zone of manipulation. The algorithm relies on images taken independently from de-localized cameras, e.g. at the end-effector of a second manipulator. Through the implementation of a Kalman filter, the algorithm can estimate the movements of the features in the image plane due to the relative movements between the camera and the target and then calculate the torques to be provided to the joints of the manipulator by adopting a visual servoing control strategy. Simulations results in two different scenarios have been presented to show an adequate behaviour of the presented approach in on-orbit-servicing operations.

Keywords: Space robotics · On-Orbit servicing · Visual servoing · Impedance control

1 Introduction

We are now entering a new and exciting phase that is changing the paradigms of exploitation of near-Earth space and its resources. In the sixties and seventies, space activities were carried on primarily for governmental or military purposes, intended more to assert the technical and strategical supremacy of one nation over the others. From the eighties up to the end of the twentieth century, the need for word-wide services led to the raise of telecommunications and commercial players into the space race scene. The race for space exploitation is now changing again, with private actors developing a whole new series of activities and economic business opportunities [1]. The change is exponentially growing due to a sensible increase of the number of launch opportunities, the reduction of the overall missions' costs and numerous investments for making space the new domain for carrying on and supporting word-wide commercial and economic activities. This necessarily is leading to an exponential growth of the objects populating near-Earth regions. According to the United Nations Office for Outer Space Affairs [2], only in 2021 more than 1700 objects were launched into space. Initially, most of the

© Springer Nature Switzerland AG 2022
P. Galambos et al. (Eds.): ROBOVIS 2020/ROBOVIS 2021, CCIS 1667, pp. 114–130, 2022.
https://doi.org/10.1007/978-3-031-19650-8_6

failures occurred during launch and early operations phases, but nowadays, many more failures occur once the satellites are operating in orbit. Even if no failures occur, the mission's lifetime is limited by the amount of fuel and other consumable items carried onboard by spacecraft. For example, in some applications, once the fuel necessary to perform station keeping and attitude maneuvers is finished, the satellite is forced to finish its mission and be dismissed, even if all the other systems would be able to continue to carry on their nominal activities for longer time. Recent studies show that repairing or refuelling these satellites would reduce costs significantly [3].

For this reason, agencies are interested in the field of in-orbit servicing. Another aspect to consider is that a large quantity of such newly inserted in orbit objects is destined to increase space debris population. Thus, numerous current research activities and under development missions are exploring and assessing the feasibility of active debris removal strategies [4].

Some of the mission concepts for on-orbit servicing and active debris removal utilize robotic manipulators for performing complex operations, such as grasping, manipulation, refuelling, inspections and many others. Space environmental conditions, such as free-floating and frictionless conditions, impose new challenges for the control of such robotic systems: classical strategies for Earth-based manipulators are generally not applicable to space-based manipulators. In addition, most of the foreseen on-orbit operations in future missions impose strict requirements in terms of precision and accuracy of the robotic arm movements, and in some cases, these operations will need to be performed with a high level of autonomy. Most of the missions carried out in the last two decades had robotic operations mainly under teleoperation or manual control (e.g. robotic arms in the International Space Station). Teleoperation of space robotic assets are currently limited by the eventual delays in communications and strict requirements necessary to maintain constant communication between the robotic manipulator and the operators. These issues become even more critical when the spacecraft operates far from Earth (i.e., in deep space and planetary exploration missions). This way of using on-orbit robotic systems is destined to disappear in favour of more autonomous systems that will decide and carry-on operations based on in-situ measurements and evaluation of the necessary operations to be performed without any human-in-the-loop.

Robotic on-orbit service (OOS) and active debris removal (ADR) missions are generally composed of three elements. The servicing spacecraft, a robotic manipulator, attached to the service spacecraft and, finally, the target spacecraft to be served. In active debris removal missions, the target spacecraft is replaced by the space debris element that needs to be removed from a certain orbital position. One of the challenges in OOS and ADR missions is represented by the uncooperativeness of the target objects, either because they have reached the end of their useful life or because they have faulty or uncontrolled parts [5]. These missions are also characterized by a set of standard phases that span from the launch and early operations when the servicing spacecraft is inserted in orbit, orbital manoeuvres to reach the target's orbit, a rephasing and approach phase that allows for having the service spacecraft in close proximity to the target, a synchronization phase that enables to minimize the relative velocity with respect target's motion, the rendezvous and docking/grasping phase and the subsequent phase where all the robotic operations are performed as well as the disengagement operations that terminates the specific operations to a specific target [6].

This paper focuses on the control strategies for driving the robotic manipulator once the approach and synchronization phases have been already accomplished by the service spacecraft and the final rendezvous/grasping phase needs to be performed. Having a reliable and robust control becomes of vital importance in such a phase, as it is extremely important to avoid unintentional collisions that could cause damage or determine the mission failure [7].

The relative position between the spacecraft and the target must be continuously monitored to avoid collisions [8]. Among the possible means to know the relative position between spacecraft, we have opted for using cameras as a sensor because of their reliability and versatility than other types of sensors [8]. There are three main options for the location of the camera system within the service spacecraft. The first option considers a fixed camera installed on the main spacecraft's body in a favourable position to oversee the operations and movements performed by the robotic manipulator. The second possible option uses an eye-in-hand configuration, where the camera is placed at the manipulator's end effector. The third and final option uses a camera installed on an auxiliary mobile reconfigurable structure. The latter is the option that we consider in this work. The problem presented by the first option is the risk of occlusions produced by the manipulator itself, preventing the realization of visual control. The second option improves this aspect since the camera moves together with the robot's end-effector but does not eliminate the possibility of occlusions in specific configurations. The adopted option offers a higher degree of versatility with the possibility of moving the camera constantly to have the best possible view that allows for each operation in any task performed by the robotic arm [9, 10]. This article focuses on the specific scenario where the service spacecraft is equipped with two robotic arms. The first of the arms will be in charge of performing the manipulation tasks, while the second one carries on a camera at its end-effector that moves to guarantee an optimal observation of the robotic operations and avoids eventual occlusions of the observed scene [11].

The paper proposes a new approach where both the service spacecraft and the target are in free-floating conditions at a sufficient distance so that the manipulator is able to perform its grasping and manipulation operations [12]. The visual servoing controller part is a well-known controller [14] for manipulator control using information obtained from cameras. In this type of control, it is not necessary to perform a 3D reconstruction of the target position to guide the robot since it only uses information extracted from the images captured by the camera. The proposed controller obtains the error directly from the image plane, directly giving torques to be applied in each of the manipulator's joints as a result. In this way, it is not necessary to either estimate the relative pose of the target with respect to the servicing spacecraft as well as to solve any complex inversion of the kinematic and dynamics of the manipulators for obtaining torques to be provided by servomotors. This last feature offers advantages, especially for the guidance of free-floating space robots, with eventual actions on the main body of the service spacecraft directly calculated by the controller itself, as already done by the authors in [7]. Visual servoing is also applied for the control of free-floating robots based directly on images, with an eye-in-hand configuration in [15] or, as done in [16], for the guidance of a spacecraft during a rendezvous manoeuvre. In this paper, the scenario proposed in [11] is considered where a camera installed at the end of the second manipulator is used to observe the target features. These features are used by the controller to calculate the control actions independently of the camera position. However, the present study focuses on the estimation problem of the eventual trajectories of the visual features, which might move due to both the motion of the manipulators of the servicing spacecraft as well as the motion of the target. The proposed approach uses Kalman filter as a tool for the estimation of the movements of the visual features in the image plane. Such estimations can be included within the visual servoing controller to obtain a robust and reliable tool that allows for moving and catching targets that are also moving with respect to the servicing spacecraft. This paper explores such an approach and provides simulations for demonstrating the viability of the methodology.

The rest of the article is organized as follows. Section 2 presents a description of the scenario, including the architecture of the service spacecraft and the key characteristics of the manipulators installed on it. Section 3 describes the visual servo control of the manipulator in detail, focusing on the estimation of the movements of the visual features and of the target motion via a Kalman filter implementation. Such estimations will then be used within ad-hoc build visual servoing controllers that track specific trajectories in the image in the specific free-floating base case. This is described in Sect. 4 with a resulting control law that will be then used to drive the robotic manipulator in test case simulation scenarios. The results obtained from the simulations are presented in Sect. 5. Finally, Sect. 6 summarize the main findings obtained in the present investigation.

2 Robotic Spacecraft

This section presents the main details of the robotic spacecraft and the on-orbit servicing scenario considered in this paper. A servicing spacecraft is equipped with two robotic arms: the main dynamic parameters of the servicing spacecraft and the robotic arms are indicated in Table 1 and Table 2, respectively (both robotic arms have the same dynamic parameters). One of the robotic arms (robotic camera) presents a camera at its end-effector and extracts the visual features from a target spacecraft to perform the guidance of the other robotic arm (robotic manipulator). Image extraction and processing are not addressed in this paper, and it is supposed that these can be performed so that the controller can get and track a pattern with m points of the target spacecraft.

Figure 1 represents the on-orbit servicing scenario considered in this paper. As previously indicated, a set of m visual features are extracted from the target using the robotic camera, C. With B is represented the coordinate frame at the servicing spacecraft centre of mass, and E represents the coordinate frame at the end of the manipulator robot. Finally, an earth-centred inertial coordinate frame, called I is used.

Table 1. Dynamic parameters of the servicing spacecraft.

Mass (Kg)	Inertia(kg·m^2)		
	I_x	I_y	I_z
2550	6200	3550	7100

Table 2. Dynamic parameters of the servicing spacecraft.

		Inertia		
Arms	Mass (Kg)	I_x	I_y	I_z
Link1	35	2	0.2	2
Link2	22	3	0.2	3
Link3	22	3	0.2	3
Link4	12	0.1	0.2	0.4
Link5	12	0.1	0.2	0.3
Link6	10	0.2	0.25	0.3

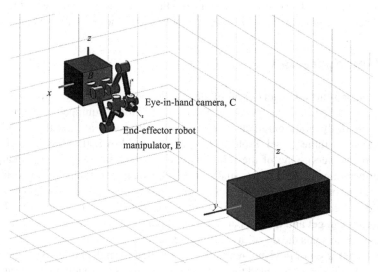

Fig. 1. Servicing spacecraft and extracted visual features.

3   Visual Servoing of a Manipulator and Estimation of the Target Motion in the Image Space

An image-based visual servoing system directly uses visual features extracted from the images obtained by the camera to generate control actions of the manipulator to track and converge progressively toward the desired features in the image plane. This approach differs from position-based controllers in that it is not necessary to calculate the 3-D pose of the observed object. This way, the control is performed directly in the image space. This paper assumes that the image processing algorithms can always extract specific points as visual features of the target. This set of points is represented with the variable s. The visual controller must apply the control actions in such a way that set s progresively reaches the value of the desired features, s_d. In this way, an error function is defined, and the objective of the controller is to reduce the value of such an error function progressively. In the next paragraphs, classical visual servoing systems are modified to allow the manipulator guidance when the visual features are obtained from a mobile camera (the robotic camera in this paper). Additionally, the estimation of the target motion is included in the next section to improve the controller behaviour during the tracking.

3.1 Visual Controller Using the Robotic Camera

In the previous paragraphs, the main properties of the employed image-based controller are described. However, in order to guide the manipulator robot, some modifications must be performed in the previous approach. The classical image-based controller considers that an eye-in-hand camera is employed. However, the camera is located at the end of the robotic camera in our case. To overcome this problem, a virtual camera located at the end of the manipulator robot is considered. This virtual camera will be employed to simulate the use of an eye-in-hand camera at the manipulator robot. This controller presents several improvements with respect the one described in our previous work [11]. The presented approach allows to determine the 3D pose of the target spacecraft frame with respect to the robotic camera only using image information. Additionally, the pose of the characteristic points with respect to the virtual camera can be obtained. Finally, this last information is projected in the image space to obtain the visual features employed by the visual servoing system. Therefore, the visual servoing can be performed independently on the point of view. These steps will be described in the next paragraphs.

First, we consider M_T^C as extrinsic parameters of the real camera located at the end of the robotic camera (pose of the target spacecraft frame with respect to the robotic camera frame). A target 3D point, P_{Pi}^T, can be expressed in the robotic camera coordinate frame as:

$$P_{Pi}^C\left(x_P^C, y_P^C, z_P^C\right) = M_T^C P_{Pi}^T \tag{1}$$

Considering a pin-hole camera projection model, the point P_P^C, expressed with respect to the camera reference frame, is projected onto the image plane at the 2D point p_i. This point is computed from the camera focal length, f, as:

$$p_i = (x_i, y_i)^T = \left(f\frac{x_{Pi}^C}{z_{Pi}^C}, f\frac{y_{Pi}^C}{z_{Pi}^C}\right)^T \tag{2}$$

Finally, the units of (2) specified in terms of metric units are scaled and transformed in pixels coordinates relative to the image reference frame, as:

$$s_i = \left(f_{ix}, f_{iy}\right)^T = (u_0 + f_u x_i, v_0 + f_v y_i)^T \tag{3}$$

where $s_i = s_i(r(t)))$, and $r(t)$ is the relative pose between the camera and inertia frame and (f_u, f_v, u_0, v_0) are the camera intrinsic parameters. The intrinsic parameters considered are the position of the optical center (u_0, v_0), , and $(f_u = s_x, f_v = s_y)$ represent the focal length in terms of pixels, where s_x and s_y are the scale factors relating pixels to distance.

In order to perform the manipulator robot guidance using the virtual camera, the following steps have been implemented:

1. First, $s = (s_1, s_2, \cdots, s_m)^T$ is considered as the extracted visual features by the robotic camera. From these visual features, the pose of the target spacecraft frame with respect to the robotic camera, M_T^C must be obtained (estimation of the camera extrinsic parameters). The estimation of these extrinsic parameters will be done by the definition of the following error function:

$$e = s_v - s \qquad (4)$$

where s have been defined as the extracted visual features and s_v is the image position of the same features computed by back-projection employing the estimated extrinsic parameters. Therefore, it is required to define a control function that reduces the previous error function by modifying the extrinsic parameters. Please note that when this error function is zeroed, the estimated extrinsic parameters will be the real ones of the camera. To enable this, the time derivative of the error function is computed as:

$$\dot{e} = \dot{s}_v - \dot{s} = \frac{\partial s_v}{\partial r} \frac{\partial r}{\partial t} = L_s \frac{\partial r}{\partial t} \qquad (5)$$

where L_s is the interaction matrix used in classical image-based visual servoing systems [14]. A proportional control law is defined to reduce the error function. Specifically, an exponential decrease of the error, e, is imposed by $\dot{e} = -\lambda_1 e$, being λ_1 a positive gain. Therefore, the following control action is obtained:

$$\frac{\partial r}{\partial t} = -\lambda_1 L_s^+ e \qquad (6)$$

2. Using the previous step, the pose of the target spacecraft frame with respect to the robotic camera is obtained M_T^C. From the spacecraft kinematics, it is also possible to obtain the relative position between the robotic camera and the virtual camera located at the end of the manipulator robot, M_C^{VC}. The homogeneous transformation matrix between the target spacecraft T and the virtual camera, VC, can easily be obtained as $M_T^{VC} = M_C^{VC} M_T^C$.

3. A kinematic model of the features extracted from the target spacecraft is known so the 3D position of each of the characteristic points with respect the frame T is known, P_i^T. Using this information and the matrix M_T^{VC}, the pose of the characteristic points with respect to the virtual camera is equal to $P_i^{VC} = M_T^{VC} P_i^T$. Considering $(x_i^{VC}, y_i^{VC}, z_i^{VC})$ the coordinates of the previous pose, Eqs. (2) and (3) can be used to obtain the value of the visual features in pixel coordinates in the image space, s_i. These features will be the extracted features at each iteration of the task.

4. In order to guide the manipulator robot, an image-based visual servoing system can be applied. This approach allows the tracking of a given trajectory by using visual information. This control action can be performed from the visual features s_i and the desired

positions of these features s_{id}, i. e., the value of these features in the desired location to be achieved. From the previous features, it is possible to define the set of observed and desired visual features as $s = (s_1, s_2, \cdots, s_m)^T$ and $s_d = (s_{1d}, s_{2d}, \cdots, s_{md})^T$ respectively, and the control action as:

$$v^{VC} = -\lambda_2 L_s^+ (s - s_d) \tag{7}$$

where v^{VC} are the velocities to be applied with respect to the virtual camera and λ_2 a positive control gain.

3.2   Estimation of the Target Spacecraft Motion in the Image Space

The visual servoing system presented in the previous section does not take into account the eventual movements of the target satellite. This section extends the previous visual servoing system to include the estimation of the target spacecraft's motion and better track the trajectories in the image space when the target is in motion. To do this, it is necessary to estimate the variations in the image error due to the motion of the target spacecraft and include it in the computation of the control actions.

The expression that relates the control action with respect to the virtual camera coordinate frame, the image error and the image error estimation due to the motion of the target spacecraft is:

$$v^{VC} = \left(\frac{\partial \widehat{e_s}}{\partial r} \right)^+ \left(-\lambda e_s - \frac{\partial \widehat{e_s}}{\partial t} \right) \tag{8}$$

where $e_s = s - s_d$ is the image error that needs to be minimized. The estimation of the motion velocity of the target spacecraft using an eye-in-hand camera system can be obtained from the camera velocities measurements and the error function. Therefore, from Eq. (8) we can obtain the value of the estimation of the error variation due to the motion of the target spacecraft (note that the proportional control action allows for obtaining an exponential decrease of the error function and, therefore, $\dot{e}_s = -\lambda e_s$):

$$\frac{\partial \widehat{e_s}}{\partial r} = \dot{e}_s - \frac{\partial \widehat{e_s}}{\partial t} v^{VC} \tag{9}$$

To obtain the value of the estimation of the motion at each iteration, a discretization of Eq. (9) can be done, obtaining the following expression:

$$\left(\frac{\partial \widehat{e_s}}{\partial t} \right)_k = \frac{e_k - e_{k-1}}{\Delta t} - \frac{\partial \widehat{e_s}}{\partial r} v^{VC} \tag{10}$$

where Δt can be obtained by computing the delay at each iteration. Additionally, the term $\frac{\partial \widehat{e_s}}{\partial r}$ is equal to the identity matrix, and therefore (10) can be simplified in the following relationship:

$$\left(\frac{\partial \widehat{e_s}}{\partial t} \right)_k = \frac{e_k - e_{k-1}}{\Delta t} - v^{VC} \tag{11}$$

Therefore, Eq. (11) can be used to measure the image error variation due to the movement of the target spacecraft. Specifically, two sources of error can be identified as an error. On the one hand, the estimator depends on the precision in the image processing. On the other hand, errors in the measurement in the camera motion, v^{VC}., can also produce errors in the estimation provided by Eq. (11). In the next section, a target spacecraft motion estimator is proposed by using a Kalman filter.

3.3 Target Spacecraft Motion Estimation

Different approaches can be used to filter the measurement error obtained when the image error variation due to the target motion is estimated. One of these approaches is approaches are the ones based on Kalman filters [17]. These filters, do not generate correct estimations when abrupt changes in the state vector are obtained (these abrupt changes are considered noise and the filter requires several iterations for the convergence). In this section, the formulation of a Kalman filter is presented to be applied to the specific case presented in this paper, i. e., the estimation of the motion of the target spacecraft.

In a general case, the equations of the model state and measurement can be considered as:

$$x_{(k+1)} = Fx_{(k)} + v_{(k)}$$
$$z_{(k)} = Hx_{(k)} + w_{(k)}$$

(12)

where:

- F is the state transition matrix. This matrix relates the state in the previous iteration k-1 with the current state k (without noise).
- H is the measurement matrix, which relates the state with the measurement.
- It is assumed that the random variables v and w are independent. v is the noise process, and it is supposed to be with white centered noise and with covariance matrix Q. w is the measurement noise. It is supposed to be with white centered noise and with covariance matrix R.

The target motion components are not correlated; therefore, two independent Kalman filters are applied to each of the components $\left(\frac{\partial \widehat{e_{sx}}}{\partial t}, \frac{\partial \widehat{e_{sy}}}{\partial t} \right)$. In the next paragraphs the subscript s (e.g., in $\frac{\partial \widehat{e_s}}{\partial t}$) is used to represent generically any of the components, x, y. The equations of the state model and measurement of the Kalman filter are:

$$\begin{pmatrix} \left(\frac{\partial e_s}{\partial t} \right)_{k+1} \\ \eta_{k+1} \end{pmatrix} = F \begin{pmatrix} \left(\frac{\partial e_s}{\partial t} \right)_k \\ \eta_k \end{pmatrix} + \begin{pmatrix} 0 \\ v_{(k)} \end{pmatrix}$$

(13)

$$\left(\frac{\partial \widehat{e_s}}{\partial t} \right)_{k+1} = H \begin{pmatrix} \left(\frac{\partial e_s}{\partial t} \right)_{k+1} \\ \eta_{k+1} \end{pmatrix} + w_{(k)}$$

(14)

where $\left(\dfrac{\partial \widehat{e}_s}{\partial t}\right)_k$ is the variation of the error due to the target spacecraft motion. This term needs to be measured by using Eq. (11). Therefore, the prediction of the state vector is given by:

$$\left(\frac{\partial \widehat{e}_s}{\partial t}\right)_{k+1|k} = \left(\frac{\partial \widehat{e}_s}{\partial t}\right)_{k|k} \tag{15}$$

with the matrices F and H being:

$$F = \begin{pmatrix} 1 & 1 \\ 0 & \rho \end{pmatrix} \tag{16}$$

$$H = \begin{pmatrix} 1 & 0 \end{pmatrix} \tag{17}$$

where ρ is the correlation grade between the successive accelerations of the target (this parameter changes between 0 and 1). In this case, the prediction and estimation equations of the Kalman filter are respectively:

$$\begin{pmatrix} \left(\dfrac{\partial \widehat{e}_s}{\partial t}\right)_{k+1|k} \\ \widehat{\eta}_{k+1|k} \end{pmatrix} = F \begin{pmatrix} \left(\dfrac{\partial \widehat{e}_s}{\partial t}\right)_{k|k} \\ \widehat{\eta}_{k|k} \end{pmatrix} \tag{18}$$

$$\begin{pmatrix} \left(\dfrac{\partial \widehat{e}_s}{\partial t}\right)_{k+1|k+1} \\ \widehat{\eta}_{k+1|k+1} \end{pmatrix} = \begin{pmatrix} \left(\dfrac{\partial \widehat{e}_s}{\partial t}\right)_{k+1|k} \\ \widehat{\eta}_{k+1|k} \end{pmatrix} + K_{k+1} \gamma_{k+1} \tag{19}$$

where γ_{k+1} is the innovation between the measurement and the previous prediction. The covariance matrices of the error prediction and estimation, the gain and measure innovation are given by:

$$\begin{aligned}
P_{k+1|k} &= F P_{k|k} F^T + Q \\
P_{k+1|k+1} &= (I - K_{k+1}H) P_{k+1|k} \\
K_{k+1} &= P_{k+1|k} H^T \left(H P_{k+1|k} H^T + R\right)^{-1} \\
\gamma_{k+1} &= \left(\frac{\partial \widehat{e}_s}{\partial t}\right)_{k+1} - \left(\frac{\partial \widehat{e}_s}{\partial t}\right)_{k+1|k}
\end{aligned} \tag{20}$$

4 On-Orbit Robot Manipulator Visual Servoing

This section describes the robot manipulator dynamics and the controller designed to perform the tracking of image trajectories. First, the dynamics of the robot manipulator can be defined by the following equation:

$$\begin{bmatrix} F_b \\ \tau \end{bmatrix} = \begin{bmatrix} M_{bb} & M_{bm} \\ M_{bm}^T & M_{mm} \end{bmatrix} \begin{bmatrix} \ddot{x}_b \\ \ddot{q} \end{bmatrix} + \begin{bmatrix} c_b \\ c_m \end{bmatrix} \tag{21}$$

where $\ddot{q} \in \Re^n$ is the set of accelerations of the manipulator joints, $\ddot{x}_b = \begin{bmatrix} \dot{v}_b^T & \dot{\omega}_b^T \end{bmatrix}^T \in \Re^6$ represents the linear and angular accelerations of the service spacecraft with respect the inertial coordinate frame, $M_{bb} \in \Re^{6 \times 6}$ is the inertia matrix of the spacecraft, $M_{bb} \in \Re^{6 \times n}$ is the coupled inertia matrix of the spacecraft and the robot manipulator, $M_{bb} \in \Re^{n \times n}$ is the inertia matrix of the robot manipulator; c_b and $c_m \in \Re^6$ represents a velocity/displacement-dependent, non-linear terms for the spacecraft and robot manipulator, $F_b \in \Re^6$ is the force and moment exerted on the service spacecraft, and $\tau \in \Re^n$ is the applied joint torque on the manipulator. This paper assumes that no control action is applied to the base spacecraft, therefore, $F_b = 0$. Additionally, free-floating conditions are considered: the base spacecraft moves when the manipulator performs a motion. With these considerations Eq. (21) can be written as:

$$M_{mm}^* \ddot{q} + H^* = \tau \tag{22}$$

where $M_{mm}^* \in \Re^{n \times n}$ represents the generalized inertia matrix of the manipulator and service spacecraft and $H^* \in \Re^n$ represents the generalized Coriolis and centrifugal matrix:

$$M_{mm}^* = M_{mm} - M_{bm}^T M_{bb}^{-1} M_{bm} \tag{23}$$

$$H^* = c_m - M_{bm}^T M_{bb}^{-1} c_b \tag{24}$$

Additionally, the linear and angular momenta of the robot manipulator and base spacecraft $\left(\ell^T, \psi^T \right)^T \in \Re^6$ are:

$$\begin{bmatrix} \ell \\ \psi \end{bmatrix} = M_{bb} \dot{x}_b + M_{bm} \dot{q} \tag{25}$$

where $\dot{q} \in \Re^n$ are the manipulators' joint velocities, and $\dot{x}_b = \begin{bmatrix} v_b^T & \omega_b^T \end{bmatrix}^T \in \Re^6$ represents the linear and angular velocities of the service spacecraft in the inertial coordinate frame. The relationship between the time derivatives of the joint positions, $\dot{q}$, and the corresponding end-effector's absolute linear and angular velocities can be obtained by the manipulator Jacobian, $J_m \in \Re^{6 \times n}$, and the Jacobian matrix of the service spacecraft, using the following relationship:

$$\dot{x}_e = J_m \dot{q} + J_b \dot{x}_b \tag{26}$$

To obtain the equation that relates joint velocities and the velocities of the manipulator end effector we can combine Eqs. (26) and (25), obtaining the following equation:

$$\dot{x}_e = J_g \dot{q} + \dot{x}_{ge} \tag{27}$$

where:

$$J_g = J_m - J_b M_{bb}^{-1} M_{bm} \tag{28}$$

$$\dot{x}_{ge} = J_b M_{bb}^{-1} \begin{bmatrix} \ell \\ \psi \end{bmatrix} \tag{29}$$

In Eq. (27), J_g is the Generalized Jacobian Matrix which relates the joint velocities of the manipulator arm and the end effector velocities. Additionally, $\dot{x}_{ge}$, is an offset velocity due to the non-zero momentum.

The previous differential kinematics is required to be extended to determine the relationship between image and joint coordinates. As previously indicated, the interaction matrix, L_s, relates the velocities of the extracted visual features in the image space, $\dot{s}$, and the end effector motion, $\dot{x}_e$. Taking into account this last relationship, Eq. (27) can be expressed as:

$$\dot{s} = L_s J_g \dot{q} + L_s \dot{x}_{ge} = L_J \dot{q} + \dot{s}_{ge} \tag{30}$$

where L_J is the product of the interaction matrix and the robot Jacobian. This matrix relates joint velocities and the time derivative of the extracted visual features. Additionally, $\dot{s}_{ge}$ is the projection in the image space of the velocity $\dot{x}_{ge}$. Therefore, the control action given in Eq. (7) can be extended taking into account the free-floating conditions and the estimation of the motion of the target spacecraft by:

$$\dot{q} = -\lambda_3 L_J^+ \left(e_s - \frac{\partial \widehat{e_s}}{\partial t} - \dot{s}_{ge} \right) \tag{31}$$

5   Results

This section presents the main results obtained in the application of the proposed controller to perform the manipulator guidance considering the on-orbit servicing scenario detailed in Sect. 2. The initial position of the target spacecraft is $(0,10,0)$ m with respect to the base spacecraft coordinate frame. The base spacecraft is left free to move in a free-floating condition when the robotic arms operate. No external forces are applied to the base spacecraft. Two different kinds of maneuvres are presented in this paper. In the first one, the robotic manipulator uses visual information extracted from the target spacecraft to perform a motion in only single direction (x or z with respect the T coordinate frame), maintaining the distance with respect to the target spacecraft. The second experiments use visual information to perform more complex motions which require displacements in several directions.

5.1   Visual Controller to Guide the Manipulator in a Single Movement

In this case, the visual information obtained by the robotic camera is used to guide the robotic manipulator in just one direction. As previously indicated, the visual information to be fed to the controller is based on the recognition and tracking of four visual feature points extracted from the target spacecraft. The coordinates of the initial features extracted by the camera in both the maneuvres under analysis are

$s_i = \begin{bmatrix} s_{ix} \\ s_{iy} \end{bmatrix}^T = \begin{bmatrix} 452 & 556 & 572 & 468 \\ 556 & 572 & 468 & 452 \end{bmatrix}^T$. To obtain a displacement along y-direction the

desired features to be included in Eq. (31) are the following ones:

$$s_d = \begin{bmatrix} s_{dx} \\ s_{dy} \end{bmatrix}^T = \begin{bmatrix} 452 & 556 & 572 & 468 \\ 631 & 648 & 543 & 527 \end{bmatrix}^T \tag{32}$$

Analogously, to obtain a displacement along z-direction, the following features will be considered as the desired ones:

$$s_d = \begin{bmatrix} s_{dx} \\ s_{dy} \end{bmatrix}^T = \begin{bmatrix} 529 & 633 & 649 & 545 \\ 556 & 572 & 468 & 452 \end{bmatrix}^T \tag{33}$$

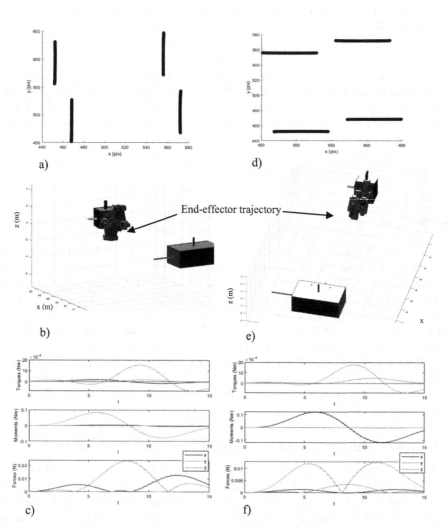

Fig. 2. a) image trajectory of the extracted visual features (displacement in y-direction). b) 2d trajectory of the servicing spacecraft (displacement in y-direction). c) Joint applied torques, and force and moments in the base spacecraft (displacement in y-direction). d) image trajectory of the extracted visual features (displacement in z-direction). e) 2d trajectory of the servicing spacecraft (displacement in z-direction). f) Joint applied torques, and force and moments in the base spacecraft (displacement in z-direction).

The results obtained in the application of the controller using both sets of desired visual features are indicated in Fig. 2. Figure 2a, and Fig. 2d represents the image trajectory of the four visual features. From the analysis of such figures, the visual features describe straight trajectories from the initial to the desired features. In both cases, the desired visual features are achieved. However, in order to show more clearly the motion performed by the servicing spacecraft, the 3D trajectories described by the robot manipulator are shown in Fig. 2b, and Fig. 2e, respectively. The trajectory described by the robotic manipulator is in blue in both figures. The manipulator end-effector correctly performed displacements along y and z directions, maintaining a constant distance with respect to the target spacecraft. Finally, Fig. 2c, and Fig. 2f represents the manipulator joint torques and the force and moments applied to the base spacecraft due to the motion of the manipulator.

5.2 Visual Controller to Guide the Manipulator Following Complex Motion Directions

The second simulation assesses the applicability of the proposed strategy when the desired motion implies a simultaneous displacement in several directions. As previously indicated, the visual information extracted from the target spacecraft is based on the four visual feature points of the target seen and extracted from the images captured by the camera. The coordinates of the initial features extracted by the camera are the same indicated in the experiments in Sect. 5.1, while the desired features to be included in Eq. (31) are the following:

$$s_d = \begin{bmatrix} s_{dx} \\ s_{dy} \end{bmatrix}^T = \begin{bmatrix} 374\ 478\ 494\ 390 \\ 480\ 496\ 392\ 375 \end{bmatrix}^T \tag{34}$$

By considering these last visual features, a movement of the end effector is obtained along both y- and z-directions simultaneously while keeping fixed the distance of the base of the spacecraft and the target spacecraft. Additionally, another case can be considered by setting as desired visual features the following ones:

$$s_d = \begin{bmatrix} s_{dx} \\ s_{dy} \end{bmatrix}^T = \begin{bmatrix} 546\ 656\ 673\ 563 \\ 594\ 613\ 500\ 486 \end{bmatrix}^T \tag{35}$$

If these last visual features are used, the manipulator robot performs an approach to the target spacecraft with a displacement along both y- and z- directions simultaneously. The results obtained in the application of the controller using both sets of desired visual features are indicated in Fig. 3 and Fig. 4. The 3D trajectories described by the robot manipulator in both experiments are represented in Fig. 3. Figure 4a, and Fig. 4c represents the image trajectory of the four visual features in the image plane. The visual features describe a straight right trajectory from the initial and the desired features but, differently from Fig. 2a, and Fig. 2d, their trajectories move along the diagonal of the image plane. In both cases, the desired visual features are achieved. As shown in Fig. 3a, the manipulator performs a displacement in a plane parallel to the target spacecraft, maintaining a fixed distance with respect to the target. As it is shown in Fig. 3b, in this last trajectory the manipulator robot also performs an approach to the target, achieving the desired pose. Finally, Fig. 4b, and Fig. 4d represents the manipulator joint torques, and the force and moments applied to the base spacecraft due to the motion of the manipulator.

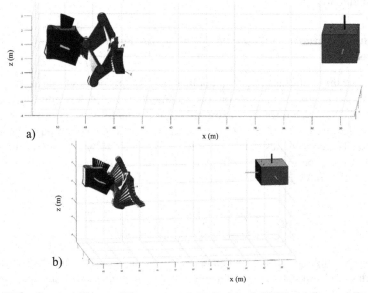

Fig. 3. a) 3D trajectory of the servicing spacecraft (trajectory 1). b) 3D trajectory of the servicing spacecraft (trajectory 2).

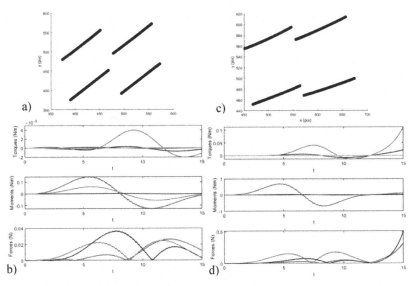

Fig. 4. a) image trajectory of the extracted visual features (trajectory 1). b) Joint applied torques, and force and moments in the base spacecraft (trajectory 1). c) image trajectory of the extracted visual features (trajectory 2). d) Joint applied torques, and force and moments in the base spacecraft (trajectory 2).

6   Conclusions

The paper presented a visual servoing algorithm suitable for on-orbit servicing and manipulation. The algorithm is applicable to a spacecraft equipped with two-arm manipulator. The two arms are dedicated to manipulation and observation tasks, respectively.

A visual servoing controller independent from the observed scene's point of view was consequently developed. The virtual features could be virtually reconstructed following a specific pattern seen on the target body and consequently assumed attached to the end effector of the operating manipulator. A Kalman filter was implemented to estimate the movements of the visual features due to the target satellite motion as well as these due to the intrinsic movement of the service spacecraft due to the manipulator operations.

Numerical results show that the so-developed controller was able to drive the manipulator in such a way to make the virtual features match the real features on the target body even when the target was relatively moving with respect to the base of the sercicing spacecraft.

Further studies will assess the robustness of the proposed controller against environmental torques and forces, evaluate the performance of the controller with different frame rates of the camera, and compare the results with other tracking controllers.

References

1. Froehlich, A. (ed.): On-Orbit Servicing: Next Generation of Space Activities. SSP, vol. 26. Springer, Cham (2020). https://doi.org/10.1007/978-3-030-51559-1

2. United Nations Office for Outer Space Affairs, https://www.unoosa.org/oosa/osoindex, Accessed 18 Feb 2022
3. Liu, Y., Zhao, Y., Tan, C., Liu, H., Liu, Y.: Economic value analysis of on-orbit servicing for geosynchronous communication satellites. Acta Astronaut. **180**, 176–188 (2021). https://doi.org/10.1016/j.actaastro.2020.11.040
4. Flores-Abad, A., Ma, O., Pham, K., Ulrich, S.: A review of space robotics technologies for on-orbit servicing. Prog. Aerosp. Sci. **68**, 1–26 (2014). https://doi.org/10.1016/j.paerosci.2014.03.002
5. Moghaddam, B.M., Chhabra, R.: On the guidance, navigation and control of in-orbit space robotic missions: a survey and prospective vision. Acta Astronaut. **184**, 70–100 (2021). https://doi.org/10.1016/j.actaastro.2021.03.029
6. Felicetti, L., Gasbarri, P., Pisculli, A., Sabatini, M., Palmerini, G.B.: Design of robotic manipulators for orbit removal of spent launchers' stages. Acta Astronaut. **119**, 118–130 (2016). https://doi.org/10.1016/j.actaastro.2015.11.012
7. Ramón, J.L., Pomares, J., Felicetti, L.: Direct visual servoing and interaction control for a two-arms on-orbit servicing spacecraft. Acta Astronaut. **192**, 368–378 (2022). https://doi.org/10.1016/j.actaastro.2021.12.045
8. Cassinis, L.P., Fonod, R., Gill, E.: Review of the robustness and applicability of monocular pose estimation systems for relative navigation with an uncooperative spacecraft. Progr. Aeros. Sci. **110**, 100548 (2019). https://doi.org/10.1016/j.paerosci.2019.05.008
9. Peng, J., Xu, W., Liu, T., Yuan, H., Liang, B.: End-effector pose and arm-shape synchronous planning methods of a hyper-redundant manipulator for spacecraft repairing. Mech. Mach. Theory **155**, 104062 (2021) https://doi.org/10.1016/j.mechmachtheory.2020.104062
10. Wang, H., Guo, D., Xu, H., Chen, W., Liu, T., Leang, K.K.: Eye-in-hand tracking control of a free-floating space manipulator. IEEE Trans. Aerosp. Electron. Syst. **53**(4), 1855–1865 (2017). https://doi.org/10.1109/TAES.2017.2674218
11. Ramon, J., Pomares, J., Felicetti, L.: On-orbit free-floating manipulation using a two-arm robotic system. In: Proceedings of the 2nd International Conference on Robotics, Computer Vision and Intelligent Systems - ROBOVIS, pp. 57–63 (2021). https://doi.org/10.5220/0010712100003061
12. Xu, R., Luo, J., Wang, M.: Kinematic and dynamic manipulability analysis for free-floating space robots with closed chain constraints. Rob. Auton. Syst. **130**, 103548 (2020). https://doi.org/10.1016/j.robot.2020.103548
13. Ma, G., Jiang, Z., Li, H., Gao, J., Yu, Z., Chen, X.: Hand-eye servo and impedance control for manipulator arm to capture target satellite safely. Robotica **33**, 848–864 (2015). https://doi.org/10.1017/S0263574714000587
14. Chaumette, F., Hutchinson, S.: Visual servo control. I. Basic approaches. IEEE Rob. Autom. Mag. **13**(4), 82–90 (2006)
15. Alepuz, J.P., Emami, M.R., Pomares, J.: Direct image-based visual servoing of free-floating space manipulators. Aerosp. Sci. Technol. **55**, 1–9 (2016). https://doi.org/10.1016/j.ast.2016.05.012
16. Pomares, J., Felicetti, L., Pérez, J., Emami, M.R.: Concurrent image-based visual servoing with adaptive zooming for non-cooperative rendezvous maneuvers. Adv. Space Res. **61**(3), 862–878 (2018). https://doi.org/10.1016/j.asr.2017.10.054
17. Salehian, M., RayatDoost S., Taghirad, H.D.: Robust unscented Kalman filter for visual servoing system. In: The 2nd International Conference on Control, Instrumentation and Automation, pp. 1006–1011 (2011). https://doi.org/10.1109/ICCIAutom.2011.6356799

Semantic Segmentation of Marine Species in an Unconstrained Underwater Environment

Gordon Böer[1]($\boxtimes$) and Hauke Schramm[1,2]

[1] Institute of Applied Computer Science, Kiel University of Applied Sciences, Kiel, Germany
{gordon.boeer,hauke.schramm}@fh-kiel.de
[2] Department of Computer Science, Faculty of Engineering, Kiel University, Kiel, Germany

Abstract. A non-invasive Underwater Fish Observatory (UFO) was developed and deployed on the seafloor to perform continuous recording of stereo video and sonar data as well as various oceanic parameters at a high temporal sampling rate. The acquired image data is processed to automatically detect, classify and measure the size of passing aquatic organisms. An important subtask in this processing chain is the semantic segmentation of the previously detected animals. Within this publication, a former segmentation system, that only considered a binary classification of fish and background, is extended to a multi-class segmentation system by including an additional species. Since the images usually contain a lot of background, the semantic segmentation is a problem with a high class imbalance, which demands special care in the choice of loss functions and evaluation metrics. Therefore, three different loss functions, namely Dice loss, Focal loss and Lovasz loss, which are well suited for class-imbalance problems, are investigated and their effect on the final mean intersection-over-union (IoU) on a separate test set is explored. For the given dataset, the model trained with a Focal loss performed best achieving an average, class specific IoU of 0.982 for the background class, 0.828 for the *Aurelia aurita* and 0.678 for the *Gadus morhua*.

Keywords: Underwater imagery · Marine species detection · Marine animal segmentation · Deep learning

1 Introduction

In the broad field of marine research, scientific surveys are the primary tool for gaining insights into the abundance, reproduction and growth rates or the distribution of marine species. Traditional vessel-based surveys, while providing invaluable information, are undertaken with judicious consideration because of the high personnel and financial resource requirements. For this reason, research institutions, seeking insight into the state of the ocean, are turning to next-generation technologies which can supplement the existing survey based methods and allow for continuous and cost-effective long-term monitoring of various ocean parameters. These modern approaches include the use of underwater cameras for example, stationary cameras installed in meaningful locations for permanent operation [11,16,21], or mobile cameras can be attached to fishing nets [33,40] and underwater robots [45], for example, or hand-held by divers [25]. It is safe

© Springer Nature Switzerland AG 2022
P. Galambos et al. (Eds.): ROBOVIS 2020/ROBOVIS 2021, CCIS 1667, pp. 131–146, 2022.
https://doi.org/10.1007/978-3-031-19650-8_7

to say, that underwater imaging has become a standard tool in marine research helping marine biologists to answer many scientific questions.

The work presented in this study is embedded in a larger project, which aims to develop methods and algorithms that can be used for the identification and biomass estimation of fish using the sensors installed on stationary and mobile Underwater Fish Observatories (UFOs).

The aim of a previous work of the authors [9] was to investigate the applicability of deep learning methods for segmentation and contouring of fish, detected in real-world underwater scenes. The algorithm presented therein was an important software part for an Underwater Fish Observatory (UFO) developed with the aim of estimating fish biomass for a fish stock assessment, using non-invasive sensor technology. A successful semantic segmentation is an important prerequisite for the automatic determination of morphometric characteristics, e.g. the lengths and widths of a fish, which in turn can be used to determine fish weight [39]. Two different segmentation models were investigated, namely the PSPNet [46] and DeepLabV3 [10], which lead to the conclusion, that the PSPNet performed best, achieving an average pixel accuracy of 96.8% and intersection-over-union (IoU) of 73.8% between the predicted and the target mask. However, this first study did considered a binary segmentation problem, i.e. separating fish of the species *Gadus morhua*, commonly known as cod, from the background. The work presented here extends the PSPNet towards multi-class segmentation by providing the possibility to segment another underwater species, namely the *Aurelia aurita*, which is known as moon jellyfish. Furthermore, three different loss functions, namely the Dice loss [30], Focal loss [27] and Lovasz [7] loss, which are well suited for class-imbalance problems, are investigated and their effect on the final IoU averaged on a separate test set is explored.

The main contributions of this work are:

– The training and evaluation of the PSPNet for the semantic segmentation of images depicting *Gadus morhua* and the *Aurelia aurita* in an unconstrained underwater scenery.
– The investigation of three different loss functions, the Dice, Focal and Lovasz loss, for their applicability to the task at hand.

2   Related Work

The semantic segmentation of images is an important area of research in computer vision and its importance is unquestioned in many application areas like biomedical imaging [19], pose estimation [15], remote sensing [24] or autonomous driving [38]. As in many areas of computer vision, state-of-the-art algorithms to date are based on deep learning architectures, well established ones being Fully Convolutional Networks [28], Mask R-CNN [17], U-Net [32], PSPNet [46] or SegNet [6]. Regarding the segmentation of marine species in digital images, several efforts have been published so far. Generally speaking, the published works fall in two broader categories, the segmentation of animals in air, e.g. fish on a photo-table [13,23,44], or the segmentation of living animals being observed in their natural habitat, in basins or nets. Since the later category is closer to our own application field, we will focus on those works.

During the last two decades various traditional computer vision algorithms have been applied to extract segmentation masks for fish, like Otsu thresholding, edge detection, Grabcut or matrix decomposition [5,31,37]. However, all these algorithms do not benefit from the recent advances possible with novel deep learning methods, as these techniques automatically learn important features based on a given dataset instead of manually selecting them based on expert knowledge.

In a recent effort, Li et al. [26] published a dataset by the name of MAS3K, consisting of 3,103 images with ground-truth segmentation masks for 37 different species of marine animals, among others including fish, jellyfish, seal, crab as well as a larger portion of camouflaged animals. Additionally they proposed a segmentation network, called the Enhanced Cascade Decoder Network (ECD-Net). The ECD-net uses a pretrained ResNet-50 [18] as backbone, followed by several feature enhancement and cascade decoder modules which are trained using a mixture loss. The authors compare their method to various other segmentation models and report superior results on the published MAS3K data. Since the ECD-Net achieved good results on very challenging images from an unconstrained water environment, it is very relevant for our own work. However, the model as published, is quite complex with 207 million trainable parameters and therefore not suited for the application on limited hardware devices. It may be possible to replace the original ResNet encoder with a MobileNetV2 [34] to make it usable in an embedded system, but this investigation is not part of the presented study.

The stereoscopic camera system "Deep Vision" [33] can be installed at the opening of a trawl net and captures videos of the fish swimming through. In a recent work [14], the stereo-data captured with this system was processed to automatically determine the length of the visible fish. This involved using a Mask R-CNN to detect to detect fish and perform a semantic segmentation, followed by a refinement step to distinguish between individual overlapping fish. The authors report an average IoU of 84.5% for an independent test set of 200 images. The deep-vision system records the fish in an obscured, well-lit enclosure, and therefore the recorded animals show unnatural behavior in front of a rather uniform background, so the results obtained may not be directly transferable to unconstrained underwater scenarios.

3   Materials and Methods

3.1   The Underwater Fish Observatory

In an ongoing effort of German universities and marine engineering companies, an Underwater Fish Observatory (UFO) was developed, which is publicly funded by the Federal Ministry for Food and Agriculture in Germany. The UFO is a stationary, cabled sensor platform that operates on the seafloor and is capable of recording a variety of sensor data at high temporal resolution and continuously for several months. The sensors used include a low-light stereo camera, an imaging sonar, a CTD (conductivity, temperature, pressure) probe, an acoustic Doppler current profiler (ADCP), and a fluorometer. Over the period of several months, the first prototype of the UFO sensor platform was deployed at seafloor level in the North Sea, about 45 nautical miles east of the island of Sylt, and in the Kiel Fjord, an inlet of the Baltic Sea in northern Germany. During the measurement campaigns, the primary goal was to conduct a continuous recording of stereo video and sonar data as well as various oceanic parameters at a high temporal sampling rate. In total, the raw data set spans approximately 240 days, resulting in nearly 3000 h hours of video footage, as the cameras where not operated during the night hours. The first prototype of the UFO, which was deployed in the Kiel Fjord, is depicted in Fig. 1.

Fig. 1. The Underwater Fish Observatory (UFO), shortly before deployment in the Kiel Fjord.

3.2 Camera Setup

A primary goal of the UFO is to be as non-invasive as possible to allow the recording of underwater organisms in their natural behavior. This requirement limits the usability of active lighting, as it creates an undesirable attraction for fish [29]. Therefore, all stereo videos were captured using a custom-built stereo rig consisting of two Photonis "Nocturn XL" cameras. These cameras use a monochrome Lynx CMOS image sensor optimized for low-light scenarios and allowed recordings without active lighting from dawn to dusk, which was verified to a maximum water depth of 22 m in the north sea. The stereo system has a baseline of 120 mm and is housed in a custom designed underwater case with a flat view port. The stereo camera is essential for the calculation of the distance and sizes of objects in real world units. However, this 3D reconstruction is only possible if the cameras are calibrated, which is done with the help of a diver who places a calibration target in different positions and angles in front of the cameras. During the operation of the UFO, the two H.264 encoded camera streams are continuously recorded on external hard disks with an optical resolution of 1280×1024 pixels at a frame rate of up to 20 fps, using a standard consumer PC.

3.3 Image Data

The image data used in this paper represents a small subset of the complete optical data suitable for automatic analysis by computer vision algorithms. For example, abiotic measurements or sonar data are not in the scope of this publication. The dataset does include many bounding-box annotations, which can be used to train a detection system, however the current work focuses on a smaller portion of the data for which segmentation masks have been annotated as well. Unlike the previously published version of the dataset [9], the data now contains samples for two species, namely the *Gadus morhua*, also known as cod, and the *Aurelia aurita* or moon jellyfish, both of which are commonly found in the Baltic Sea. In total, the number of images in the dataset of *Gadus morhua* amounts to 1548 images and *Aurelia aurita* to 1405 images, respectively. All images have been manually labeled with semantic segmentation masks using CVAT [35], where pixels, belonging to one of the considered animals are marked as belonging to the species, everything else as background. In other words, the segmentation task at hand is considered multi-class segmentation but not instance segmentation. In most images, the background pixels outnumber the foreground pixels, so special measures must be taken to deal with problems resulting from a high class imbalance. Each image, randomly chosen from the dataset, contains only individuals from the same species, but there may be several individuals of the same species in the same image. Since these species are two completely different animals, the diversity and difficulty of the dataset has increased considerably as compared to the previous version. It should also be noted, that the jellyfish can exhibit different shapes due to its contractile movement pattern and may also appear translucent sometimes, all of which adds another layer of complexity. Furthermore, the images contain examples with different distances to the camera and difficult viewing conditions, resulting in occluded and only partially visible animals. For illustration, Fig. 2 shows some examples of dataset images with the respective segmentation ground-truth.

Fig. 2. Example images with the respective segmentation ground-truth as contained in the used dataset. The dataset contains examples of the two species, single and multiple individuals per image, at different distances from the camera, and only partially visible animals.

Since the images used are consecutive frames extracted from video sequences, the dataset contains several fairly similar samples. For a jellyfish moving slowly past the camera, for instance, the successive video frames, although not exactly the same, have only minor visual differences. Without special care, this characteristic becomes problematic when the subsets used for training and the final performance evaluation of the model are randomly selected, since very similar images may end up in the data splits, which in turn may lead to an overly optimistic assessment of the algorithm's capabilities. Therefore, the test set has been aggregated from videos that were recorded on a different day than the training set. Using this strictly separated test set, we aim to fairly assess the generalization ability of the used segmentation model. From the remaining images which are used for training, we take out a small subset of 10% per class, randomly selected, to compute validation metrics and apply a learning rate adaption during the training phase. The described measures lead to the data split as described in Table 1.

Table 1. Number of images per species used for training, validation and testing of the segmentation model.

Species	Number of images		
	Training	Validation	Test
Gadus morhua	1034	114	400
Aurelia aurita	820	91	494

3.4 PSPNet

In a future phase of the UFO project, the developed algorithms will be used on a remotely operated underwater vehicle to detect fish and estimate their size during exploration. Therefore, it is of great importance to develop a system that can run on limited hardware, which is typically used in mobile platforms due to limited installation space and power consumption. In a previous investigation [9] it was found, that the PSPNet is a suitable segmentation model which can produce good segmentation results using a limited amount of model parameters, by replacing the originally used ResNet encoder backbone by a MobileNetV2 [34]. Since the presented work is dealing with a multiclass segmentation, the PSPNet configuration had to be extended, by (1) increasing the size of the output layer and (2) by using multi-class versions of the employed loss functions and evaluation metrics.

In the original implementation of PSPNet, a pre-trained ResNet was employed in combination with a dilated network strategy to extract the feature maps. As was mentioned above, the ResNet was interchanged with MobileNetV2 in the proposed system. The spatial pyramid pooling (SPP) module in PSPNet first downsamples the feature maps from the encoder at 4 different scales (1×1, 2×2, 3×3 and 6×6), all of which are afterwards upsampled and fused together. The integrated feature maps from the SPP module are concatenated along with the feature maps from the encoder. The decoder, followed by a bilinear upsampling layer with a scale of 8, then converts the concatenated feature maps to the segmentation output. The SPP module eliminates the requirement for a fixed input size.

3.5 Intersection-over-Union (IoU)

The Intersection-over-Union(IoU), also called the Jaccard index [20], is a commonly used metric for evaluating the quality of detection and segmentation predictions which is well suited for problems with a class imbalance. Given the targeted segmentation mask for an image, the IoU provides a measure of the overlap between this mask and a predicted segmentation. The IoU ranges from 0.0 to 1.0., where a value of 0.0 denotes no overlap and 1.0 a perfect overlapping segmentation. Given the classification results per pixel, T_p as true positives, F_p as false positives and F_n as false negatives, the IoU is calculated as:

$$IoU = \frac{T_p}{T_p + F_p + F_n} \tag{1}$$

The underwater data used in this study usually contains many background areas, which leads to very high IoU values when calculated naively, since the background can usually be classified very reliably. However, since our main focus is to correctly segment the previously detected animals rather than the entire visible scene, we omit the background class when averaging the IoU value for an image. We adopt this approach to arrive at a realistic performance estimate that is not glossed over by the (in our case) simple background class.

3.6 Optimization Criteria

Special care has to be taken when dealing with datasets that exhibit a high class imbalance. Therefore, three different loss functions were investigated, namely the Dice loss [30], Focal loss [27] and Lovasz loss [7], all of which are suited for segmentation tasks of this kind. In all cases, the network parameters were optimized using the Adam backpropagation algorithm [22].

Dice Loss. The Dice loss DL, which originated from the Sørensen-Dice [12,36] coefficient, is a widely used metric to calculate the overlap between two samples which evaluates the performance of a semantic segmentation model. Given a prediction p and target mask y for an image, the Dice loss per class $c \epsilon C$ is calculated as

$$DL(p,y) = \frac{1}{|C|} \sum_{c\epsilon C} \frac{2\sum_i^N y_i p_i}{\sum_i^N p_i^2 + \sum_i^N y_i^2} \tag{2}$$

, with p_i being the predicted class per image pixel and y_i the respective target class for the same pixel. Note that Eq. 2 simply calculates the mean value of the separate losses per class.

Focal Loss. The Focal loss [27] is considered to be an improved version of the Cross-entropy loss. The main idea of the Focal loss is to utilize a weighting scheme that dampens the contribution of easy data samples to the loss calculation, and thereby allows the model to focus on difficult examples. This weighting is added by the term $-(1 - p_t)^\gamma$, which increases the calculated loss FL for classifications with a low probability p_t. In semantic segmentation, p_t is usually calculated by applying a *softmax* function to the final classification vector per pixel. It can be seen, that when γ becomes 0, the loss function becomes the standard Cross-entropy $FL(p_t) = -log(p_t)$. On the contrary, the larger γ is chosen, the more it will increase the loss for low p_t values.

$$FL(p_t) = -(1 - p_t)^\gamma log(p_t) \tag{3}$$

For all conducted experiments, we have chosen a value of $\gamma = 2$.

Lovasz Loss. The Lovasz loss LL is a loss function specifically designed for semantic segmentation, which aims to optimize the mean IoU during model training. The loss is computed by utilizing the *softmax* function f, that provides the class probabilities for each image pixel, which are supplied to $m(c)$, to calculate class specific pixel errors, which in turn are used to construct the loss surrogates ΔJ_c.

$$LL(f) = \frac{1}{|C|} \sum_{c \in C} \overline{\Delta J_c}(m(c)) \qquad (4)$$

Further details about the calculation of the Lovasz loss can be found in the original publication [7].

4 Experiments

4.1 Setup

Despite the different loss functions, the same hyperparameter configuration were used for all presented results. For all experiments, an input dimension of 1280×1024 pixels, which is equivalent to the full image size, an initial learning rate of 0.0001, a batch size of 8 and trained for a maximum of 120 epochs. In addition, a learning rate adaption was employed to allow for a better convergence, i.e. starting with a higher learning rate and gradually decreasing it. To control when the learning rate should be decreased, after each training epoch, the average IoU is calculated on the evaluation set. If the calculated IoU does not increase significantly, i.e. by at least 0.001 within 20 epochs, the learning rate is reduced by a factor of 0.1.

The models have been implemented with PyTorch [42] and were trained and evaluated on a NVIDIA TITAN XP GeForce RTX 2080 TI GPU. The training configuration and evaluation was supported by Hydra [41] and Weights & Biases [8].

4.2 Results

The training of the different models was monitored using different standard metrics such as pixel-level accuracy or classification recall. However, in our opinion, the IoU value is the most meaningful metric to compare the training, since it allows for an intuitive insight into the quality of the segmentation and its improvement over the course of a training run. We furthermore do not consider the background class when averaging the IoU for an image, due to the reasons described above. Although the loss curves allow a qualitative assessment of the training process, e.g. whether the optimization converges, they are not suitable for a direct comparison, especially when different loss functions are used. The final model for each of the three configurations, which is afterwards used on the test data, was based on the best mean IoU as achieved on the validation data during training. The following Fig. 3 visualizes the training loss and the averaged IoU, as computed on the validation data after each training epoch. A look at the loss curves reveals, that the loss for each configuration decreases continuously and eventually reaches a plateau. The comparison of these curves leads to the conclusion, that using the Dice loss leads to slightly better segmentation result at the end, although the focal loss seems to achieve a better parameter optimization early on. As far as training is concerned, the Lovasz loss does not seem to have a clear advantage over the other loss variants for our data set.

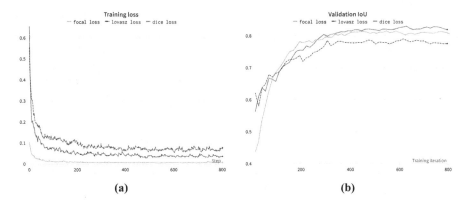

Fig. 3. Training loss and averaged IoU computed on the validation set, excluding the background class, for the 3 different loss functions

The averaged IoU values for the validation and test set, as achieved by the three different model variants, are summarized in Table 2. For this table, the IoU was calculated in two variants, with and without taking into account the background class. In addition, the class-specific IoUs are listed to express the performance of the models for each class. The best IoU value on the validation data, with and without considering the background class, was obtained with the Dice loss, followed in both cases by the Focal loss, while the model using the Lovasz loss performed the worst. However, the performance of all three models on the validation set is quite similar. The different performances of the models become even more apparent when looking at the test results. Here, the model optimized with the Focal loss performs best in all cases and is well ahead of the other two loss functions. This observation carries over to the class specific losses, where again the Focal loss performs best in all cases.

Table 2. The IoU results achieved by the three different configurations on the test and evaluation set, as well as the class specific averages.

loss	$\overline{IoU}_{noBG}$		$\overline{IoU}_{withBG}$		$\overline{IoU}_{class}$		
	Val	Test	Val	Test	Background	Jellyfish	Cod
Dice loss	**0.836**	0.461	**0.985**	0.68	0.97	0.784	0.454
Focal loss	0.822	**0.623**	0.983	**0.785**	**0.982**	**0.828**	**0.678**
Lovasz loss	0.818	0.438	0.981	0.646	0.922	0.807	0.422

4.3 Discussion

It can be observed, that all models perform similarly well on the validation data. However, on the test set, the Focal loss performs best, beating the other two models by a considerable margin. It can be assumed that all models perform well on the validation dataset because it resembles a random subset of the training data and is very similar to it. The test set, however, was recorded on a completely different day and therefore includes completely different underwater scenes, making it a perfect benchmark for the generalization capabilities of the trained models. Given the highly dynamic nature of moving animals recorded in an unconstrained environment, as is the case in this dataset, each new video sequence may naturally contain a lot of variation that has not been seen in the training data. Typical dynamic effects which cause this variation are:

- The movement of animals results in images showing them from different perspectives, e.g. from the front or from the side.
- Difficult visibility conditions, especially during the dark hours of the day or when water is very turbid due to suspended sediment or strong currents.
- Different lighting of the scene due to atmospheric conditions, e.g. the difference between cloudy and sunny days.

Given this, it is not surprising that models perform significantly worse on test data than on validation data. Although objective evaluation metrics such as the IoU are a good starting point for ranking one algorithm against another, looking at individual examples where the model failed allows a better assessment of strengths and weaknesses in most cases.

In Fig. 4 several examples from the test set are illustrated, where the PSPNet trained with the focal loss failed to deliver a good result. The illustration shows the input image, the predicted segmentation, the ground-truth and the difference between them for each example. The difference between the predicted and the target mask is highlighted by white pixels. In all of these examples it is apparent, that the background class (black color in the ground-truth mask) is predicted very well in most cases. This was to be expected since the average IoU scores for this class are very high among all models. The background class most likely can be segmented very well, because it does not show too much variation, in contrast to the other classes.

The example in Fig. 4(a) shows an image with a low signal-to-noise ratio. These are typically images which were recorded at twilight, i.e. when the sun was below the horizon. In this example, the model did not provide a consistent segmentation mask, but was only able to segment individual parts of the fish. The poor result is probably caused by the poor visibility, which has not been seen in the training set. However, since the human annotator was able to unambiguously the fish, we are confident that the model will be able to learn this type of representation if it is provided with comparable training data.

A bad example for the segmentation of a jellyfish can be seen in Fig. 4(b), where the segmentation is also not continuous and has several missing parts, that have been classified as background. In our opinion, this error is due to the translucent nature of the jellyfish, which can cause parts of the animal to strongly resemble the background, similar to looking through a pane of glass. It can be argued that some of these errors

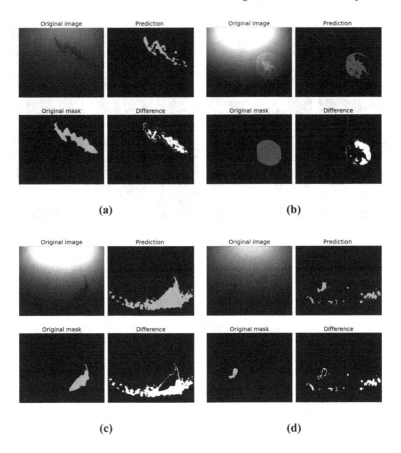

Fig. 4. Illustration of bad segmentation results from the test set, as generated by the PSPNet trained Focal loss.

could have been avoided by post-processing steps such as morphological closing, and indeed this would have been part of our standard processing pipeline. However, with this work we wanted to evaluate the pure segmentation module only, without any error correction, which we hope to avoid through proper end-to-end training anyway.

A major source of errors seems to be the lower image region, which is less well illuminated by the lighting from the surface, which explains the poor visibility in the lower part of the image. These errors can be seen in Fig. 4(c) and (d), where the model incorrectly predicted several of those regions as belonging to class cod. A similar example is given in Fig. 5, however here the segmentation results of each model are visualized to express how the different models deal with this kind of data. This example clearly shows that the model trained with Focal loss produces much fewer wrong classifications for this difficult example. This could be an indication that the training data contained few examples similar to the image shown here. Since the focal loss produces a larger error for difficult examples, i.e. if the model has a high uncertainty in these image regions, it has a larger impact on the parameter optimization. The other loss functions, on the

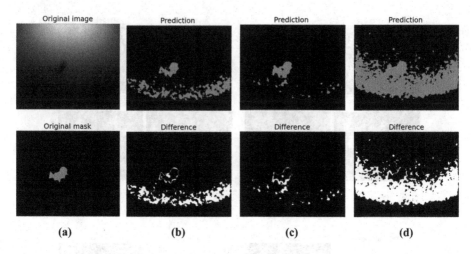

Fig. 5. Comparative illustration of the segmentation results for a difficult input image (a), as generated by the 3 models with Dice loss (b), Focal loss (c) and Lovasz loss (d).

other hand, do not weight difficult examples differently and therefore have a harder time learning this representation when there are only a few examples. However, a more detailed investigation of this possible explanation is not part of this paper.

Finally, Fig. 6 shows two of the best segmentation results obtained on the test set for both classes. The IoU for these two images is close to 1.0, indicating a near perfect match. The remaining errors occur at the boundaries of the animals, a behavior that is common in semantic segmentation, as the boundary regions are often highly ambiguous due to the difficulty in annotating them. However, there are approaches that address this type of problem and attempt to minimize the inconsistencies between and within classes in the boundary regions [43].

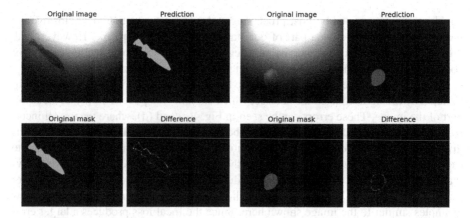

Fig. 6. Illustration of good segmentation results from the test set, achieved with PSPNet that has been trained with Focal loss.

4.4 Conclusion

In the current work we have extended our previous segmentation system [9] based on the PSPNet to a multi-class segmentation problem, to allow for the semantic segmentation of living animals from the species *Aurelia aurita* and *Gadus morhua* on single images, that have been recorded underwater in an unconstrained environment. The dataset is characterized by a high class imbalance, because the number of pixels belonging to scene background mostly dominate the other classes. For this reason three different loss functions, the Dice loss, the Focal loss and the Lovasz loss, which are well suited for class imbalance problems, were investigated by studying their impact on the final segmentation result, i.e. the average IoU for each model on a separate and challenging test set. The strength and weaknesses of the current segmentation model have been illustrated using selected examples from the test set. We found that the PSPNet trained with a Focal loss performed best, achieving an average class specific IoU of 0.982 for the background class, 0.828 for the *Aurelia aurita* and 0.678 for the *Gadus morhua*.

In the future, we plan to extend the current system with more training data selected from a large pool of unlabeled data using active learning approaches. By doing so, we aim to enable the segmentation of more species and improve the segmentation performance on challenging examples such as images with difficult viewing conditions. In a subsequent work, the generated segmentation masks will be used to extract morphometric features, such as fish length, and to locate specific key points on the fish outline. These outlines can be used to improve a stereo matching algorithm, which in turn is needed to automatically calculate the size of an animal in real world units. We plan to deploy the developed algorithms on an embedded device to be used in remotely operated and autonomous underwater vehicles that complement a network of stationary UFO underwater sensors.

Acknowledgements. This work was in part financially supported by the German Federal Ministry of Food and Agriculture (BMEL), grant number 2819111618. The planning and construction, the sensor integration and the operation of the UFO has been realized by the MacArtney Germany GmbH [2]. All species identifications of imaged underwater organisms, as well as the biological accompanying studies, were carried out by the Helmholtz Centre for Ocean Research Kiel [1]. The administrative project coordination and validation of biophysical data was done by the Thuenen institute [4]. The recording of the camera data was realised using the CamIQ software, which has been supplied by the rosemann software GmbH [3].

References

1. Geomar helmholtz centre for ocean research kiel. https://www.geomar.de/, Accessed 28 Mar 2022
2. Macartney germany gmbh. https://www.macartney.de/, Accessed 28 Mar 2022
3. rosemann software gmbh. https://www.camiq.net, Accessed 28 Mar 2022
4. Thuenen institute. https://www.thuenen.de, Accessed 28 Mar 2022
5. Abdeldaim, A.M., Houssein, E.H., Hassanien, A.E.: Color image segmentation of fishes with complex background in water. In: Hassanien, A.E., Tolba, M.F., Elhoseny, M., Mostafa, M. (eds.) AMLTA 2018. AISC, vol. 723, pp. 634–643. Springer, Cham (2018). https://doi.org/10.1007/978-3-319-74690-6_62

6. Badrinarayanan, V., Kendall, A., Cipolla, R.: Segnet: a deep convolutional encoder-decoder architecture for image segmentation. IEEE Trans. Pattern Anal. Mach. Intell. **39**(12), 2481–2495 (2017)
7. Berman, M., Triki, A.R., Blaschko, M.B.: The lovász-softmax loss: a tractable surrogate for the optimization of the intersection-over-union measure in neural networks. In: Proceedings of the IEEE Conference on Computer Vision and Pattern Recognition, pp. 4413–4421 (2018)
8. Biewald, L.: Experiment tracking with weights and biases (2020). https://www.wandb.com/softwareavailablefromwandb.com
9. Böer., G., Veeramalli., R., Schramm., H.: Segmentation of fish in realistic underwater scenes using lightweight deep learning models. In: Proceedings of the 2nd International Conference on Robotics, Computer Vision and Intelligent Systems - ROBOVIS, pp. 158–164. INSTICC, SciTePress (2021). https://doi.org/10.5220/0010712700003061
10. Chen, L.C., Papandreou, G., Schroff, F., Adam, H.: Rethinking atrous convolution for semantic image segmentation. arXiv preprint arXiv:1706.05587 (2017)
11. Dearden, P., Theberge, M., Yasué, M.: Using underwater cameras to assess the effects of snorkeler and scuba diver presence on coral reef fish abundance, family richness, and species composition. Environ. Monit. Assess. **163**(1), 531–538 (2010)
12. Dice, L.R.: Measures of the amount of ecologic association between species. Ecology **26**(3), 297–302 (1945)
13. Fernandes, A.F.: Deep learning image segmentation for extraction of fish body measurements and prediction of body weight and carcass traits in nile tilapia. Comput. Electron. Agric. **170**, 105274 (2020)
14. Garcia, R.: Automatic segmentation of fish using deep learning with application to fish size measurement. ICES J. Marine Sci. **77**(4), 1354–1366 (2020)
15. Güler, R.A., Neverova, N., Kokkinos, I.: Densepose: dense human pose estimation in the wild. In: Proceedings of the IEEE Conference on Computer Vision and Pattern Recognition, pp. 7297–7306 (2018)
16. Harvey, E.S., Santana-Garcon, J., Goetze, J., Saunders, B.J., Cappo, M.: The use of stationary underwater video for sampling sharks. In: Shark Research: Emerging Technologies and Applications for the Field and Laboratory, pp. 111–132 (2018)
17. He, K., Gkioxari, G., Dollár, P., Girshick, R.B.: Mask R-CNN. CoRR abs/1703.06870 (2017). http://arxiv.org/abs/1703.06870
18. He, K., Zhang, X., Ren, S., Sun, J.: Deep residual learning for image recognition. In: Proceedings of the IEEE Conference on Computer Vision and Pattern Recognition, pp. 770–778 (2016)
19. Isensee, F., Jaeger, P.F., Kohl, S.A., Petersen, J., Maier-Hein, K.H.: nnu-net: a self-configuring method for deep learning-based biomedical image segmentation. Nat. Methods **18**(2), 203–211 (2021)
20. Jaccard, P.: The distribution of the flora in the alpine zone. 1. New Phytologist **11**(2), 37–50 (1912)
21. Kawabata, K., et al.: Underwater image gathering by utilizing stationary and movable sensor nodes: towards observation of symbiosis system in the coral reef of okinawa. Int. J. Distrib. Sensor Netw. **10**(7), 835642 (2014)
22. Kingma, D.P., Ba, J.: Adam: a method for stochastic optimization. arXiv preprint arXiv:1412.6980 (2014)
23. Konovalov, D.A., Saleh, A., Efremova, D.B., Domingos, J.A., Jerry, D.R.: Automatic weight estimation of harvested fish from images. In: 2019 Digital Image Computing: Techniques and Applications (DICTA), pp. 1–7. IEEE (2019)
24. Längkvist, M., Kiselev, A., Alirezaie, M., Loutfi, A.: Classification and segmentation of satellite orthoimagery using convolutional neural networks. Remote Sens. **8**(4), 329 (2016)

25. Letessier, T.B., Juhel, J.B., Vigliola, L., Meeuwig, J.J.: Low-cost small action cameras in stereo generates accurate underwater measurements of fish. J. Exp. Marine Biol. Ecol. **466**, 120–126 (2015)
26. Li, L., Dong, B., Rigall, E., Zhou, T., Donga, J., Chen, G.: Marine animal segmentation. IEEE Trans. Circ. Syst. Video Technol. **32**, 2303–2314 (2021)
27. Lin, T.Y., Goyal, P., Girshick, R., He, K., Dollár, P.: Focal loss for dense object detection. In: Proceedings of the IEEE International Conference on Computer Vision, pp. 2980–2988 (2017)
28. Long, J., Shelhamer, E., Darrell, T.: Fully convolutional networks for semantic segmentation. In: Proceedings of the IEEE Conference on Computer Vision and Pattern Recognition, pp. 3431–3440 (2015)
29. Marchesan, M., Spoto, M., Verginella, L., Ferrero, E.A.: Behavioural effects of artificial light on fish species of commercial interest. Fisher. Res. **73**(1–2), 171–185 (2005)
30. Milletari, F., Navab, N., Ahmadi, S.A.: V-net: fully convolutional neural networks for volumetric medical image segmentation. In: 2016 Fourth International Conference on 3D Vision (3DV), pp. 565–571. IEEE (2016)
31. Qin, H., Peng, Y., Li, X.: Foreground extraction of underwater videos via sparse and low-rank matrix decomposition. In: 2014 ICPR Workshop on Computer Vision for Analysis of Underwater Imagery, pp. 65–72. IEEE (2014)
32. Ronneberger, O., Fischer, P., Brox, T.: U-net: convolutional networks for biomedical image segmentation. In: Navab, N., Hornegger, J., Wells, W.M., Frangi, A.F. (eds.) MICCAI 2015. LNCS, vol. 9351, pp. 234–241. Springer, Cham (2015). https://doi.org/10.1007/978-3-319-24574-4_28
33. Rosen, S., Holst, J.C.: Deepvision in-trawl imaging: sampling the water column in four dimensions. Fisher. Res. **148**, 64–73 (2013)
34. Sandler, M., Howard, A., Zhu, M., Zhmoginov, A., Chen, L.C.: Mobilenetv 2: inverted residuals and linear bottlenecks. In: Proceedings of the IEEE Conference on Computer Vision and Pattern Recognition, pp. 4510–4520 (2018)
35. Sekachev, B., et al.: opencv/cvat: v1.1.0 (2020). https://doi.org/10.5281/zenodo.4009388
36. Sorensen, T.A.: A method of establishing groups of equal amplitude in plant sociology based on similarity of species content and its application to analyses of the vegetation on danish commons. Biol. Skar. **5**, 1–34 (1948)
37. Spampinato, C., Giordano, D., Di Salvo, R., Chen-Burger, Y.H.J., Fisher, R.B., Nadarajan, G.: Automatic fish classification for underwater species behavior understanding. In: Proceedings of the First ACM International Workshop on Analysis and Retrieval of Tracked Events and Motion in Imagery Streams, pp. 45–50 (2010)
38. Treml, M., et al.: Speeding up semantic segmentation for autonomous driving (2016)
39. Wilhelms, I., et al.: Atlas of length-weight relationships of 93 fish and crustacean species from the north sea and the north-east atlantic. Technical report, Johann Heinrich von Thünen Institute, Federal Research Institute for Rural . . . (2013)
40. Williams, K., Lauffenburger, N., Chuang, M.C., Hwang, J.N., Towler, R.: Automated measurements of fish within a trawl using stereo images from a camera-trawl device (camtrawl). Methods Oceanogr. **17**, 138–152 (2016)
41. Yadan, O.: Hydra - a framework for elegantly configuring complex applications. Github (2019). https://github.com/facebookresearch/hydra
42. Yakubovskiy, P.: Segmentation models pytorch (2020). https://github.com/qubvel/segmentation_models.pytorch
43. Yu, C., Wang, J., Peng, C., Gao, C., Yu, G., Sang, N.: Learning a discriminative feature network for semantic segmentation. In: Proceedings of the IEEE Conference on Computer Vision and Pattern Recognition, pp. 1857–1866 (2018)

44. Yu, C., et al.: Segmentation and measurement scheme for fish morphological features based on mask r-cnn. Inf. Process. Agric. **7**(4), 523–534 (2020)
45. Zarco-Perello, S., Enríquez, S.: Remote underwater video reveals higher fish diversity and abundance in seagrass meadows, and habitat differences in trophic interactions. Sci. Rep. **9**(1), 1–11 (2019)
46. Zhao, H., Shi, J., Qi, X., Wang, X., Jia, J.: Pyramid scene parsing network. In: Proceedings of the IEEE Conference on Computer Vision and Pattern Recognition, pp. 2881–2890 (2017)

Social Embodiment of Companion Robots in Smart Spaces: IoRT for Independent Living

Chanzo Muema[1]([✉]), Steven Lawrence[2], Taif Anjum[3], and Amir Shabani[1]

[1] University of the Fraser Valley, Abbotsford, BC V2S 7M7, Canada
Chanzo.Muema@student.ufv.ca, Amir.Shabani@ufv.ca
[2] University of Waterloo, Waterloo, ON N2L 3G1, Canada
Steven.Lawrence@uwaterloo.ca
[3] University of British Columbia, Kelowna, BC V1V 1V7, Canada
Taif.Anjum@ubc.ca

Abstract. With the rapid increase of interest in independent living along with the continual growth of the global aging population, there is a significant need for developing technological solutions that are trustworthy, functional, and scalable. Towards this vision, we developed a novel framework that provides an organic, evolving, and immersive assistive interaction between human, robot, and their environment. Our contribution is in the system design and the computing aspect of the proposed solution. At the system level, we are utilizing the concept of the Internet of Robotic Things (IoRT) to integrate smart personal devices and smart space automation technologies with social companion robot(s) and mixed/augmented reality smart glasses. At the computing level, we propose utilizing advancements in the field of Artificial Intelligence (AI) and Machine Learning (ML) towards providing task assistance in daily activities, smart space control, and improving emotion and mood through Affective Computing. We provide details of our IoRT system integration and quantitative experimental results on Facial Emotion Recognition (FER) which is one of the core components for Affective Computing. We improved FER utilizing Deep Learning on the edge and then deployed it on our Social Companion Robot (SCR) called Miro. We integrated the SCR with a Mixed Reality smart glass (Microsoft Hololens 2) and smart home automaton hub (Google). While the smart automation controller is directly in charge of controlling the environment (e.g., lighting, temperature), the robot can increase the control level with a more context-aware decision providing a socially embodied control.

Keywords: Human-robot-interaction · Internet of Robotic Things (IoRT) · Social companion robots · Smart home automation · Social embodiment · Affective computing · Mixed/augmented reality · Independent living

© Springer Nature Switzerland AG 2022
P. Galambos et al. (Eds.): ROBOVIS 2020/ROBOVIS 2021, CCIS 1667, pp. 147–171, 2022.
https://doi.org/10.1007/978-3-031-19650-8_8

1   Introduction

Humanity's life expectancy is increasing at an unprecedented pace, which means the global population will outperform itself every year. According to the World Health Organization (WHO), by 2030, globally, one out of every six people will be aged 60 years or over [51]. Furthermore, between 2020 and 2050, the number of people aged 80 years or older will triple to 426 million [51]. The rapid increase of the global aging population is concerning as there is a critical shortage of caregivers in the work force [11].

Independent living can be challenging for older adults, whether it is in their own residence or long-term care facilitates. The COVID-19 pandemic has brought forth the necessity for advanced assistive technologies to support our aging population as well as their caregivers. The goal of assistive technologies is not to replace humans, but to relieve the pressure from over-worked staff and caregivers while making it easier for them to focus better on their human-to-human tasks. A poll [3] by AGE-WELL Canada surveyed 2,026 Canadians aged 50 and older found that 50% of Canadians aged sixty-five and above are comfortable paying for technologies to improve their mental and physical health, while two-thirds are prepared to pay for technologies that help them to stay home as they grow older. It is worth noting that seventy-two percent of this age group are comfortable using current technology. Seniors are increasingly using technologies such as online appointments, shopping, and social media applications to cope with their daily life duties and stay connected with loved ones during the ongoing pandemic [3]. Moreover, Ambient/Active Assisted Living (AAL) technologies [28] have shown to be effective in support of independent living and overcoming motor and cognitive barriers.

Additionally, robotic technologies such as SCRs can assist older adults in daily tasks such as taking medication, eating healthy meals, getting dressed, exercising, and tracking their vital signs [1]. Furthermore, using Computer Vision (CV) and Natural Language Processing/Understanding (NLP/NLU), they can check for signs of depression, loneliness, cognitive impairments (e.g., Alzheimer's and Parkinson's disease) [12,53], physical impairments (e.g., difficulty walking, pain during movement), and pain detection (even in people who have difficulty expressing pain due to paralysis or severe dementia) [6,9,40]. Pain, in particular, tends to be under-reported and not treated, resulting in agitation and aggression.

Based on the IoRT framework [2,44], SCRs can be integrated with other personal and environmental smart devices in the space and become an active participant in different scenarios for information sharing, control of the environment, and assisting the occupants in their daily life tasks. In fact, integrating smart home systems and sensors with SCRs can improve the quality of life for older adults in both care home facilities and their own homes. This integration with the environment will allow SCRs to apply Affective Computing (i.e., recognize and respond to human affect) comprehensively. For example, using AI combined with social inference [20], SCRs can learn the personal temperature and light setting preferences for each individual in a living environment and modify the setting according to their mood to improve their emotional state. This interaction can be a response towards the human counterpart's emotion detected through FER and assessing the scene/situation. More specifically, SCR's bi-directional communication with smart devices along with Augmented Reality/Mixed Reality (AR/MR) enables the fusion of information from different modalities and hence the convergence of real data with digital and virtual data towards a better inference. To assure privacy, security protocols could be engineered in these communications, specifically as the system is connected to the central monitoring station of a service provider for remote health/security monitoring. When it comes to video communication, encoding or obfuscating personal/identifiable parts of the scene (e.g., face obfuscation) along with prompting the user for approval are among strategies towards engineering privacy.

In our previous work [5], we presented the integration of SCRs with MR smart glasses (e.g., Microsoft's HoloLens) to add an additional layer of functionality ensuring reliability and trustworthiness of the system when adopted at scale in senior homes or long-term care facilities. Here, we argue that the same integration could be beneficial for independent living, hence improving the acceptance rate and the adoption of the technology at a much larger scale. In fact, despite all the progress made in the field of AI and robotics, the public has a fear of leaving robots in charge of making (critical) decisions for their loved ones when they are alone and not in a proper state of mind or ability [7]. Hence, a timely intervention by a professional/expert is required when it comes to vital/critical tasks and decision making, more specifically.

Our proposal of integrating SCR with home automation and AR has multi-tier benefits in several avenues including the development of human-centered AI solutions for advanced AAL offerings which should increase the technology adoption and acceptance rate. More specifically, when used by the elder (i.e., end-user), the integrated solution provides an immersive experience with a higher degree of independence, hence a higher degree of engagement. This is accomplished by increasing their control level of the environment through learning their preferences for different situations or setting of temperature/lighting (personalized or command-based), AI-powered companionship of a mobile robot, and an interface to enable the user to be in the loop of decision making through smart glasses or human-robot interactions such as conversation.

With the robot at the center of our integration platform, our solution offers an operational assist system and an information assist system. The operational assist system combines a SCR robot with an environmental control system for the convenience of users. An information assist system connects the space with remote locations for communication.

Moreover, when used at scale across separate homes, such an integration added to the existing monitoring/security services provides an immersive experience for the operator/expert in the loop to be more proactive and engaging in the situation with both the robot and the user. It is worth noting that having a company in charge of monitoring provides more accountability and trust for the service recipients (i.e., both the elders and their loved ones). In fact, combining artificial intelligence of the robot with human ethics (applied by the operator) provides better engagement.

Microsoft's HoloLens can be connected to a group of Social Companion Robots. The caretaker/administrator wearing the smart glasses can monitor the SCR's behavior and actions in case of a malfunction. The caretaker/administrator can override the SCR's actions and resolve any issues that arise. For example, if the SCR makes a false alert, the caretaker/administrator can override the alert. Important information such as vital readings, mood, food/medicine intake schedule/history, exercise schedule/history and sleep data can be available to the caretaker/administrator for monitoring purposes if permitted by the older adult.

The older adults will be anonymized and the caretaker/administrator will have no information about that individual. However, if the older-adult wishes to speak to the caretaker/administrator they can instruct the SCR to turn on its camera and microphone in order to communicate with the user/expert. This integration will allow for a central control unit for all the SCRs.

For individual uses of SCRs in residences, the smart glasses will allow easy access to the caregiver or family members to check up on the older adults and monitor their health and well-being.

The main idea of our system is to connect multiple devices (smart glasses, smart home devices, and sensors) with SCRs to enhance the older adult's experience. Integrating environmental control as part of human-robot interaction makes the realization of affective computing with SCRs more realistic, comprehensive, and effective. The proposed system integrates AR smart glasses (Microsoft's HoloLens 2) with the SCR Miro. Our prototype successfully demonstrated bi-directional audio and video communication between the two devices. Additionally, the SCR (Miro) can be controlled remotely through AR smart glasses (Microsoft's HoloLens 2). We further propose off-loading Deep Learning inferences to the edge using edge hardware accelerators.

The remaining portion of this chapter is organized as follows. Section 2 reviews related work, Sect. 3 covers our proposed framework, Sect. 4 discusses the Integration of AR Smart Glass with SCRs. Section 5 presents a computation off-loading method for performing Deep Learning inferences on the edge. Section 6 discusses the smart home integration with Miro. Section 7 covers the remote and local supervision of SCRs through Microsoft's HoloLens 2. Section 8 presents the conclusion and future work.

2   Related Work

A study was conducted in older adults living in independent residences to identify the unique challenges of aging in place in Canada from the perspectives of older adults with self-reported cognitive decline and informal caregivers [25]. Some of the main themes identified were emotional challenges/low mood, memory decline, difficulty with mobility/physical tasks, social isolation, and difficulties with activities of daily living [25]. Cognitive decline is a predominant issue to elders who experience change in their social roles, and physical capabilities [15]. This decline triggers an onset of negative side effects, mainly, a decline in quality of life, and mental state [15]. Aging in place is a concept that describes older adults' desire to remain and live in their own homes without needing to be institutionalized when health care needs change [50]. When older adults are institutionalized due to age or declining cognitive ability, there is a negative impact on their quality of life as well as economic consequences on their family and society. [10]. Furthermore, the desire to age in place creates increased stress on informal caregivers (family, friends, etc.) that provide unpaid assistance with day-to-day tasks. Approximately 3.8 million Canadians over the age of 45 provide informal care to an adult over the age of 65; a quarter of these carers are older adults themselves [48]. With off-the-shelf robots available at increasingly affordable prices, they pose as an inclusive solution to provide support to the ageing population to live at home longer and provide ongoing support to help mitigate these issues.

Many researchers are looking to robots to provide assistive support both physically and mentally to the aging populations. Robots such as "Miro", "Paro", "Hector", and "Ifbot" have demonstrated benefits for cognitive training, speech engagement, and overall high therapeutic effects [15,17]. Although the WHO stated delivering person-centered integrated care and the development of smart, physical, social, and age-friendly environments will improve the quality of life for older adults [4,51], research groups remain focused more so on adding assistive features and not the integration and operations of smart spaces. Whereas, our work is towards centralized operation with AR and intelligent robots. Additionally, we are looking at increasing the robot's embodied intelligence by integrating multi-modal sensory information from multiple sources, adding more processing power, and actuating control of the smart space devices. This will allow for decision-making and action selection to be based on the cognitive state of individuals in the smart space, and hence make the robot to be a socially embodied intelligent agent and the environment to be a socially amenable space. Below we will look a related work primarily focused towards these topics.

2.1   Centralized Operation and Integration

Smart spaces are gaining more popularity as they are being seen in homes, cities, factories, and commercial offices [23,26]. More and more people are looking to smart space technology to have fully connected homes and workplaces. The work by Pahl *et al.* [34] looks towards middleware architecture to help merge communication between these heterogeneous devices to allow for a homogeneous user experience and central operation. Advancements in smart space technologies are allowing for this data from environmental sensors and physiological sensors to be obtained and processed in real-time, increasing the perception of intelligent agents such as robots [2].

The review by Simoens *et al.* [44] on the IoRT highlights the various advantages robot integration with smart spaces can provide for both domestic and industrial applications. For such integration, some researchers look to cloud-based solutions such as ROSLink [18] and MAVLink [19]. Whereas, others such

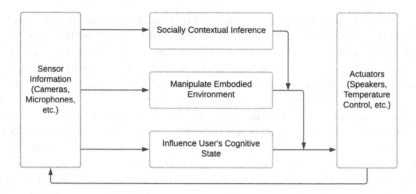

Fig. 1. Subsumption of decision making determined by cognitive state of users.

as Uchechukwu *et al.* [49] focused on local integration with ROS to connect a robot for centralized-decision making. The latter is similar to our work by prioritizing local integration, however, our work emphasizes edge computation and decision making determined by the cognitive state of the smart space users, whereas, their focus was on collision avoidance. For such inferences, various physiological and environmental sensors can be used. Figure 1 shows how our system's socially contextual inference is subsumed by the goal of influencing the smart space user's cognitive state.

Research has shown the critical features that should be monitored in the ageing population are physiological parameters, body functions, and changes to daily life activities and routines including social and environmental factors [4,45]. Changes in a person's daily activities are a good indicator of an underlying physical or mental issue. Nevertheless, detecting this change is very important. With the use of smart devices and physiological sensors, researchers can establish a fairly accurate baseline in health and well-being [29], sleep quality [39], stress level [42], and cognitive decline [4]. These devices and sensors are an integral component of a smart space. However, research appears to focus more on specific components and not on mass integration and operation. We are working towards an architecture allowing for the integration of such devices with a centralized SCR to mediate minor to medium issues via environment interaction and raise alerts for more severe cases.

2.2 Embodied Intelligence and Social Embodiment

Below is a minimal definition of embodiment discussing the physical properties that are required. Using this definition we can discuss how to increase the degree of embodiment. To do so, we will increase the number of incoming and outgoing channels of perturbation for the robot, furthering its structural coupling [24] with the environment. Although simply fulfilling this definition does not equate to interesting behavior, we will demonstrate via integration with smart space devices we can achieve quantitatively different coupling relationships leading to intelligent, purposeful behavior.

"A system X is embodied in an environment E if perturbatory channels exist between the two. That is, X is embodied in E if for every time t at which both X and E exist, some subset of E's possible states have the capacity to perturb X's state, and some subset of X's possible states have the capacity to perturb E's state." [38, pp. 2]

Social embodiment further examines the influence of the sensory, motor, and perpetual cues in the environment on the thoughts, affect, and behavior [20]. In fact, years of evolution have allowed humans to evolve their perception enough to infer abstract concepts such as the cognitive/emotional state of an individual, environment, and social context, to name a few. It has been proved to be challenging to have intelligent agents such as robots perceive and infer such situations, although researchers are making progress. Jing *et al.* [15] propose a cognitive-emotional model designed to target eldercare robots to detect, extract, and recognize emotional features to determine the participant's current cognitive state which is used to regulate the cognitive state of the robot and adjust the parameters of a smart home environment. This model, however, assumes off-boarding computation and cloud communication, which bring arise issues such as network latency and privacy/security concerns. In contrast, our architect is built to promote computation on the edge and local communication to existing smart devices with the capability to engineer privacy when it is connected to the cloud. The results of their work show that cognitive state can increase in a smart environment with their cognitive model [15], although the test appears to be limited with only fifteen participants spending ten minutes in the environment. The work by Johnson *et al.* [16] focused on introducing the KSERA (Knowledgeable SErvice Robots for Aging) system to enhance the behavior of a humanoid robot named NAO and hence developing a user-centered social assistive robot (SAR). KSERA system provides mainly assistance to elders through a user-centered interface with the NAO robot, centralizing both the operational assistance (i.e., control of the environment) and information assistant (e.g., communication with the outside world through video conferencing with loved ones). By enhancing NAO's behavior by increasing its environment perception and expressibility (i.e., perturbatory channels), its acceptance rate had been increased. In fact, NAO was deemed more 'likable' and participants exhibited a preferred path of communication through the robot instead of individual smart space devices. This study shows the importance of (social) embodiment and centralization of the control around robots for improving user experience and hence increasing the technology acceptance rate by elder adults. Robotic Smart Home (RSH) project [46] in Japan is another similar project which also studies the architectural design of the living space along with activity assist robots (AAR) to create an optimal home environment for elders.

Regarding context recognition, the work of Yang *et al.* [52] has demonstrated interesting results using their proposed deep learning model for detecting context and recognizing situations considered private and/or embarrassing. Recognizing such context will allow for actions to be mitigated to preserve the user's privacy. A vital component to consider in the design of smart spaces is overall acceptability. Acceptance of smart home technology in the elder community is contingent on minimizing lifestyle change [35]. Research shows resistance to technology that takes control away from users, promotes a lazy lifestyle, or infringes privacy [35]. We hope to aid in the acceptance of such monitoring devices by introducing a centralized SCR that will give a sense of companionship as opposed to simple ambient monitoring.

In line with the KSERA project with their humanoid robot NAO and the RSH project with their activity assist robot, our framework is based on the social companion robot Miro being the central integration point of the space devices and also the interaction point with the user/elder for both the operational/control assistant and also information/communication assistant. However, our proposal of connecting SCRs to a security/health monitoring service provider and the use of mixed/augmented reality by their operator is a unique setting. As argued in our previous work [5], this setting could provide a priority in resource management and hence improve the efficiency of the provided services, more specifically in emergency situations with limited available staff/resources.

3   Proposed Framework

Our proposed system is to deploy SCRs to the personal dwellings of elderly adults in need of partial or full-time care to facilitate individual monitoring and personalized interactions through speech and vision. To address privacy concerns surrounding the video, image, and audio data, each SCR can have a system in place to analyze sensitive data for the most relevant data (key frames) and only communicate the aggregated data to the central interface accessed by the caregiver or operator. To address the cloud/internet cyber security concerns, an encrypted

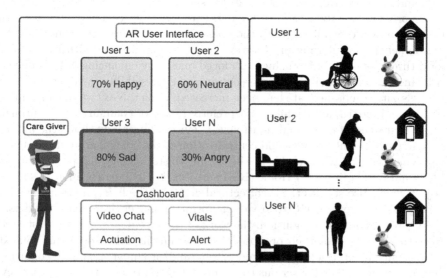

Fig. 2. AR-based system integrated with SCRs for older adult care in long-term care facility [5].

virtual proxy tunnel can be implemented between the central monitoring system's network and the SCR. As seen in Fig. 2, the caregiver with AR system can monitor the analyzed status of the elders and provide necessary support through the SCR without needing to be present in the elder's room. This allows the caregiver wearing the AR system to effectively and efficiently interact with multiple SCRs through one centralized interface. Our proposed system would also allow for the remote administration and support of care facilities implementing the AR-based system integrated with SCRs. Figure 3 demonstrates such an environment.

For our application, the use of emotion recognition through an SCR's interface can make the experience more interactive and engaging for the user while being a strong tool to provide feedback on the user's well-being. However, performing deep learning training and inferences in embedded systems such as SCRs is challenging due to the computational cost of deep learning algorithms. In such cases, researchers utilize the cloud to perform the computation. However, cloud computing comes with issues regarding privacy, latency, cost, and more. To circumvent these issues, our framework leverages hardware accelerators to perform on-the-edge inferences in real-time. For an overview of the complete framework see Fig. 4.

4 Integrating AR Smart Glass with SCRs

Our proposed AR-based system for monitoring a group of social robots in both care home facilities and personal dwellings requires deploying a group of SCRs with the following constraints:

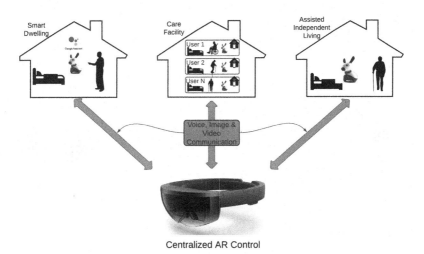

Fig. 3. Centralized administration of SCRs at the service provider office through MR/AR.

1. Remotely controlling functions of the robot to assist the elderly while ensuring optimal performance.
2. Non-intrusive monitoring and reporting to a centralized caregiver or system administrator.
3. Bi-directional communication to facilitate voice interaction between the caregiver and elderly.

Having a centralized monitoring platform for a group of SCRs is imperative for our application. The platform will be used to remotely monitor and receive environmental and other sensing data from visual, speech, haptic, and thermal sensors. A video/voice chat option allows live interaction between the caregiver and the older adult based on the sensor data (e.g., SCR detects that the older adult is in emotional or physical distress). Furthermore, the SCR can report and recommend intervention based on this sensor data (e.g., the elderly adult has skipped medication, meals, etc.).

4.1   Establishing Bidirectional Communication Between ROS and AR Smart Glass

The framework used to establish bi-directional communication between the SCR (Miro) and the HoloLens 2 is Unity and RosSharp using a Microsoft environment and the RosBridge-suite to facilitate the connection to our Ubuntu environment. RosSharp is a set of open-source software libraries and tools written in C#

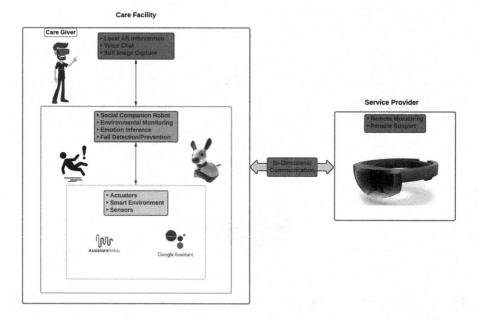

Fig. 4. SCR provides context-aware control of the smart space/home and has bi-directional communication with the AR/MR of the service provider.

Table 1. System Development tools [5].

Development stack
Microsoft visual studio 2019
RosSharp
Mixed reality toolkit
ROS-bridge suite
Miro development kit
Client stack
HoloLens 2
Miro-e
Server stack
Ubuntu 18.04 bionic beaver
ROS noetic

for communicating with ROS environments through .NET applications (Unity). RosBridge-suite is a collection of programs (Web socket, JSON API, etc.) for communicating between ROS and non-ROS programs. Using RosBridge-suite we can exchange data (text, audio, image, etc.) between ROS nodes. The System development tools are presented in Table 1.

Figure 5 outlines the proposed system architecture - the left side represents the AR user interface (HoloLens 2) with Unity running in a Windows environment. The right side represents Miro's Ubuntu 18.04 environment.

Roscore and RosBridge are instantiated in the Ubuntu environment that the Miro is interacting with. Roscore is a collection of nodes and programs that are prerequisites to ROS-based systems. It is used to send data through topics that the Miro can subscribe or publish to in order to access or send data.

From the Unity environment, simulated ROS message types can be sent to the Websocket hosted on the Ubuntu machine. These messages are then translated through the RosBridge and published to ROS topics. In order to establish this full bi-directional link, we created a unity project and imported RosSharp, the Mixed Reality Toolkit, and configured the RosBridge client for use with Unity.

4.2 Developing a HoloLens Application in Unity

The Augmented Reality application for Hololens is created using the unity engine. To exchange messages between the HoloLens 2 and ROS, a Universal Windows Platform (UWP) application must be running on the headset. To accomplish this we used the Mixed Reality Toolkit prefabs as well as the following Unity features:

1. TextMeshPro for displaying a text representation of our FER data and building a simple user interface (UI)

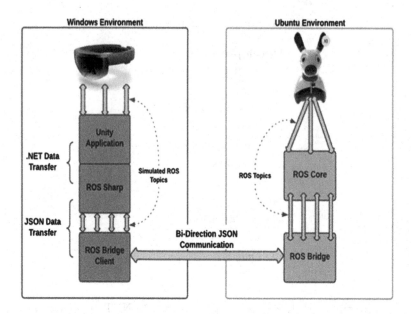

Fig. 5. HoloLens-Miro end-to-end System Architecture [5].

2. A two-dimensional canvas for displaying still images
3. An audio source asset to play audio streamed from a ROS environment

The UI has buttons corresponding to various functions on the Miro (motor actuation, LED toggling, etc.), as well as a button for capturing image data and a button to start voice communication. The predicted emotion from our FER model is displayed on top of the user interface, and still images are captured and displayed on the two-dimensional canvas above the interface and the audio is streamed through the built-in speakers in the HoloLens headset.

4.3   Publishing to ROS Topics

ROS topics are named buses over which nodes can exchange messages. Each topic is constrained by the message type used to publish it (text, image, etc.) and subscribed nodes can only receive messages with a matching type. We can create custom topics for both Miro and Unity to publish and subscribe to. The Unity project must be subscribed to the Miro topic that it intends to send and receive messages on and vice versa. The Miro has various topics including illumination, kinematic joints, camera, microphones, etc. We can publish to these Miro topics to trigger corresponding functions on the Miro such as wagging its tail, moving, illuminating an LED, etc.

To begin the process of publishing and subscribing to topics, Roscore is initialized with the master node as the Ubuntu machine. Then we connect the RosBridge-Client Node and Miro's ROS node to the master node. Once both nodes are linked to the master node we can exchange messages over the topics. We use a script that allows Miro to listen for data to be published to the subscribed topics. Once a publish request is received, the specific command for that topic is executed. The Miro is always listening for publish requests and matches the type of topics it is subscribed to. A similar process takes place when executing commands to the HoloLens 2; a publish request is sent to RosSharp topics in Unity from Miro's ROS node.

4.4   Audio and Image Streaming Through ROS Topics

For our proposed environment to be an effective centralized monitoring system, it is imperative that a centralized operator/caregiver can directly interact with the older adult receiving care. A line of direct vocal communication between the operator and adult in care allows for immediate action or intervention to be taken when the older adult is in distress. For example, based on FER data, we can have the Unity interface alert the caregiver that the adult is in emotional distress. The caregiver can then capture a still image of the room through the Miro's cameras. Miro can then be moved to the adult's location through the interface and then voice chat can be initiated to gauge the responsiveness of the adult in distress or to reassure them that assistance is on the way.

The Miro has a named topic for every kinematic control surface and environmental sensor contained within the robot. Through Unity, we can create an audio playing object and have it subscribed to the microphone topic published by Miro. Similarly, an object with an image mesh can be created in Unity to receive the image data from the camera topics published by Miro. The system can continuously pull live images from the room at a frequency that the caregiver/controller sets. To capture the microphone input from the HoloLens, a new topic must be created within unity to convert from the HoloLens's audio data type to a format Miro can interpret. Miro can then subscribe to this created topic and play audio recorded from the HoloLens microphone. Through the UI the caregiver can choose to initiate one-way or two-way audio communication with the Miro or receive image data from the cameras.

5   Deep Learning Inference on the Edge

FER has been a topic of interest in the computer vision community for many applications, specifically within affective computing. Standard ML algorithms and their variations have been extensively used for FER classification. Our past research shows that Deep Learning techniques with Convolutional Neural Networks (CNNs) have proven to outperform standard ML algorithms for image and video classification in FER [5]. However, Deep Learning training and inferences are computationally expensive and typically performed using powerful and expensive computers or servers. Most mobile robots such as Miro have limited onboard resources such as processor, memory, and battery. We previously explored methods for offloading the computational load and found that cloud solutions are not viable due to network security vulnerabilities [5,8]. Furthermore, network latency and instability can disrupt cloud-based computing [8]. We require an affordable flexible solution that is secure due to the sensitive data being processed onboard [30].

Apart from Graphics Processing Units (GPUs), system-on-chip architectures that utilize the power of Application-Specific Integrated Circuits (ASICs), Field-programmable Gate Arrays (FPGAs) and Vision Processing Units (VPUs) can also be used for inference at the edge. Our investigation shows that several products satisfy the need for Deep Learning inference on the edge with respect to our cost, latency, and security requirements:

1. The Edge TPU by Google is an ASIC exclusively for inference achieving 4 Tera Operations Per Second (TOPS) for 8-bit integer inference. It only runs models trained on Tensorflow on a host PC and then needs to be converted to Tensorflow lite. It requires further conversion to a Coral-specific format to comply with the hardware requirements. Google's Coral Dev Board featuring Edge TPU is priced at $169 (USD) for the 4GB RAM version.
2. The Intel Neural Compute Stick 2 is a System-on-Chip built on the Myriad X VPU, optimized for computer vision with a dedicated neural compute engine for hardware acceleration of deep neural network inferences. It has a max performance of 4 TOPS, similar to the Edge TPU. However, it requires a host PC since the device is distributed as a USB 3.0 stick. It also requires the model to be converted to an Intermediate Representation (IR) format that can slow down the development process. This device is priced at $68.95 (USD) excluding the cost of a host PC
3. NVIDIA's Jetson series is a group of embedded machine learning platforms that aims to balance computational power with energy efficiency. They feature CUDA-capable GPUs for efficient machine learning inferences. Their cheapest and lightest model is the Jetson Nano TX1 with a peak performance of 512 single-precision (SP) Giga floating-point operations per second (GFLOPS). They cost $129 (USD) for the 4GB version.

Unlike the EDGE TPU and Neural Compute Stick 2 (NCS2), Jetson Nano does not require a host PC, models do not require any conversion, is not restricted to any specific machine learning framework, and is the cheapest option. Jetson Nano is essentially a small Linux computer that can run any model trained on a more powerful system with little to no changes. This flexibility was important to us as it will speed up the development process. Due to the flexibility of Jetson Nano which all other devices lack we decided to choose Jetson Nano as our primary edge accelerator to off-load deep learning inference, see Fig. 6.

5.1   Analysis of Compute Time

We analyzed the inference time of Neural Compute Stick 2 and Jetson Nano. Table 2 shows the different inference times for FER using two CNN architectures

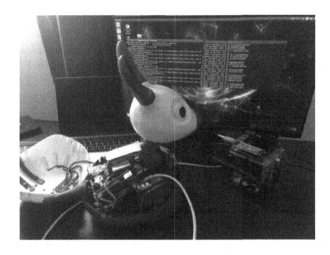

Fig. 6. Hardware Integration of Miro-e and Nvidia's Jetson Nano via Ethernet port for efficient Deep Learning inference at the edge. The final prototype we will have the Jetson Nano board on Miro-e's body [5].

Table 2. Latency time comparison for dataset training (DCNN vs MobileNet).

	Intel xeon silver	Intel xeon silver + NCS2	Raspberry Pi 3(B+) + NCS2	Jetson nano (TF)	Jetson nano (TF-TRT)
DCNN	43 ms	14.23 ms	16.17 ms	264 ms	57 ms
MobileNet	46 ms	14.31 ms	16.05 ms	200 ms	53 ms

respectively. We took an average of 10,000 inferences for each device. The first column shows the average inference time using only the Intel Xeon silver CPU with 128 GB of RAM. The second and third column shows the inference time for the NCS2 with the host PC as the Intel Xeon Silver 4110 CPU @ 2.10 GHz and Raspberry Pi 3(B+) respectively. The third and fourth column represents the inference time for Jetson Nano with only TensorFlow and TensorFlow-TensorRT (TF-TRT) respectively. TF-TRT is a Tensorflow integration that optimizes deep learning inference on NVIDIA GPUs. Our experiments show that NCS2 outperforms Jetson Nano even with the TF-TRT optimizer. However, the flexibility of Jetson Nano outweighs the low latency for our application.

While the EDGE TPU and Neural Compute Stick 2 presented the best lowest latency, they both require a host PC. However, the Jetson Nano has the lowest compute time but does not require a host PC, models don't require conversion, it is not restricted to a specific ML framework, and it is the lowest in cost including the host PC. We determined that the latency in the Jetson Nano was a worthwhile trade-off because of our system's functional requirements.

In previous experiments, we found that while the Miro's onboard computer (Raspberry Pi 3(B+)) can also perform these computations on its own, its computational power is significantly less than that of the Jetson Nano TX1 [5].

5.2   CNN Architecture for FER

In our recent studies, we found that publicly available FER datasets were heavily age-biased. We introduced a data augmentation technique for FER using face aging augmentation. To increase the age diversity of existing FER datasets we used GAN based face aging augmentation technique to include representation of our target age group (older adults). We conducted comprehensive experiments for both intra-dataset [21] and cross-dataset [5] that suggest face aging augmentation significantly improves FER accuracy.

To implement FER, we utilize two Deep Learning architectures, specifically, CNNs because of their great promise for image classification. For the purpose of FER, several studies showed that CNNs outperform other state-of-the-art methods [21, 27, 36]. For our experiments, the two architectures used were; MobileNet, a lightweight CNN developed by Google and a simple CNN which we will refer to as Deep CNN (DCNN) [14]. Our DCNN classifier includes six convolutional 2D layers, three max-pooling 2D layers, and two fully connected (FC) layers. The Exponential Linear Unit (ELU) activation function is used for all the layers. The output layer (FC) has nodes equal to the number of classes (in this case, six classes) with a Softmax activation function. To avoid overfitting, Batch Normalization (BN) was used after every convolutional 2D layer, and dropouts were used after every max-pooling layer. Both BN and dropout were used after the first FC layer.

A lightweight model such as MobileNet is required for our application of FER in embedded systems at the edge such as SCRs. MobileNet has 14 convolutional layers, 13 depth-wise convolutional layers, one average pooling layer, an FC layer, and an output layer with the Softmax activation function. BN and Rectified Linear Unit (ReLU) are applied after each convolution. MobileNet is faster than many popular CNN architectures such as AlexNet, GoogleNet, VGG16, and SqueezeNet while having similar or higher accuracy [14]. The main difference between DCNN and MobileNet is that the latter classifier leverages transfer learning by using pre-trained weights from ImageNet. Throughout every experiment, MobileNet contained 15 frozen layers from ImageNet. An output layer was added with nodes equal to the number of classes and softmax is used as the activation function. We used both DCNN and MobileNet classifiers with implementations from [43]. The Nadam optimizer was used along with two callbacks, 'early stopping' to avoid overfitting. For reducing the learning rate when learning stops improving, we used 'ReduceLRonPlateau'. The data is normalized prior to being fed into the neural networks as neural networks are sensitive to un-normalized data. Both the models we deployed onto Miro (MobileNet and DCNN) were trained with both original and face age augmented images.

5.3   Miro and Jetson Nano Integration: Deep Learning Inference on the Edge

We used ROS to establish a connection between the Jetson Nano and Miro. The connection can be established either by Ethernet or wireless (Wi-Fi) connection. In order to main network security, we decided to restrict Miro's access to the internet and hard-wired the Jetson directly to the Raspberry Pi via Ethernet.

Fig. 7. Real-time FER with Miro on the edge [5].

A compatible environment was required for both Jetson Nano and Miro. ROS Noetic is required in order to interface with Miro. This version of ROS is only compatible with Ubuntu 20.04 Focal Fossa. However, Ubuntu 18.04 is the latest version that is compatible with ROS. To overcome this we used a Docker image on Ubuntu 18.04 with ROS noetic built from source. We then installed Tensorflow, OpenCV, and other necessary Python and ROS libraries. Finally, we installed the Miro development kit on the Jetson Nano and established a direct connection through the Ethernet port, and communication was facilitated by ROS libraries. We successfully performed real-time FER with both MobileNet and DCNN models without any noticeable lag.

Taking advantage of Miro's camera topics, we are able to write a script to display the left-eye camera and right-eye camera and view Miro's real-time video feed. Each frame of the feed can be used to detect and track faces in real-time. Once the face is detected, is it then cropped, re-sized to 48×48, converted to grayscale, and passed onto our trained FER model for emotion prediction. Figure 7 demonstrates our real-time FER through Miro.

6 Smart Home Integration with Miro-e

In our recent studies, we stated what differentiates SCRs from other assistive technologies is the interaction component. The robot needs to interact with the human counterpart in a natural human-like manner. More specifically, it needs to recognize and respond to human emotion. Furthermore, we stated that our system should be learning from the user's habits and become more personalized over time [5]. In our system, our SCR needs to be able to interact with a user's environment in response to FER input. Using the Google Assistant SDK, Miro can interact with a user's smart home environment in response to environmental

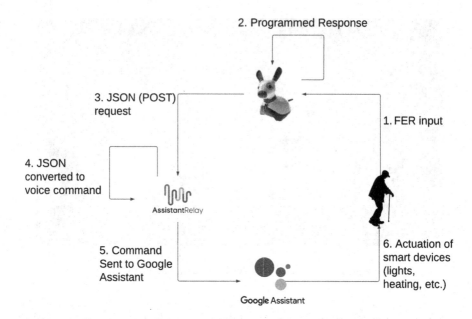

Fig. 8. FER input inferring an affective response in a smart environment.

and sensory data. For example, if Miro notices that the user is sad, based on previously learned or programmed information, the Miro can send a command to a Google Home speaker to play a song that typically makes the user happy. Moreover, a robot equipped with natural language processing/understanding (NLP/NLU) or a robot integrated with another smart device with such capability could engage in a series of Q&A with the user to better understand the root cause of the issue. It can then come up with a better decision or action in response to ease the situation and improve the emotional state of the user.

In a smart home environment deployed using Google Assistant's Google Home, smart devices (lights, speakers, televisions, etc.) can be controlled using mobile devices, voice commands, and gesture-based inputs [37]. Our Miro can act as a control for these smart devices by interacting with the Google Assistant environment and sending the Google Home queries based on FER data gathered with the google assistant SDK using Assistant Relay. Assistant Relay is an open-source Node.js server that can expose the Google Assistant SDK in an existing Google Assistant environment as a REST API [13]. The API accepts HTTP POST requests on a local network address and relays the text in the request as a command to the Google Home unit. The server runs in the same environment as ROS Bridge to facilitate local network interaction between Miro and the Google Home. Figure 8 shows the order of events as FER data is passed from Miro to the Google Assistant environment.

Our proposed system leverages the FER system in place to send a command to a Google Home based on a list of pre-programmed responses. Miro receives FER input from the adult in care, and based on the inferred emotion, it sends a POST request to Assistant Relay. Assistant Relay interprets and converts the request into a voice command piped directly to the Google Home. Finally, Google Home interacts directly with the smart devices in the system. For example, Miro could recognize that a user is angry, and send a command to the thermostat to lower the temperature and change the lights to a calming color to diffuse the situation.

7 Remote and Local Supervision of SCRs Through Microsoft's HoloLens 2

In our previous studies, we addressed the security concerns involving communication over the internet [5]. We opted for a design that hardwired Miro to the network via Ethernet to limit access to external networks [5]. However, to meet the goal of remotely controlling multiple SCRs in different geographical locations (the homes of older adults) we must design a system for securely communicating information over the internet. Furthermore, our previously proposed AR-based control system did not address the need to control multiple SCRs simultaneously.

7.1 Centralisation: Controlling an SCR from a Remote Location

Our goal is to connect two networks in different geographical locations to facilitate remote control of SCRs. We determined that a virtual private network (VPN) would be necessary to communicate remotely. VPNs are a means of creating secure communications over public network infrastructure. They employ encryption to ensure information is kept private and confidential [22]. There are various standards of VPN: SSL, IPSec, SSH, Layer 2, etc. Furthermore, the use of a VPN requires the use of a firewall to facilitate the connection between two networks. A firewall is a physical network device that behaves as a gateway between external networks [22]. We must select a cost-effective firewall that supports a scaling solution for remote control of multiple SCRs.

Our primary concern when communicating over remote networks is the security of the data that is being sent and received. For this reason, we chose to use the Layer 2 Tunneling Protocol (L2TP) in conjunction with Internet Protocol Security (IPSec). L2TP is a method of data encapsulation before it is sent, and IPSec wraps the data in encryption securing the packets being sent over the internet [22].

When considering a firewall, we focussed on finding an open-source and freely accessible platform that supports the L2TP/IPSec VPN standard. We looked at the three following platforms:

1. The pfSense project is a free network firewall distribution, based on the FreeBSD operating system with a custom kernel including third party free software packages for additional functionality [31].
2. NethServer is a CentOS-based Linux distribution for servers. The product's main feature is a modular design that makes it simple to turn Linux into a mail server and filter, web server, groupware, firewall, web filter, IPS/IDS or VPN server [32].

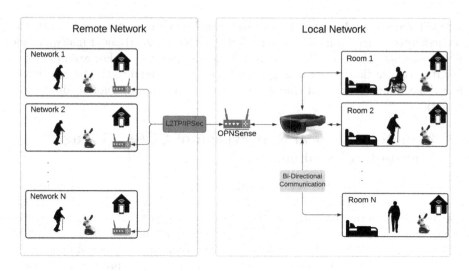

Fig. 9. Centralised AR control of local and remote SCRs.

3. OPNsense is an open-source, easy-to-use, and easy-to-build FreeBSD-based firewall and routing platform [33].

OPNSense and pfSense offer the same functionality, whereas Nethserver is more modular in its use cases. We chose OPNSense as a platform because it had readily available virtualization images, supported open source development, and came with many out-of-the-box configurations for IPSEC/L2TP.

To establish a connection between our AR Smart Integrated environment and a remote Miro, we set up a virtual machine on PCs located on both the AR Headset's network and Miro's. Next, we imported the OPNSense virtual image and configured the IPSec/LT2P VPN as outlined in OPNSense's documentation [33]. We then allowed the firewalls to forward the network traffic generated by Miro and the headset through the tunnel [33]. With both firewalls communicating, we were able to successfully send commands to Miro across the VPN. Figure 9 shows our proposed network topology with secure bi-directional communication between remotely and locally networked social companion robots.

7.2 Scaleability: Controlling Multiple SCRs Simultaneously

ROS topics are designed to be broadcast to all nodes subscribed. As such there is no way to utilise the same topic to issue two different commands simultaneously to two different SCRs [41]. Uniquely identifiable topics must be deployed through ROS scripts in order to maintain individual control of each SCR.**EXPAND**

8 Conclusion

Given the rise of the global aging population, it is imperative to develop systems for age-friendly smart environments to support our aging population for both independent living and in long-term care facilities. Furthermore, research suggests that independent living evokes feelings of security and familiarity, as well as attachment and social connectedness, giving older adults a sense of identity, independence, and autonomy [25]. Integrating SCRs with smart environments can improve the quality of life for older adults. With the use of personalized machine learning, SCRs can behave analytically and learn the preferences of the older adults such as their preferred temperature, lighting intensity, and even activate robotic vacuum cleaners (e.g., Roomba [47]) according to their preferred time.

Founded on the IoRT framework with social embodiment, we proposed a centralized AR-based system for interfacing and bi-directional communication through SCRs. More specifically, we developed a seamless communication between Microsoft HoloLens 2 and the Miro robot that facilitates bi-directional voice communication as well as image capture through the SCR's sensors. To facilitate the remote control of SCRs located outside of the AR's network (i.e., SCR in the homes), we implemented a Layer 2 IPSec VPN. This integration serves as an efficient platform for monitoring the health and well-being of the adult in care, responding more effectively to distressful situations (e.g., hurt, unresponsive, etc.), and controlling the robot for assisting the older adult from any geographical location.

For more natural interactions between the robot and user, we developed an improved Deep Learning based FER technique for affective computing. To overcome Miro's limited computational power, we off-loaded the Deep Learning inference to on the edge hardware accelerators. To achieve this we integrated Miro with Nvidia's Jetson and successfully performed our FER algorithms on the edge. Furthermore, our method minimizes the cost, network latency and privacy/cybersecurity concerns of alternative options which require cloud and internet connectivity.

We augmented our FER technique by integrating smart home technology to facilitate social inference and further the system's affective computing. Using the Google Assistant framework and Assistant relay, Miro is able to process a user's emotion and influence a change in the user's smart environment based on the emotion recognized (eg. play a happy song when the user is angry). To achieve this, we created a table of pre-programmed commands that Miro can send to Assistant Relay based on the list of recognizable emotions encapsulated by our FER technique. Assistant Relay can then forward the command to a Google Home to actuate smart elements in a user's environment. This form of affective computing facilitates our model of assisted independent living by allowing Miro to assist based on user behaviors. It is worth noting that while smart personal devices and space automation technologies can monitor and control a variety of things in a personalized smart space, having them integrated with the robot (SCR) enables a higher level of intelligence in control with a more context-aware and situation-aware decision providing socially embodied control [20]. In this case, the SCR and MR can recognize different events and changes in their surroundings while autonomously acting and reacting appropriately.

Our future work will include reducing the amount of external hardware required for our SCR to be deployed in each location; Currently, each Miro needs a paired PC at each remote location. We seek to remove the need for a separate PC and integrate our software stack on-board. Another research direction is a bi-directional system of consent to facilitate a non-invasive video chat application. We currently have one-way still image transmission and not video chat due to privacy concerns surrounding freely accessible cameras in personal dwellings. Furthermore, we can implement methods of face obfuscation in images and video to mitigate privacy concerns. Another field of consideration is to assess the usability, acceptance rate, and benefits of our systems. Finally, we can study human factors in the interface design and add more functionalities for communication, alert, and health analysis to the interface.

References

1. Abou Allaban, A., Wang, M., Padır, T.: A systematic review of robotics research in support of in-home care for older adults. Information **11**, 75 (2020)
2. Afanasyev, I., et al.: Towards the internet of robotic things: analysis, architecture, components and challenges. In: 2019 12th International Conference on Developments in eSystems Engineering (DeSE), pp. 3–8. IEEE (2019)
3. Age Well Canada: COVID-19 has significantly increased the use of many technologies among older Canadians: poll (2020). https://agewell-nce.ca/archives/10884, Accessed 19 Feb 2022
4. Anghel, I., et al.: Smart environments and social robots for age-friendly integrated care services. Int. J. Environ. Res. Public Health **17**(11), 3801 (2020)
5. Anjum, T., Lawrence, S., Shabani, A.: Augmented reality and affective computing on the edge makes social robots better companions for older adults. In: International Conference on Robotics, Computer Vision and Intelligent Systems, vol. 2, pp. 196–204 (2021)
6. Atee, M., Hoti, K., Parsons, R., Hughes, J.D.: A novel pain assessment tool incorporating automated facial analysis: interrater reliability in advanced dementia. Clin. Intervent. Aging **13**, 1245 (2018)
7. Bar-Cohen, Y., Hanson, D., Marom, A.: The Coming Robot Revolution: Expectations and Fears About Emerging Intelligent, Humanlike Machines. Springer, Heidelberg (2009). https://doi.org/10.1007/978-0-387-85349-9
8. Chen, C., et al.: Deep learning on computational-resource-limited platforms: a survey. Mobile Inf. Syst. (2020)
9. Chen, Z., Ansari, R., Wilkie, D.: Automated pain detection from facial expressions using FACS: a review. arXiv preprint arXiv:1811.07988 (2018)
10. Dupuis-Blanchard, S., Gould, O.N., Gibbons, C., Simard, M., Éthier, S., Villalon, L.: Strategies for aging in place: the experience of language-minority seniors with loss of independence. Glob. Qual. Nurs. Res. **2**, 1–9 (2015)
11. Fleming, K.C., Evans, J.M., Chutka, D.S.: Caregiver and clinician shortages in an aging nation. In: Mayo Clinic Proceedings, vol. 78, pp. 1026–1040. Elsevier (2003)
12. Fraser, K.C., Meltzer, J.A., Rudzicz, F.: Linguistic features identify alzheimer's disease in narrative speech. J. Alzheimer's Dis. **49**(2), 407–422 (2016)
13. Hesp, G.: Documentation: Assistant relay (2020). https://assistantrelay.com/docs/next/introduction/

14. Howard, A.G., et al.: Mobilenets: efficient convolutional neural networks for mobile vision applications. arXiv preprint arXiv:1704.04861 (2017)
15. Jing, H., Lun, X., Dan, L., Zhijie, H., Zhiliang, W.: Cognitive emotion model for eldercare robot in smart home. China Commun. **12**(4), 32–41 (2015)
16. Johnson, D.O., et al.: Socially assistive robots: a comprehensive approach to extending independent living. Int. J. Social Rob. **6**(2), 195–211 (2014)
17. Johnson, M.J., et al.: Task and design requirements for an affordable mobile service robot for elder care in an all-inclusive care for elders assisted-living setting. Int. J. Social Rob. **12**(5), 989–1008 (2020)
18. Koubaa, A., Alajlan, M., Qureshi, B.: ROSLink: bridging ROS with the internet-of-things for cloud robotics. In: Koubaa, A. (ed.) Robot Operating System (ROS). SCI, vol. 707, pp. 265–283. Springer, Cham (2017). https://doi.org/10.1007/978-3-319-54927-9_8
19. Koubâa, A., Allouch, A., Alajlan, M., Javed, Y., Belghith, A., Khalgui, M.: Micro air vehicle link (mavlink) in a nutshell: a survey. IEEE Access **7**, 87658–87680 (2019)
20. Lakens, D.: Grounding social embodiment. Social Cogn, **32**, 168–183 (2014)
21. Lawrence, S., Anjum, T., Shabani, A.: Improved deep convolutional neural network with age augmentation for facial emotion recognition in social companion robotics. J. Comput. Vision Imaging Syst. **6**(1), 1–5 (2020)
22. Liu, D., Miller, S., Lucas, M., Singh, A., Davis, J.: Firewall Policies and VPN Configurations. Elsevier Science, Amsterdam (2006)
23. Liu, H., et al.: A review of the smart world. Fut. Gener. Comput. Syst. **96**, 678–691 (2019)
24. Maturana, H.R., Varela, F.J.: Autopoiesis and Cognition: The Realization of the Living, vol. 42. Springer, Heidelberg (2012). https://doi.org/10.1007/978-94-009-8947-4
25. Mayo, C.D., Kenny, R., Scarapicchia, V., Ohlhauser, L., Syme, R., Gawryluk, J.R.: Aging in place: challenges of older adults with self-reported cognitive decline. Can. Geriat. J. **24**(2), 138 (2021)
26. Mazzara, M., Afanasyev, I., Sarangi, S.R., Distefano, S., Kumar, V., Ahmad, M.: A reference architecture for smart and software-defined buildings. In: 2019 IEEE International Conference on Smart Computing (SMARTCOMP), pp. 167–172. IEEE (2019)
27. Mellouk, W., Handouzi, W.: Facial emotion recognition using deep learning: review and insights. Procedia Comput. Sci. **175**, 689–694 (2020)
28. Mihailidis, A., Boger, J., Czarnuch, S., Nagdee, T., Hoey, J.: Ambient assisted living technology to support older adults with dementia with activities of daily living: key concepts and the state of the art (2012)
29. Miramontes, R., et al.: Plaimos: a remote mobile healthcare platform to monitor cardiovascular and respiratory variables. Sensors **17**(1), 176 (2017)
30. Mittal, S.: A survey on optimized implementation of deep learning models on the nvidia jetson platform. J. Syst. Arch. **97**, 428–442 (2019)
31. Netgate: Getting started with pfsense software (2022). https://www.pfsense.org/getting-started/, Accessed 21 Feb 2022
32. NethServer: Home page (2022). https://www.nethserver.org/, Accessed 21 Feb 2022
33. OPNSense: About opnsense (2022). https://opnsense.org/about/about-opnsense/, Accessed 21 Feb 2022

34. Pahl, M.O., Carle, G., Klinker, G.: Distributed smart space orchestration. In: NOMS 2016–2016 IEEE/IFIP Network Operations and Management Symposium, pp. 979–984. IEEE (2016)
35. Portet, F., Vacher, M., Golanski, C., Roux, C., Meillon, B.: Design and evaluation of a smart home voice interface for the elderly: acceptability and objection aspects. Pers. Ubiq. Comput. 17(1), 127–144 (2013)
36. Pranav, E., Kamal, S., Chandran, C.S., Supriya, M.: Facial emotion recognition using deep convolutional neural network. In: 2020 6th International Conference on Advanced Computing and Communication Systems (ICACCS), pp. 317–320. IEEE (2020)
37. Purewall, S.J.: 10 cool things you can do with google home devices
38. Quick, T., Dautenhahn, K., Nehaniv, C.L., Roberts, G.: On bots and bacteria: ontology independent embodiment. In: Floreano, D., Nicoud, J.-D., Mondada, F. (eds.) ECAL 1999. LNCS (LNAI), vol. 1674, pp. 339–343. Springer, Heidelberg (1999). https://doi.org/10.1007/3-540-48304-7_45
39. Razjouyan, J., Lee, H., Parthasarathy, S., Mohler, J., Sharafkhaneh, A., Najafi, B.: Improving sleep quality assessment using wearable sensors by including information from postural/sleep position changes and body acceleration: a comparison of chest-worn sensors, wrist actigraphy, and polysomnography. J. Clin. Sleep Med. 13(11), 1301–1310 (2017)
40. Rezaei, S., Moturu, A., Zhao, S., Prkachin, K.M., Hadjistavropoulos, T., Taati, B.: Unobtrusive pain monitoring in older adults with dementia using pairwise and contrastive training. IEEE J. Biomed. Health Inf. 25(5), 1450–1462 (2020)
41. Robotics, O.: Documentation: ROS (2019). http://wiki.ros.org/Topics, Accessed 12 Feb 2022
42. Seoane, F., et al.: Wearable biomedical measurement systems for assessment of mental stress of combatants in real time. Sensors 14(4), 7120–7141 (2014)
43. Sharma, G.: Facial emotion recognition (2020). https://www.kaggle.com/gauravsharma99, Accessed 19 Feb 2022
44. Simoens, P., Dragone, M., Saffiotti, A.: The internet of robotic things: a review of concept, added value and applications. Int. J. Adv. Rob. Syst. 15(1), 1729881418759424 (2018)
45. Suzman, R., Beard, J.R., Boerma, T., Chatterji, S.: Health in an ageing world-what do we know? The Lancet 385(9967), 484–486 (2015)
46. Tanabe, S., et al.: Designing a robotic smart home for everyone, especially the elderly and people with disabilities. Fujita Med. J. 5(2), 31–35 (2019). https://doi.org/10.20407/fmj.2018-009
47. Tribelhorn, B., Dodds, Z.: Evaluating the roomba: a low-cost, ubiquitous platform for robotics research and education. In: Proceedings 2007 IEEE International Conference on Robotics and Automation, pp. 1393–1399. IEEE (2007)
48. Turner, A., Findlay, L., et al.: Informal caregiving for seniors. Health Rep. 23(3), 33–36 (2012)
49. Uchechukwu, D., Siddique, A., Maksatbek, A., Afanasyev, I.: Ros-based integration of smart space and a mobile robot as the internet of robotic things. In: 2019 25th Conference of Open Innovations Association (FRUCT), pp. 339–345. IEEE (2019)
50. Wiles, J.L., Leibing, A., Guberman, N., Reeve, J., Allen, R.E.: The meaning of "aging in place" to older people. The Gerontologist 52(3), 357–366 (2012)
51. World Health Organization: Ageing and health (2021). https://www.who.int/news-room/fact-sheets/detail/ageing-and-health, Accessed 19 Feb 2022

52. Yang, G., Yang, J., Sheng, W., Junior, F.E.F., Li, S.: Convolutional neural network-based embarrassing situation detection under camera for social robot in smart homes. Sensors **18**(5), 1530 (2018)
53. Yeung, A., et al.: Correlating natural language processing and automated speech analysis with clinician assessment to quantify speech-language changes in mild cognitive impairment and alzheimer's dementia. Alzheimer's Res. Therapy **13**(1), 1–10 (2021)

Rapid Structure from Motion Frame Selection
for Markerless Monocular SLAM

Blake Troutman(✉) and Mihran Tuceryan

Indiana University-Purdue University Indianapolis, Indianapolis 46202, USA
{bltroutm,tuceryan}@iu.edu
https://science.iupui.edu/cs/

Abstract. Simultaneous Localization and Mapping (SLAM) is a method to simultaneously map the environment and estimate the location and pose of an agent. Visual SLAM utilizes visual data from a camera to accomplish the same. Markerless visual SLAM systems that use natural features in images and make use of multiple view geometry methods require an initialization procedure that typically involves using structure from motion techniques to solve for the first pair of keyframes and subsequently triangulating the initial set of 3-space points with the resulting keyframes. Single-camera (monocular) systems that use these techniques need to select appropriate frames for the structure from motion process from the camera's pre-initialization motion, but this frame selection problem is non-trivial. This is due to the fact that frame suitability is largely determined by the cameras' baseline length and the coplanarity of the scene points, both of which are unknown prior to initialization. This work presents a set of logistic regression and neural network models that can be used to select good frames for the structure from motion process by using a small set of summary data related to the matched correspondences. These models are trained on 14 different sequences from the TUM RGB-D dataset (totaling over 23,000 samples) without the need for any ground truth pose information. The resulting models demonstrate significantly higher precision and recall than the previous state-of-the-art frame selection techniques while still being able to run in real-time and function for both coplanar and non-coplanar scene points.

Keywords: Simultaneous Localization and Mapping (SLAM) · Structure from motion · Machine learning · Model selection · Monocular vision · Stereo vision

1 Introduction

Simultaneous Localization and Mapping (SLAM) has become a standard architecture for systems that aim to estimate the pose of a camera in real-time while simultaneously mapping its environment. These systems can be used to facilitate applications of augmented/virtual reality or can even be used to aid in robot localization and navigation. Visual SLAM has a variety of implementation approaches, including approaches that focus on filtering and approaches that focus on multiple-view geometry. The latter category may also be referred to as keyframe-based SLAM, as it is popular for systems of this category to utilize a subset of the observed frames (keyframes) for various procedures of the localization and mapping process.

© Springer Nature Switzerland AG 2022
P. Galambos et al. (Eds.): ROBOVIS 2020/ROBOVIS 2021, CCIS 1667, pp. 172–189, 2022.
https://doi.org/10.1007/978-3-031-19650-8_9

Assuming that the system has no prior insight regarding the structure of the environment, a keyframe-based SLAM system will need to use observations from the camera to construct an initial map of its environment before the pose of the camera can begin to be continually estimated. Stereo SLAM systems can initialize their maps on a single frame by performing feature matching between the stereo images and using those feature matches to carry out one of a few structure from motion processes. This will result in a pair of keyframes (including their poses), a set of 3-space points, and a mapping between the observed features and their corresponding 3-space points. With this information, the system's map can be considered initialized and the system can move on to faster tracking methods that match features directly to the calculated 3-space points.

Single camera (monocular) SLAM systems can initialize their maps in a similar fashion to stereo systems; however, they must allow the camera to move for a period of time before initialization and select a pair of images from this movement to be used for the structure from motion process. This presents the problem of frame selection, as many frame pairs do not yield usable results from structure from motion processes. The major factors that determine success in a structure from motion process include the camera baseline (the Euclidean distance between the positions of the cameras) and the 3-space coplanarity of the observed points. Since both of these factors are unknown to the system before initialization, it is non-trivial how feature matches between two frames can be quickly analyzed to determine their suitability for initialization. This work provides an approach for quickly determining the initialization suitability of an image pair with respect to one of three structure from motion approaches.

1.1 New Contributions

In a previous work [27], we proposed that this problem can be solved by extracting a small set of summary features from the set of correspondences and running those features through logistic regression models. The approach is fast enough for real-time use on resource limited platforms, functions on both planar and non-planar scenes, and yields higher precision than the previous state-of-the-art approach [3]. However, the models in this previous work were trained on a very limited set of data and the labelling criteria for the training samples relied on ground truth data. Additionally, though the precision and recall of the models were shown to be significantly higher than that of the previous state-of-the-art approach, the models' validation metrics still had large room for improvement.

In this paper, we propose new models that greatly improve upon the performance of the original models, while continuing to operate in real-time and function for both planar and non-planar scenes. Specifically, new contributions include the following:

- Five models are trained for each of the three structure from motion approaches, including logistic regression models and dense neural networks with inner layer sizes of 8×8, 16×16, 32×32, and 64×64. These models achieve significantly higher precision and recall than the models presented in [27].
- Instead of training each model on data generated from a single sequence of the TUM RGB-D dataset [24], data generated from 14 different sequences is used to improve the models' performance on a wider variety of scenes and camera movements.
- Optical flow tracking [13,22] is traded out for homogeneous ORB [21] tracking to improve the system's applicability to real world SLAM systems.

– The models now use a labelling criteria that does not depend on ground truth information, enabling virtually any RGB camera sequence to be used as training data.

2   Related Work

A wide variety of monocular SLAM systems have emerged over the past couple of decades. The first successful application of purely monocular SLAM was introduced in 2007 as MonoSLAM [4]. This system uses natural landmarks in the scene for regular tracking; however, its map initialization procedure requires the use of a known fiducial marker in order to provide the system with initial feature points. This use of markers enables the system to provide pose estimation on each frame, even before new scene points are populated into the map. Using markers during map initialization can also enable the system to determine an accurate real-world scale for subsequent map points, as shown in [30]. Numerous visual SLAM systems [1,11,12,14,29] leverage markers outside of the initialization process by using their known scene locations to perform pose estimation throughout the entire runtime of the system. In these cases, no map initialization is necessary because the map is predetermined before runtime.

Though markers prove useful in solving the visual SLAM problem, they add constraints to the applicability of any system that uses them. For instance, if the system depends on markers for all pose estimation, then pose estimation can only take place when markers are in the system's view. Additionally, a user may want to leverage pose estimation without the scene preparation required by marker setup, so a system that depends on markers (even exclusively in map initialization) may be considered less desirable than a system that does not depend on them. Some visual SLAM systems successfully eliminate the need for markers by tracking arbitrary image patches and reconstructing the scene with structure from motion techniques [9,10,17,19,25].

The implementation of map initialization is less trivial in these systems that cannot rely on known marker locations. Structure from motion techniques are often used in these markerless systems to triangulate scene points into the map at an arbitrary scale. However, it is less obvious how monocular data from these systems can be leveraged in typical stereo structure from motion processes. Parallel Tracking and Mapping (PTAM) [9] solves this map initialization problem by requiring the end-user to move the camera in the scene and manually select two recorded frames to be used for a structure from motion reconstruction. Upon selection of the frames, the system matches FAST features [20] between them and uses these correspondences in conjunction with the five point algorithm [23] (or in later implementations, a homography decomposition [5]) to deduce the poses of the camera during these two frames. PTAM concludes initialization by using these poses to triangulate 3-space points for the observed feature correspondences. This framework is also adopted in [25]. The clear drawback of this approach is the requirement of user intervention for frame selection. [8] presents a map initialization approach that can be performed in a single frame without user intervention, but it constrains the system to operation within a typical indoor room and depends on map points that coincide with the walls in the room, so this approach is not universal.

ORB-SLAM [17], like PTAM, also uses a pair of frames recorded before initialization to perform a structure from motion reconstruction. However, ORB-SLAM also implements an automatic frame selection heuristic so the end-user is not required to select the frames manually. The system achieves this by recording a reference frame (typically the first frame) and then attempting reconstruction on each subsequent frame. There are various measurements of the reconstruction that ORB-SLAM makes in order to determine if the reconstruction will result in a usable map. Some of these measurements include the parallax of the triangulated points and the reprojection errors of the triangulated points. If these measurements indicate that the reconstruction is not suitable for subsequent tracking, then it is thrown out and the process is repeated on the next frame; otherwise, the reconstruction is retained and the system is considered initialized. The drawback of this approach is the high computation time associated with structure from motion estimation and reconstruction, making it less suitable for resource-limited platforms such as mobile phones. There are modified versions of ORB-SLAM that aim to improve its map initialization procedure, but ultimately stray from monocular SLAM by requiring RGB-D input [6].

The frame selection criteria used in ORB-SLAM is robust but computationally expensive. SLAM systems can benefit from a faster means of frame selection, but there are relatively few works that provide this. An early work by Tomono [26] presents a frame selection criteria that functions by predicting the degeneracy of the fundamental matrix before its estimation via the eight point algorithm. However, this approach lacks a strong degree of robustness, as it is only applied to fundamental matrix estimates, it cannot distinguish between degeneracies caused by insufficient translation and degeneracies caused by planar scenes, and the threshold parameter proposed in this work is dependent on the number of correspondences detected. VINS-Mono [19] uses a simpler means of detecting initialization suitability. In this system, frame-pairs are used for initialization if more than 30 features are tracked with pixel disparities (the Euclidean distance between the endpoints of a feature correspondence) over 20 pixels. Similarly, a later SLAM system [3] also uses pixel disparities for this decision, except it uses the median and standard deviation of the pixel disparities as decision criteria. However, both of these systems depend on a subsequent evaluation of the estimation accuracy and, as a consequence of their decision criteria, will fail under many cases of pure rotational movement. In our previous work [27], we greatly improved upon the accuracy achieved by the approach from [3] by making the frame selection decision with logistic regression models that use model features which summarize the set of correspondences. These models, however, were trained on a relatively small set of data and relied on available ground-truth information in order to construct training data. We mitigate these drawbacks in this work and consequently achieve higher precision and recall than the models demonstrated previously.

3   Monocular SLAM Map Initialization

Keyframe-based monocular SLAM systems typically utilize a pinhole camera model, where points in 3-space are projected into image space with the following equation:

$$\mathbf{x} = \mathbf{K} \begin{bmatrix} \mathbf{R} \ \mathbf{t} \end{bmatrix} \mathbf{X} \tag{1}$$

where $\mathbf{X}$ is a homogeneous column vector of a point in 3-space, $\mathbf{x}$ is a homogeneous column vector of the 2D projection of $\mathbf{X}$ in image space, $\mathbf{R}$ is a 3×3 rotation matrix representing the camera's orientation in 3-space, $\mathbf{t}$ is a column vector of the camera's translation in 3-space, and $\mathbf{K}$ is the 3×3 matrix containing the camera's intrinsic parameters. Specifically, $\mathbf{K}$ is defined by

$$\mathbf{K} = \begin{bmatrix} f & s & c_x \\ 0 & f & c_y \\ 0 & 0 & 1 \end{bmatrix} \tag{2}$$

where f is the focal length of the camera, s is the skew parameter, and c_x and c_y are the coordinates of the image center.

The recurrent goal of SLAM systems which utilize this model is to estimate the pose of the camera, $[\mathbf{R}\ \mathbf{t}]$, by using observed measurements of feature points, $\mathbf{x}$, and their respective estimated 3-space locations $\mathbf{X}$. However, markerless systems do not have any prior knowledge of the values of $\mathbf{X}$; these point locations must be triangulated as feature points are matched across frames with sufficient camera movement.

In markerless monocular SLAM systems, it is the responsibility of map initialization to provide an initial set of 3-space point locations, $\mathbf{X}$, to match against subsequent feature observations, $\mathbf{x}$, which will enable the system to track the camera movement in succeeding frames. To estimate a set of 3-space point locations with no prior knowledge of the camera pose, feature points are extracted and matched between two camera frames which observe the same scene but are taken from different locations in 3-space. These feature matches can then be used to estimate the camera's transformation from the first frame to the second frame via structure from motion techniques. The feature points can then be triangulated into 3-space by using $[\mathbf{I}\ \mathbf{0}]$ as the first frame pose and the aforementioned camera transformation as the second pose.

There are three standard structure from motion techniques that are commonly implemented in keyframe-based SLAM systems. Each of them uses a set of feature correspondences (a pair of 2-space image points, where these points represent the projections of a single 3-space point in the first camera and second camera, respectively) to estimate a matrix that can be used to deduce the $\mathbf{SE(3)}$ pose matrix, $[\mathbf{R}\ \mathbf{t}]$. The matrices that may be estimated include the essential matrix, the fundamental matrix, and the homography matrix.

3.1 The Essential Matrix

The essential matrix is a real, 3×3, non-zero matrix given by Eq. (3) that relates two views

$$\mathbf{E} = [\mathbf{t}]_\times \mathbf{R} \tag{3}$$

where $\mathbf{E}$ is the essential matrix, $\mathbf{R}$ is the rotation of the second view with respect to the first view's orientation, and $[\mathbf{t}]_\times$ is defined by

$$[\mathbf{t}]_\times = \begin{bmatrix} 0 & -t_z & t_y \\ t_z & 0 & -t_x \\ -t_y & t_x & 0 \end{bmatrix} \tag{4}$$

where t_x, t_y, and t_z are the translation components of the second view with respect to the first view's position.

The significance of the essential matrix in the context of structure from motion problems is that it can be used to recover the rotation matrix, $\mathbf{R}$, and translation vector, $\mathbf{t}$ through singular value decomposition (SVD). This process is summarized by the following theorem [7,28]:

Theorem 1. *Let the singular value decomposition of* $\mathbf{E}$ *be* $\mathbf{U}diag(1,1,0)\mathbf{V}^T$. *The four possible factorizations of* $\mathbf{E} = [\mathbf{t}]_\times \mathbf{R}$ *are*

$$[\mathbf{t}]_\times = \mathbf{U}\mathbf{Z}\mathbf{U}^T \text{ or } \mathbf{U}\mathbf{Z}^T\mathbf{U}^T, \quad \mathbf{R} = \mathbf{U}\mathbf{W}\mathbf{V}^T \text{ or } \mathbf{U}\mathbf{W}^T\mathbf{V}^T \tag{5}$$

where

$$\mathbf{W} = \begin{bmatrix} 0 & -1 & 0 \\ 1 & 0 & 0 \\ 0 & 0 & 1 \end{bmatrix} \quad \mathbf{Z} = \begin{bmatrix} 0 & 1 & 0 \\ -1 & 0 & 0 \\ 0 & 0 & 0 \end{bmatrix} \tag{6}$$

Of the four hypotheses for $\mathbf{R}$ and $\mathbf{t}$, the correct configuration is selected by triangulating a point via a single feature correspondence between the first camera's pose (assumed to be $[\mathbf{I}\ \mathbf{0}]$) and any of the pose hypotheses $[\mathbf{R}_i\ \mathbf{t}_j]$. Of these four cases, only the correct configuration will uphold the cheirality constraint (the constraint that requires imaged points to be in front of the cameras) for both $[\mathbf{I}\ \mathbf{0}]$ and $[\mathbf{R}_i\ \mathbf{t}_j]$. Given the triangulated point, $\mathbf{X} = [x\ y\ z\ w]^T$, between the first camera's pose, $[\mathbf{I}\ \mathbf{0}]$, and some hypothesis of the second camera's pose, $[\mathbf{R}_i\ \mathbf{t}_j]$, cheirality is upheld between both cameras if $zw > 0$ and $z'w > 0$, where z' is the third component of $[\mathbf{R}_i\ \mathbf{t}_j]\,\mathbf{X}$.

This process is described in further detail in [7].

Estimating the Essential Matrix with the Five Point Algorithm. Section 3.1 describes the relationship between the essential matrix and the pose of a secondary camera with respect to a primary camera, but the utility of the essential matrix is brought about by the addition of the fact that it can be estimated from a small set of 2D-2D feature correspondences. One of the standard approaches to solve this problem is the five point algorithm, proposed in [18].

The five point algorithm is a sophisticated algorithm that requires at least five feature correspondences to estimate the essential matrix of two cameras. It works by organizing the components of the correspondences into an $N \times 9$ matrix (were N is at least 5) and then finding four vectors that span its right nullspace. The components of the essential matrix can be described as a linear combination of these four vectors, so the algorithm concludes by solving for the coefficients of this linear combination. For explicit implementation details, see [18].

The five point algorithm is effective at estimating the essential matrix regardless of the coplanarity of the 3-space scene points, making it a strong candidate for map initialization. However, it is more sophisticated and typically more computationally demanding than alternative structure from motion algorithms. The five point algorithm is also implemented in the OpenCV computer vision library [2] and, consequentially, is utilized in this work when estimating the essential matrix.

3.2 The Fundamental Matrix

The fundamental matrix is a 3×3 rank 2 homogeneous matrix that acts as the algebraic representation of epipolar geometry. Epipolar geometry refers to the relationship between points in 3-space and the constraints of their projections in stereo imaging. Specifically, for a pair of cameras, it follows that any feature correspondence between those cameras, $(\mathbf{x}, \mathbf{x}')$, upholds the constraint

$$\mathbf{x}'^{T} \mathbf{F} \mathbf{x} = 0 \tag{7}$$

where $\mathbf{F}$ is the fundamental matrix and $\mathbf{x}$ and $\mathbf{x}'$ are homogeneous column vectors representing points in the two images.

The rotation matrix, $\mathbf{R}$, and translation vector, $\mathbf{t}$, can be recovered from the fundamental matrix by converting it to the essential matrix with

$$\mathbf{E} = \mathbf{K}^{T} \mathbf{F} \mathbf{K} \tag{8}$$

Note that Eq. (8) assumes the same intrinsic camera parameter matrix for both cameras. From this point, the pose parameters are recovered from $\mathbf{E}$ as shown in Sect. 3.1.

Estimating the Fundamental Matrix with the Eight Point Algorithm. Like the essential matrix, the fundamental matrix can also be estimated from a small set of 2D-2D feature correspondences. The eight point algorithm is a simple and reliable approach for accomplishing this task.

The eight point algorithm relies on using the epipolar constraint from Eq. (7) in conjunction with at least eight feature correspondences to estimate the fundamental matrix. It works by reformulating the constraint from Eq. (7) in terms of the components of the feature correspondence and then factoring out the components of $\mathbf{F}$. This results in a 1×9 vector being multiplied by $\mathbf{F}$ in flattened form, rather than $\mathbf{F}$ being pre- and post-multiplied by two different vectors as shown in Eq. (7). This 1×9 vector can then be stacked with 8 or more feature correspondences to yield an $N \times 9$ matrix, where N is at least 8. It follows that the components of $\mathbf{F}$ make up the right nullspace of this $N \times 9$ matrix. Since the fundamental matrix is defined up to an arbitrary scale, the SVD of this matrix can be used to solve for $\mathbf{F}$. For further details, see [7].

Estimation of the fundamental matrix is a simple and computationally cheap means of facilitating map initialization. However, the eight point algorithm is not well constrained when the feature correspondences map to points in 3-space that are coplanar [7], and it will often provide an inaccurate estimate under such a condition. The eight point algorithm is also implemented in OpenCV and is the algorithm used in this work when estimating the fundamental matrix.

3.3 The Homography Matrix

A homography matrix is a homogeneous 3×3 matrix that represents a planar projective transformation. Specifically, it takes the form

$$\mathbf{x}' = \mathbf{H} \mathbf{x} \tag{9}$$

where $\mathbf{H}$ is the homography matrix, $\mathbf{x}$ is a homogeneous column vector representing an image point, and $\mathbf{x}'$ is a homogeneous column vector representing the projection of $\mathbf{x}$ into a new image space given $\mathbf{H}$. $\mathbf{H}$ defines a projective transformation for the plane upon which $\mathbf{x}$ lies, so homographies are not defined for all possible sets of feature correspondences of points in 3-space, but rather are only defined for sets of feature correspondences that are coplanar in 3-space.

With a homography matrix, $\mathbf{H}$, the rotation matrix $\mathbf{R}$ and translation vector $\mathbf{t}$ can be extracted with a number of methods [5,15,31]. OpenCV implements the approach from [15], which proposes an analytical method for extracting the motion parameters $\mathbf{R}$ and $\mathbf{t}$ from $\mathbf{H}$. Specifically, this approach results in four solutions for the motion parameters, $\{\mathbf{R}_a, \mathbf{t}_a\}$, $\{\mathbf{R}_b, \mathbf{t}_b\}$, $\{\mathbf{R}_a, -\mathbf{t}_a\}$, and $\{\mathbf{R}_b, -\mathbf{t}_b\}$. The correct solution can be deduced through the use of the cheirality constraint mentioned in Sect. 3.1. This is the approach for homography decomposition that is used throughout this work. For specific implementation details and formulation for $\mathbf{R}$ and $\mathbf{t}$, see [15].

Estimating the Homography Matrix with Four Point Algorithm. Like the essential matrix and fundamental matrix, the homography matrix can also be estimated from a small set of 2D-2D feature correspondences. The process that accomplishes this is the four point direct linear transformation (DLT) algorithm [7]. As the name suggests, only four feature correspondences are required for this algorithm to accurately estimate a homography between the two cameras; however, the correspondences must be projections of points that are coplanar in 3-space.

The four point DLT algorithm utilizes the constraint from Eq. (9) to establish that $\mathbf{x}'$ and $\mathbf{H}\mathbf{x}$ are parallel, and thus $\mathbf{x}' \times \mathbf{H}\mathbf{x} = 0$. Much like the eight point algorithm, this new equation can be reformulated in terms of the components of the feature correspondence and then the components of $\mathbf{H}$ can be factored out. This results in a 2×9 matrix for each feature correspondence that can be multiplied with the components of $\mathbf{H}$ to produce a product of 0. With four or more feature correspondences, this matrix can be stacked into an $N \times 9$ matrix (where N is at least 8), with a right nullspace equal to the components of $\mathbf{H}$. The right nullspace of this matrix can be solved for with its SVD (in the same fashion that the components of $\mathbf{F}$ are found in the eight point algorithm), as the homography is only defined up to a non-zero scale factor. For a comprehensive explanation of this process, see [7].

Estimation of the homography matrix is straightforward and computationally inexpensive, much like the eight point algorithm described in Sect. 3.2. However, it is only effective in cases where the feature correspondences are projections of coplanar points in 3-space. This is in direct contrast to the degenerate case of the eight point algorithm; as a result, some map initialization procedures [3,17] include both the eight point algorithm and the four point algorithm to take advantage of the speed of these approaches without concern for the coplanarity of scene points.

3.4 Triangulation

The three aforementioned matrices can each be used to recover the motion from the two cameras. The second step of SLAM map initialization is to recover the structure of the scene. In a keyframe-based system, this is typically implemented by determining the positions of the feature correspondences in 3-space directly. To do this, a simple linear method for triangulation can be used.

Assuming both cameras share the same intrinsic parameter matrix, $\mathbf{K}$, then the projections in the feature correspondence $(\mathbf{x}, \mathbf{x}')$ can be modeled by the homogeneous equations

$$\mathbf{x} = \mathbf{PX} \tag{10}$$

$$\mathbf{x}' = \mathbf{P}'\mathbf{X} \tag{11}$$

where

$$\mathbf{P} = \mathbf{K}\begin{bmatrix} \mathbf{R}_0 & \mathbf{t}_0 \end{bmatrix} \tag{12}$$

$$\mathbf{P}' = \mathbf{K}\begin{bmatrix} \mathbf{R}_1 & \mathbf{t}_1 \end{bmatrix} \tag{13}$$

where $\begin{bmatrix} \mathbf{R}_0 & \mathbf{t}_0 \end{bmatrix}$ is the pose of the first camera (assumed in initialization to be $\begin{bmatrix} \mathbf{I} & \mathbf{0} \end{bmatrix}$) and $\begin{bmatrix} \mathbf{R}_1 & \mathbf{t}_1 \end{bmatrix}$ is the pose of the second camera, which will be the resulting pose from any of the structure from motion techniques outlined in Sects. 3.1, 3.2, and 3.3.

It follows from Eqs. (10) and (11) that $\mathbf{x} \times (\mathbf{PX}) = \mathbf{0}$ and $\mathbf{x}' \times (\mathbf{P}'\mathbf{X}) = \mathbf{0}$. These constraints can be used to formulate the resulting linear equation $\mathbf{AX} = \mathbf{0}$, where

$$\mathbf{A} = \begin{bmatrix} x\mathbf{p}_3^T - \mathbf{p}_1^T \\ y\mathbf{p}_3^T - \mathbf{p}_2^T \\ x\mathbf{p}'_3{}^T - \mathbf{p}'_1{}^T \\ y\mathbf{p}'_3{}^T - \mathbf{p}'_2{}^T \end{bmatrix} \tag{14}$$

and $\mathbf{p}_i^T$ and $\mathbf{p}'_i{}^T$ are the ith rows of $\mathbf{P}$ and $\mathbf{P}'$, respectively. It follows that $\mathbf{X}$ is the right nullspace of $\mathbf{A}$, which can be computed with the SVD of $\mathbf{A}$. This triangulation process can be executed for each feature correspondence to gather a set of 3-space scene points, which can be subsequently matched against and used for PnP tracking [16] later on in the system's typical tracking routine.

4   Model Configurations

Given the structure from motion approaches outlined in Sects. 3.1, 3.2, and 3.3, a SLAM system may face at least one of three different classification problems when determining when a frame pair is well-conditioned for map initialization. The classification problems can be defined as follows:

1. **Classification E:** Will the set of feature correspondences between the two images result in a usable map initialization if the motion between the cameras is solved with the five point algorithm (solving for the essential matrix)?

2. **Classification F:** Will the set of feature correspondences between the two images result in a usable map initialization if the motion between the cameras is solved with the eight point algorithm (solving for the fundamental matrix)?
3. **Classification H:** Will the set of feature correspondences between the two images result in a usable map initialization if the motion between the cameras is solved with the four point algorithm (solving for a homography)?

Since a SLAM system may only implement a subset of these initialization approaches, these classification problems are defined as binary problems. That is, the goal is *not* to select which initialization approach would be the best for a given frame pair (as many frame pairs may not be suitable for initialization under *any* approach); rather, the goal is to determine whether or not the given initialization approach would result in a usable initialization with the given frame pair.

To develop classifiers for the classification problems defined above, a logistic regression model and four neural network models of varying sizes are trained for each classification problem. Each model input consists of data that summarizes the set of feature correspondences between two frames. This input data consists of 23 features, including the number of correspondences and the mean of the pixel disparities. The pixel disparity of a feature correspondence is defined by the Euclidean distance between the 2D image points that make up the feature correspondence. Additionally, the input data includes the standard deviation of the pixel disparities, the minimum and maximum values of each component of the correspondences (x, y, x' and y', where (x, y) is the point in the first image and (x', y') is the corresponding point in the second image), the range of each component of the correspondences, and a normalized eight-vector that represents the distribution of the correspondence directions. The direction, θ, of a correspondence is defined by

$$\theta = \arctan\left(\frac{y' - y}{x' - x}\right) \tag{15}$$

The directions used in these eight features include eight angles evenly spaced between 0 and 2π. Figure 1 shows an example of the construction of the direction vector.

Five models are trained to solve each classification problem. The first model is a logistic regression model that simply takes the 23 input features through a sigmoid activation function, where the positive class is interpreted as 1 and the negative class is interpreted as 0 (see Fig. 2). The other four models are dense neural networks with two hidden layers and two-class softmax activation outputs. The layer sizes of the models include 8×8 (see Fig. 3), 16×16, 32×32, and 64×64. The inclusion of multiple models is in an effort to achieve the highest classification precision and recall for each classification problem.

(a)   (b)

Fig. 1. (a) An example of a set of motion-based feature correspondences (green lines) overlayed onto the secondary image. Note that the circled endpoint of each correspondence corresponds to the feature's location in the secondary image and the opposite endpoint corresponds to the feature's original location in the primary image. (b) Direction visualization for each correspondence. Discretizing these directions as cardinal directions (N, NE, E, SE, S, SW, W, and NW), the top-most correspondence can be considered southwest-facing while the remaining correspondences can be considered west-facing. For this set of correspondences, its directional model features would be encoded as the normalized form of $(0, 0, 0, 0, 0, 1, 3, 0)$, which is $(0, 0, 0, 0, 0, 0.32, 0.95, 0)$.

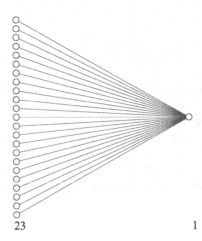

23   1

Fig. 2. Visualization of the logistic regression model. The 23 input features are each fed into the single sigmoid activation neuron to produce the classification result.

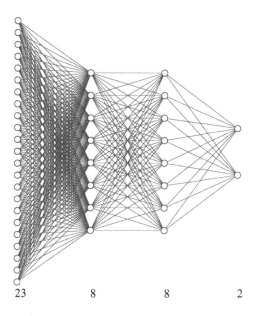

Fig. 3. Example architecture of the 8×8 neural network model. Note that the model takes 23 model inputs and processes them through 2 identically-sized layers (in the case displayed here, the hidden layers are each of size 8) which converge to the 2-class softmax output layer. The only architectural difference of the other neural network models is the size of the hidden layers; the input layer and output layer have the same size across all of the neural network models in this work.

4.1 Data Collection

The models are trained on sets of feature correspondences that are computed from the monocular images in multiple sequences of the TUM RGB-D dataset [24]. Specifically, the training sequences include:

- freiburg1_360
- freiburg1_desk
- freiburg1_rpy
- freiburg1_xyz
- freiburg2_desk
- freiburg2_dishes
- freiburg2_rpy
- freiburg2_xyz
- freiburg3_checkerboard_large
- freiburg3_large_cabinet
- freiburg3_nostructure_texture_far
- freiburg3_nostructure_texture_near_withloop
- freiburg3_structure_texture_far
- freiburg3_structure_texture_near

Sets of correspondences are extracted from each sequence by splitting the sequences into batches of sequential frames. The batch size used in a sequence is set empirically by assessing the magnitude of the typical camera motion used in the given sequence. These batch sizes include 10 frames, 30 frames, 45 frames, and 60 frames. In each batch, the first frame of the batch is compared to every other frame in the batch and features are matched between the frames to compute a single set of correspondences.

Since the end-goal is to utilize these models in a realtime SLAM system, it is helpful that features are extracted and matched in the training data in the same fashion that they are extracted and matched in the facilitating SLAM system. For this reason, a homogeneous distribution of ORB features are extracted across each frame, as this is a feature extraction approach which is actually implemented in the initialization procedures of some systems [17].

4.2   Labeling Criteria

In order to train the models, each set of correspondences has to be associated with a label indicating whether or not the correspondences are sufficient for the respective structure from motion initialization approach. Previously, we utilized the median scaled reconstruction error and normalized translation chordal distance to determine these labels [27]. The drawback of these metrics is that they require ground truth data, which limits the pool of available training data. Instead of using ground truth error metrics to determine these labels, we now label the correspondence sets using an approach similar to the initialization heuristic seen in ORB-SLAM.

This labelling approach begins by using the respective matrix estimate and correspondences to reconstruct the scene and camera poses. The parallax and reprojection errors are recorded for each triangulated point from the reconstruction. The correspondence set is labeled as the negative class if its reconstruction contains less than 50 points with parallax greater than $2°$, or if the reconstruction contains less than a minimum number of "good" points. A "good" point is a point that upholds cheirality for both cameras and has a reprojection error less than 4 pixels for both cameras. The minimum number of good points is set as the maximum between the values 50 and $0.9 \times n$, where n is the number of inliers deduced from the RANSAC scheme used to estimate the respective matrix. If the correspondence set instead results in a sufficient number of points with high parallax and a sufficient number of "good" points, then the set is labelled in the positive class.

The performance of ORB-SLAM on standard datasets suggests that this initialization criteria is robust and reliable. However, reconstructing the scene on every frame before the system is initialized is much more computationally expensive than running quick inference on a relatively small neural network. This is the significance of using models to predict the appropriateness of initialization; these models can be used to quickly filter through inevitably poor correspondence sets before investing the computation time to validate the appropriateness of initialization with the expensive aforementioned labelling algorithm.

5   Results

Table 1. Performance of logistic regression models for each classification problem after being trained on the `freiburg3/structure_texture_far` sequence and tested on the `freiburg3/structure_texture_near` sequence, using optical flow matching and the labelling criteria from [27].

Model	Accuracy	Precision	Recall	F1 Score
Logistic regression (E)	0.7326	0.4290	0.6453	0.5154
Logistic regression (F)	0.6959	0.3639	0.5822	0.4479
Logistic regression (H)	0.8343	0.3725	0.1166	0.1776

Table 2. Cross validation performance for models trained for Classification E using 80%-20% data split for training and testing, respectively.

Model	Accuracy	Precision	Recall	F1 Score
Logistic regression	0.6384	0.6556	0.6109	0.6325
Neural network (8×8)	0.7288	0.7974	0.5997	0.6846
Neural network (16×16)	0.7845	0.7684	**0.8030**	**0.7853**
Neural network (32×32)	**0.7976**	**0.8334**	0.7344	0.7808
Neural network (64×64)	0.7691	0.7806	0.7365	0.7579

Table 3. Cross validation performance for models trained for Classification F using 80%-20% data split for training and testing, respectively.

Model	Accuracy	Precision	Recall	F1 Score
Logistic regression	0.6114	0.6115	0.6223	0.6169
Neural network (8×8)	0.7462	0.7847	0.6749	0.7257
Neural network (16×16)	0.7598	0.8593	0.6182	0.7190
Neural network (32×32)	**0.8521**	**0.8691**	**0.8273**	**0.8476**
Neural network (64×64)	0.7820	0.8587	0.6723	0.7542

Table 4. Cross validation performance for models trained for Classification H using 80%-20% data split for training and testing, respectively.

Model	Accuracy	Precision	Recall	F1 Score
Logistic regression	0.6458	0.6379	0.6437	0.6407
Neural network (8×8)	0.7435	0.8136	0.6438	0.7188
Neural network (16×16)	0.7827	0.8462	0.7006	0.7665
Neural network (32×32)	0.7707	0.8851	0.6317	0.7373
Neural network (64×64)	**0.8126**	**0.8983**	**0.7127**	**0.7948**

Table 5. Validation performance for models trained for Classification E, using `freiburg3_long_office_household` as test data.

Model	Accuracy	Precision	Recall	F1 Score
Logistic regression	0.5969	0.7089	0.6001	0.6500
Neural network (8 × 8)	**0.7870**	**0.7525**	0.6468	**0.6957**
Neural network (16 × 16)	0.7226	0.6084	**0.7372**	0.6667
Neural network (32 × 32)	0.7030	0.5943	0.6638	0.6271
Neural network (64 × 64)	0.6869	0.5663	0.7181	0.6332

Table 6. Validation performance for models trained for Classification F, using `freiburg3_long_office_household` as test data.

Model	Accuracy	Precision	Recall	F1 Score
Logistic regression	0.4696	0.1897	0.5598	0.2834
Neural network (8 × 8)	0.5965	**0.8724**	0.5897	0.7037
Neural network (16 × 16)	0.5733	0.8713	0.5571	0.6797
Neural network (32 × 32)	**0.7354**	0.8312	**0.8463**	**0.8387**
Neural network (64 × 64)	0.6137	0.8716	0.6153	0.7213

Table 7. Validation performance for models trained for Classification H, using `freiburg3_long_office_household` as test data.

Model	Accuracy	Precision	Recall	F1 Score
Logistic regression	0.5857	0.6265	**0.6324**	0.6294
Neural network (8 × 8)	**0.7118**	0.7256	0.5632	**0.6341**
Neural network (16 × 16)	0.6749	0.6667	0.5343	0.5932
Neural network (32 × 32)	0.6962	**0.7257**	0.5063	0.5965
Neural network (64 × 64)	0.6277	0.5808	0.5776	0.5792

For each classification problem, the sequence data is balanced to include the same number of positive samples as negative samples. This is done to aid in training and is achieved by duplicating samples in the class of the smaller size. After duplicating samples for balancing, the set of samples is shuffled and split into training data and testing data, where training data accounts for 80% of the balanced sample set and testing data accounts for the remaining 20%. This results in the models for Classification E being trained on 23,537 samples, models for Classification F being trained on 31,619 samples, and models for Classification H being trained on 23,372 samples. This 80%-20% split also results in models for Classification E being tested on 5,885 samples, models for Classification F being tested on 7,905 samples, and models for Classification H being tested on 5,844 samples. The accuracy, precision, recall and F1 score of models trained for Classification E, Classification F, and Classification H are shown in Tables 2, 3, and 4, respectively.

Additionally, these models are tested on 2,498 samples generated from the `freiburg3_long_office_household` sequence, which the models are never exposed to via training. Validation metrics using this sequence for model testing are shown in Tables 5, 6, and 7. For comparison, the results of the logistic regression models from the previous work [27] are also displayed in Table 1. Each model is also able to run inference on an individual sample within 4 milliseconds (using a Ryzen 7 5800X CPU and GTX 1080 GPU with Deeplearning4j); this demonstrates the real-time viability of these models, despite the increased complexity of neural networks.

The results measured with the 80%-20% data split show a relatively high F1 score for the best model in each classification problem, with the 16×16 neural network reporting an F1 of 0.7853 for Classification E, the 32×32 neural network reporting an F1 of 0.8476 for Classification F, and the 64×64 neural network reporting an F1 of 0.7948 for Classification H. When moving to the results measured with the `freiburg3/long_office_household` sequence, the scores are generally lower than the scores of the 80%-20% split, as the models neither have exposure to this sequence nor to sequences of the same scene during training. However, these results still indicate a significant improvement in both precision and recall over the previous models. The F1 scores for the highest scoring models using the `freiburg3/long_office_household` sequence as test data are 0.6957, 0.8387, and 0.6341 for classifications **E**, **F**, and **H**, respectively. Interestingly, this validation set indicates (via F1 scores) that the optimal model for Classification E is the 8×8 neural network rather than the 16×16 neural network, and the optimal model for Classification H is also the 8×8 neural network, rather than the 64×64 neural network. Both test sets, however, indicate that the 32×32 neural network configuration is the best for Classification F.

6   Conclusion

Fast structure from motion frame selection remains an open problem in the context of markerless, monocular SLAM. However, this frame selection problem can be practically solved with the use of neural network models, as shown in this work. These models yield higher precision and recall than the previous models shown in [27] while remaining real-time viable and functioning with both coplanar and non-coplanar configurations of scene points. Additionally, these models indicate that the 23 pieces of correspondence summary data can be used to solve this problem, and future models could be created with either different model configurations to further improve results, or with different training data to improve the models' performance on SLAM systems operating within more specific contexts. The speed in which inference can take place on deep learning models motivates their use in future work regarding the improvement of other aspects within visual SLAM.

References

1. Arth, C., Pirchheim, C., Ventura, J., Schmalstieg, D., Lepetit, V.: Instant Outdoor Localization and SLAM Initialization from 2.5D Maps. IEEE Trans. Visual. Comput. Graph. **21**(11), 1309–1318 (2015). https://doi.org/10.1109/TVCG.2015.2459772

2. Bradski, G.: The OpenCV library. Dr. Dobb's J. Softw. Tools. **25**, 120–123 (2000)
3. Butt, M.M., Zhang, H., Qiu, X.C., Ge, B.: Monocular SLAM initialization using epipolar and homography model. In: 2020 5th International Conference on Control and Robotics Engineering, ICCRE 2020, pp. 177–182 (2020). https://doi.org/10.1109/ICCRE49379.2020.9096497
4. Davidson, A.J., Reid, I.D., Molton, N.D., Stasse, O.: MonoSLAM: real-time single camera SLAM. IEEE Trans. Pattern Anal. Mach. Intell. **29**(6), 1052–1067 (2007). https://doi.org/10.1109/TPAMI.2007.1049
5. Faugeras, O., Lustman, F.: Motion and Structure From Motion in a Piecewise Planar Environment. Int. J. Pattern Recogn. Artif. Intell. **02**, 485–508 (1988). https://doi.org/10.1142/s0218001488000285
6. Fujimoto, S., Hu, Z., Chapuis, R., Aufrère, R.: Orb slam map initialization improvement using depth. In: 2016 IEEE International Conference on Image Processing (ICIP) pp. 261–265 (2016). https://doi.org/10.1109/ICIP.2016.7532359
7. Hartley, R., Zisserman, A.: Multiple View Geometry in Computer Vision, 2nd edn. Cambridge University Press, Cambridge (2004)
8. Huang, J., Liu, R., Zhang, J., Chen, S.: Fast initialization method for monocular slam based on indoor model. In: 2017 IEEE International Conference on Robotics and Biomimetics (ROBIO), pp. 2360–2365 (2017). https://doi.org/10.1109/ROBIO.2017.8324772
9. Klein, G., Murray, D.: Parallel tracking and mapping for small AR workspaces. In: 2007 6th IEEE and ACM International Symposium on Mixed and Augmented Reality, pp. 225–234 (2007). https://doi.org/10.1007/978-3-642-24734-7-7
10. Klein, G., Murray, D.: Parallel tracking and mapping on a camera phone. In: 2009 8th IEEE International Symposium on Mixed and Augmented Reality, pp. 83–86 (2009). https://doi.org/10.1109/ISMAR.2009.5336495
11. Kobayashi, T., Kato, H., Yanagihara, H.: Novel keypoint registration for fast and robust pose detection on mobile phones. In: Proceedings - 2nd IAPR Asian Conference on Pattern Recognition, ACPR 2013, pp. 266–271 (2013). https://doi.org/10.1109/ACPR.2013.67
12. Korah, T., Wither, J., Tsai, Y.T., Azuma, R.: Mobile augmented reality at the Hollywood walk of fame. In: 2011 IEEE Virtual Reality Conference, pp. 183–186 (2011). https://doi.org/10.1109/VR.2011.5759460
13. Lucas, B.D., Kanade, T.: An iterative image registration technique with an application to stereo vision. In: Proceedings of the 7th International Joint Conference on Artificial Intelligence, Vol. 2, pp. 674–679. IJCAI 1981, Morgan Kaufmann Publishers Inc., San Francisco, CA, USA (1981)
14. Maidi, M., Preda, M., Le, V.H.: MarkerLess tracking for mobile augmented reality. In: 2011 IEEE International Conference on Signal and Image Processing Applications, ICSIPA 2011, pp. 301–306 (2011). https://doi.org/10.1109/ICSIPA.2011.6144077
15. Malis, E., Vargas, M.: Deeper understanding of the homography decomposition for vision-based control (2007)
16. Marchand, E., Uchiyama, H., Spindler, F.: Pose estimation for augmented reality: a hands-on survey. IEEE Trans. Visual. Comput. Graph. **22**(12), 2633–2651 (2016). https://doi.org/10.1109/TVCG.2015.2513408, https://hal.inria.fr/hal-01246370
17. Mur-Artal, R., Montiel, J.M., Tardos, J.D.: ORB-SLAM: a versatile and accurate monocular SLAM system. IEEE Trans. Rob. **31**(5), 1147–1163 (2015). https://doi.org/10.1109/TRO.2015.2463671
18. Nistér, D.: an efficient solution to the five-point relative pose problem. In: Proceedings of 2003 IEEE Computer Society Conference on Computer Vision and Pattern Recognition, 2003, vol. 2, pp. 2–195 (2003)

19. Qin, T., Li, P., Shen, S.: VINS-Mono: a robust and versatile monocular visual-inertial state estimator. IEEE Trans. Rob. **34**(4), 1004–1020 (2018). https://doi.org/10.1109/TRO.2018. 2853729

20. Rosten, E., Drummond, T.: Machine learning for high-speed corner detection. In: Leonardis, A., Bischof, H., Pinz, A. (eds.) ECCV 2006. LNCS, vol. 3951, pp. 430–443. Springer, Heidelberg (2006). https://doi.org/10.1007/11744023_34

21. Rublee, E., Rabaud, V., Konolige, K., Bradski, G.: ORB: an efficient alternative to SIFT or SURF. In: Proceedings of the IEEE International Conference on Computer Vision, pp. 2564–2571 (2011). https://doi.org/10.1109/ICCV.2011.6126544

22. Shi, J., Tomasi, C.: Good features to track. In: 1994 Proceedings of IEEE Conference on Computer Vision and Pattern Recognition (1994). https://doi.org/10.1016/j.jastp.2018.01. 001

23. Stewenius, H., Engels, C., Nister, D.: Recent developments on direct relative orientation. ISPRS J. Photogramm. Remote. Sens. **60**, 284–294 (2006). https://doi.org/10.1016/j. isprsjprs.2006.03.005

24. Sturm, J., Engelhard, N., Endres, F., Burgard, W., Cremers, D.: A benchmark for the evaluation of RGB-D slam systems. In: Proceedings of the International Conference on Intelligent Robot Systems (IROS), October 2012

25. Sun, L., Du, J., Qin, W.: Research on combination positioning based on natural features and gyroscopes for AR on mobile phones. In: Proceedings - 2015 International Conference on Virtual Reality and Visualization, ICVRV 2015, pp. 301–307 (2015). https://doi.org/10. 1109/ICVRV.2015.55

26. Tomono, M.: 3-D localization and mapping using a single camera based on structure-from-motion with automatic baseline selection. In: Proceedings - IEEE International Conference on Robotics and Automation, pp. 3342–3347 (2005). https://doi.org/10.1109/ROBOT.2005. 1570626

27. Troutman, B., Tuceryan, M.: Towards fast and automatic map initialization for monocular slam systems. In: Proceedings of the 2nd International Conference on Robotics, Computer Vision and Intelligent Systems - ROBOVIS, pp. 22–30. INSTICC, SciTePress (2021). https:// doi.org/10.5220/0010640600003061

28. Tsai, R.Y., Huang, T.S.: Uniqueness and estimation of three-dimensional motion parameters of rigid objects with curved surfaces. IEEE Trans. Pattern Anal. Mach. Intell. PAMI. **6**(1), 13–27 (1984). https://doi.org/10.1109/TPAMI.1984.4767471

29. Ufkes, A., Fiala, M.: A markerless augmented reality system for mobile devices. In: Proceedings - 2013 International Conference on Computer and Robot Vision, CRV 2013, pp. 226–233 (2013). https://doi.org/10.1109/CRV.2013.51

30. Xiao, Z., Wang, X., Wang, J., Wu, Z.: Monocular ORB SLAM based on initialization by marker pose estimation. In: 2017 IEEE International Conference on Information and Automation, ICIA 2017, pp. 678–682, July 2017. https://doi.org/10.1109/ICInfA.2017. 8078992

31. Zhang, Z., Hanson, A.R.: 3d reconstruction based on homography mapping. In: ARPA Image Understanding Workshop, pp. 0249–6399 (1996)

Detecting Tool Keypoints with Synthetic Training Data

Bram Vanherle$^{(\boxtimes)}$ (ID), Jeroen Put, Nick Michiels (ID), and Frank Van Reeth (ID)

Hasselt University - tUL - Flanders Make, Expertise Centre for Digital Media,
Hasselt, Belgium
{bram.vanherle,jeroen.put,nick.michiels,frank.vanreeth}@uhasselt.be

Abstract. In this paper an end-to-end technique is presented to create a deep learning model to detect 2D keypoint locations from RGB images. This approach is specifically applied to tools, but can be used on other objects as well. First, 3D models of similar objects are sourced form the internet to avoid the need for exact textured models of the target objects. It is shown in this paper that these exact 3D models are not needed. To avoid the high cost of manually creating a data set, an image generation technique is introduced that is specifically created to generate synthetic training data for deep learning models. Special care was taken when designing this method to ensure that models trained on this data generalize well to unseen, real world data. A neural network architecture, Intermediate Heatmap Model (IHM), is presented that can generate probability heatmaps to predict keypoint locations. This network is equipped with a type of intermediate supervision to improve the results on real world data, when trained on synthetic data. A number of other tricks are employed to ensure generalisation towards real world images. A dataset of real tool images is created to validate this approach. Validation shows that the proposed method works well on real world images. Comparison to two other techniques shows that this method outperforms them. Additionally, it is investigated which deep learning techniques, such as transfer learning and data augmentation, help towards generalization on real data.

Keywords: Object keypoint detection · Deep learning · Synthetic data generation

1 Introduction

Working in modern manufacturing industry requires a lot of technical knowledge from operators. The complexity of object being assembled increases and the amount of different types of objects is growing as well. The recent advances in computer vision systems, can help these operators before, during and after the assembly process. They can help train operators, give customized instructions during assembly, predict and prevent errors or can be used to analyze their workflow afterwards. One component of such visions systems is the detection

© Springer Nature Switzerland AG 2022
P. Galambos et al. (Eds.): ROBOVIS 2020/ROBOVIS 2021, CCIS 1667, pp. 190–207, 2022.
https://doi.org/10.1007/978-3-031-19650-8_10

Fig. 1. The goal of this paper is to detect the image locations of certain keypoints of tools under varying, as shown in this image. Keypoint locations are actual detections by our model.

of tool keypoints. This is required as it is often important to know what part of a physical tool has touched a certain part or surface. Figure 1 shows some keypoints detected from images of tools. A big challenge in the detection certain parts of a tool is that the appearance of the tool can vary tremendously. This can be due to variations in lighting, pose, occlusions and backgrounds. In recent years deep convolutional neural networks have established themselves as one of the best methods for interpreting images under a lot of varying conditions. CNNs are efficient due to their spatial invariance while also being excellent at extracting information from images thanks to their automatic feature learning. We therefore use deep learning for detecting these tool keypoints. The method we use, generates heatmaps that indicate the probability a keypoint is at a certain pixel.

The biggest difficulty when solving problems with supervised learning is collecting a dataset. As the size of the state of the art models keeps growing, more and more data is needed to train them. A traditional dataset consists of two main parts: input images and target labels. Traditionally input images are either collected from the internet or photographs are specifically taken for the target problem. The former is usually not an option when trying to solve a domain specific problem and the latter can take a human quite some time. The target labels can also be collected from the internet if they are accompanied by images, otherwise they have to be manually made by humans, which can be very costly. Another problem with human generated labels or images is that bias can be introduced, since humans can be very subjective. To avoid both the cost of collecting data and introducing bias, we opt to use synthetic training data for our method.

While this is an easy method to generate data, models trained on synthetic data do suffer from a problem. A model trained on synthetic data will suffer from a drop in performance when applied to real images. This is because the real images are sampled from a different domain than the synthetic images, this is called the domain gap. The data generation method presented in this paper is modified to improve the generalization towards real images. Additionally, the proposed neural network architecture is adapted to perform better when trained on synthetic data. We also apply a number of techniques to mitigate the domain

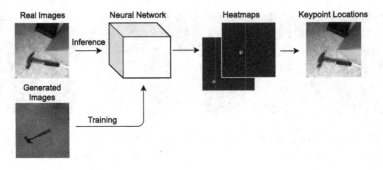

Fig. 2. A full overview of the proposed technique [22].

gap. An overview of our approach is shown in Fig. 2. To validate our data generation technique and neural network architecture we have assembled a dataset of real images of tools and annotated these manually[1]. Our models trained on purely synthetic data are validated on this real dataset. We also compare the performance of existing methods Simple Baselines [24] and Stacked Hourglass Networks [15] to our method. Furthermore, we investigate the impact of the different techniques to bridge the domain gap applied in our method.

This paper is an extension of our previous work [22] where we already approached the problem of finding tool keypoints with synthetic data. This paper includes some improvements over the previous one. In our previous work we simulated occlusions in the training data by pasting cutouts from objects images randomly on our images. This lead to unrealistic looking images which could lead to lower accuracy due to the network focusing on artifacts from the cut and pasting. We therefore now add distractor objects to the 3D scene and render these. This introduces occlusions and more randomness, while avoiding unrealistic looking training data with artefacts, this is detailed further in Sect. 3. This paper and our previous work uses intermediate supervision to boost higher level feature learning. In the previous work however, there was an imbalance between the higher and lower level feature losses due to differing heatmap sizes. That is resolved in this paper by introducing a weighting term in the loss function as described in Sect. 4.2. Furthermore, we also conduct a number of extra experiments to analyze the impact of certain techniques with respect to training on synthetic data described in Sect. 5. Finally, we have also made our dataset of synthetic and real tools publicly available.

2   Related Work

Both keypoint detection and using synthetic training data for deep learning are two popular topics in computer vision research. Here we highlight some prominent research in these two areas.

---

[1] https://bvanherle.github.io/synthetic_tools.

2.1 Keypoint Detection

In classic computer vision, keypoint detection is usually done by creating a feature descriptor such as SIFT [14] or SURF [1] from the keypoint on a source image. The keypoint is then found on a target image by matching this descriptor to locations in the image. These methods focus on local features and fail to consider the global context of the image, hence why they don't generalize well to unseen data and fail under variations of pose, lighting and texture.

In more recent works there has been a shift to Deep Learning to avoid these issues. Object landmark detection is not a problem that is often considered on its own. Usually it is part of the solution for other problems such as: 6DoF Pose estimation, Human Pose Estimation and Object detection. Localizing landmarks can be done in several ways, the most common approaches are: regression of coordinates, pixelwise voting and heatmap generation.

Early works would use a CNN to detect image features, followed by fully connected layers that directly regress the (x, y) coordinates of the keypoints. An example of such a method is DeepPose [19] for human pose estimation. This is difficult for the network to learn, as it needs to learn how to output numeric values of the location of activations in its feature map.

This lead to the creation of networks that regress heatmaps for each keypoint. Keypoint locations are computed from the maxima of these heatmaps. These methods are easier to train since they can directly use the spatial information in the up-sampled feature maps to generate heatmaps. This method has been used for 6DoF Pose Estimation [16], Object Detection [13] and mainly for Human Pose Estimation [15, 23, 24].

In these methods the value of the heatmap at a certain location is directly computed by the activations of the feature map at that position. This makes it difficult for the network to detect keypoints when objects are occluded or truncated. For this reason Pixelwise-Voting network [17] was introduced. This type of network learns, for each keypoint, to generate unit vectors at each pixel pointing to that keypoint. Those unit vectors are then used to vote for keypoint locations using RANSAC [6]. This forces the network to focus on local features and spatial relations between object parts, and allows it to infer the position of invisible parts.

The method proposed in this paper falls under the category of heatmap generating models. Although the pixel-wise voting method can handle occlusions better, the RANSAC voting adds extra computational complexity at runtime which is to be avoided in a real-time system. Existing heatmap models often have fast inference times, but rely on real images with annotations as training data. Our method removes this need by offering a data generation method and a deep learning model that performs well, when trained on synthetic images.

2.2 Synthetic Training Data

Models trained on synthetic data, applied to real images, suffer from the domain gap. This is because the domain of rendered images differs form the domain of real photographs and there are several ways to reduce this domain gap.

A first research track focuses on making the domain of the synthetic images match more closely to that of the real images. This can be done by trying to make the rendering more realistic via physically based rendering [10] or by adapting the synthetic images as if they were taken by the same sensor as the images in the real domain [7]. PBR rendering can be very compute intensive and requires detailed and correct textures of the target models. Camera sensor modelling can be very helpful, but only if it is known beforehand what camera will be used.

To avoid the problem that rendered images do not look realistic enough, some methods use a set of existing images to generate more training data. This is done via compositing, an object is taken from one image and pasted at a random position on a random image. From this the label can be inferred. This process can be programmed [5] or a network can be trained to do this [21]. The problem with this approach is that foreground images are sampled from a limited set, leading to a lack of variety in the dataset. Also, not all types of annotations can be inferred from these composited images, such as depth.

These approaches try to bridge the domain gap by moving the training domain as close as possible to the target domain. A different approach tries to make the training domain as wide as possible and thus improving the probability images from the target domain are recognized. This is achieved by making the training images as random as possible. The method is called domain randomization [20]. All parameters such as, lighting, textures, positions, poses are fully randomized. The images do not necessarily look realistic, but this is not necessary for this method.

Another approach is domain adaptation, here images from one domain are transformed to look as if they came from the other domain. If done properly, this improves the accuracy of the final model, since it is trained on images from the same domain as the target images. This can either be done by transforming the synthetic images to the real domain before training [3] or by transforming the real images to synthetic ones before inference [26].

Our approach to bridging the domain gap is a combination of a number of techniques. We try to accurately render 3D models whilst also making the constructed scenes as random as possible. We use transfer learning to make the model more robust to real world images and also use data augmentation to introduce more randomness.

3   Training Data

To quickly generate large, unbiased and correct datasets we have developed a data generation tool. The output of this tool is a set of input images and target labels. For this paper we output 2D keypoint image locations, but different types of annotations are also supported. Using models trained on synthetic data on real world data can lead to significant losses in accuracy. The data generation process is designed specifically to achieve good performance on deep learning tasks. This section details this process.

Fig. 3. A few of the different 3D models of hammers used to train the neural networks in this paper.

3.1   Generating Scenes

Earlier methods of synthetic data generation used simple cut-and-past techniques [5], where a foreground object was cut from an image and randomly pasted on a random background image. This can lead to unrealistic images as the lighting is not consistent and artifacts can be created around the edges. Additionally, not all annotations can be derived from this type of image composition, e.g. depth and pose information. We therefore opt to construct a 3D scene and render it to generate an image. This gives a more realistic effect and allows us to export each type of annotation.

To be able to generate a 3D scene and render it properly, textured 3D models are needed. These are usually not readily available. Acquiring them can be done manually via 3D modelling software, but this is very cumbersome. An alternative is making a 3D scan, but this requires expensive hardware. To avoid the need for an exact 3D copy of the target object, we propose using a set of similar objects of the same type. This will force the network to learn about the type of object in general, which will ensure it generalizes to the unseen target objects. Figure 3 shows some of the different models of hammers used in this paper. Models trained on synthetic data can suffer from the domain gap, as the images it sees during inference time look different from the training set. One way we combat this is by using domain randomization [20]. By randomizing as many aspects of the training data as possible we force the training domain to be bigger, increasing the chance the target domain is included. The domain gap exists on two levels: visually and contextually. The visual domain gap implies that images look differently from the target images: the lighting is not realistic, camera noise is different or the textures are not the same. Whereas the contextual domain gap refers to the fact that the scenes depicted in the synthetic images differ from the scenes of the target images. We use randomness to combat both types of domain gap.

Having 3D models available we can construct the scenes needed to generate training images and their corresponding labels. A random model is selected and placed in a predefined region of interest in the scene with a random position and rotation. The model keeps it original texture, but in some cases the texture is randomly adapted by changing the hue. To determine the position of the camera its distance r to the region of interest is selected randomly from uniform

Fig. 4. Some examples of the synthetically generated images produced by our method.

distribution, a random point on the sphere defined by r and the center of the region of interest is selected to place the camera. The camera is rotated to look at the center of the region of interest. A random environment map is selected and given a random intensity. This is used as a background and to compute lighting and reflections. Optionally, a point light is placed on a random location with random properties. Finally, a number of random objects from ShapeNet [2] are selected and placed in the scene to simulate occlusions.

3.2 Rendering

Besides randomness, visual fidelity is also important when generating training images [10]. We therefore use raytracing to generate the training images. But since large quantities of images are needed, a full path tracing approach would be too slow. We therefore use a hybrid approach between rasterization and raytracing, to find a good trade-off between speed and realism. This allows us to generate about 200 images per minute. Some renderings are shown in Fig. 4.

4   Method

To find the keypoints of some object in an image, we generate a probability P map of shape (w, h, N) with w and h the width and height of the image and N the number of keypoints. P_{xyn} thus gives the probability the n-th keypoint is at pixel (x, y) of the image. The exact keypoint locations for keypoint n can be computed from its probability map P_n by finding the index of $max(P_n)$.

To generate these heatmaps a neural network is used. The task of generating heatmaps, nicely aligns with the structure of a convolutional neural network. A CNN generates a feature map, which contains information about the features present in an image while encoding their position as well. This spatial information allows the network to easily learn to generate probabilities at the location of the keypoints.

The values in probability map P_n for keypoint n during training are computed by constructing a 2D Gaussian:

$$P_n(x, y) = A \exp\left(-\left(\frac{(x - x_n)^2 + (y - y_n)^2}{2\sigma^2}\right)\right) \tag{1}$$

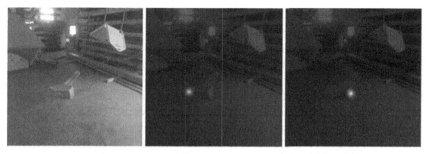

(a) Heatmaps generated for the hammer image on the left.

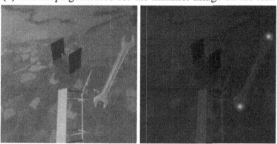

(b) Heatmap generated for the wrench image on the left.

Fig. 5. Examples of heatmaps generated for different tools.

with A a constant amplitude, (x_n, y_n) the pixel location of keypoint n and $\sigma = width/64$. The amplitude A is set so that $P_n(x_n, y_n) = 1$. Figure 5a shows the heatmaps that are generated on the keypoint locations of the hammer in the image.

Generally, a separate probability map is generated for each keypoint, but in some cases keypoints can belong to the same semantic class. This makes them indistinguishable for the neural network, as is the case for the two ends of a wrench. This is confusing for the network to learn, causing bad performance. We solve this by grouping keypoints of the same class together, combining their probability maps in one map. An example of this is shown in Fig. 5b.

4.1 Network Architecture

A Fully Convolutional Neural Network is trained to generate these probability maps. The base of the network is a ResNet50 [8] feature detector. Due to its smaller size it offers fast execution speed while still achieving good accuracy.

ResNet50 finds features by using consecutive Residual Blocks and pooling operations. Due to these pooling operations the input image of size $(224, 224, 3)$ is downscaled to a feature map of size $(7, 7, 2048)$. To be able to accurately recover keypoint locations this feature map is upsampled repeatedly to a $(224, 224, N)$ probability map.

For this upsampling we introduce an upsampling block. The feature map is first upsampled using nearest neighbour interpolation. Because a lot of spatial information is lost in the $(7, 7)$ feature map we use skip connections to recover this spatial information. After the feature map is upsampled, the feature map from the corresponding ResNet layer is concatenated to the feature map. The concatenation operation is followed by two convolutions. These convolutions are done to process the concatenated feature map to identify new features, useful for the final probability maps. These convolutions have a size of three and stride one, they are followed by a LeakyReLU activation and Batch Normalization [11] is used to increase training speed and stability. There is Dropout [18] between the two convolutions to promote generalization. An overview of this upsampling block is shown in Fig. 6. The upsampling is repeated five times to increase the feature map resolution to $(224, 224)$. The first upsampling block uses 256 filters, this amount is divided by two for each subsequent upsampling block. To transform the feature map in a probability map, a final convolution is applied. This is a convolution of size two and N filters, with N the number of desired probability maps. Finally, a Sigmoid activation is used to ensure the probabilities are in the $[0, 1]$ range. This is illustrated in Fig. 7.

Training is done using the ADAM [12] optimizer with a learning rate of $1.5e^{-4}$. If the loss plateaus for 10 epochs the learning rate is scaled by 0.1. A batch size of 32 is used. The network stops training after showing no improvement for 20 epochs and trains for a maximum of 100 epochs. The loss on the validation set is measured at each epoch and the model with the lowest validation error is kept.

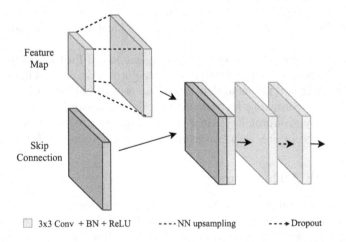

Fig. 6. Illustration of the upsampling block [22].

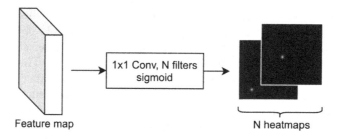

Fig. 7. The final layer of the network, transforming the feature maps to probability maps.

4.2   Training on Synthetic Data

Training on synthetic data can lead to a loss in accuracy. To avoid this we have already adapted our data generation strategy, but there are also certain techniques that can be applied to the network architecture and training process that can benefit the generalization on unseen real data. This section outlines the actions we have taken.

Data Augmentation. Data augmentation plays an important part in training models on synthetic data. First one of the following transformations is applied: affine scale, affine translate, affine rotate, affine shear, perspective transform and horizontal flip. These transformations are also applied to the corresponding probability maps. This type of augmentation helps improve general robustness in the model as increases the diversity in the training set.

Next, zero to two of the following augmentations are applied to modify the colors of the image: Gaussian blur, add, multiply, additive noise, motion blur and grayscale. There is often a big difference in the way objects look in synthetic images and the way they look in real images, as rendering cannot perfectly simulate real life lighting or material properties, the noise introduced by a camera sensor or the noise and artefacts introduced by storing images. The aforementioned augmentations help alleviate this by making the model more robust to different appearances of objects in images.

Transfer Learning. Transfer learning is very useful when training on synthetic data, as it allows us to use part of a model that already knows how to interpret real world images. This is done by initalizing the ResNet feature detector with weights trained on ImageNet [4] as described by Hinterstoisser et al. [9]. These weights are then frozen during training, so that they remain unchanged. The layers after the feature detection are not frozen, and will learn the features necessary to find the tool keypoints. Feezing the first layers during training ensures the network will not learn lower level features specific to the synthetic data and will instead be able to interpret real world images at inference time.

Intermediate Feature Boosting. In the architecture described so far, there exists the risk that the network lazily focuses on the lower level features. This is due to the fact that at the last upsampling step, a skip connection is used to concatenate the first features of the feature detection network. This is something we try to avoid, as lower level features, such as texture, can differ tremendously between real and synthetic data. The higher level features, such as shape, do match between synthetic and real data. We therefore introduce a modification to our architecture to boost the learning of these higher level features.

Intermediate supervision is used to force the network to learn good features that assist in localizing the keypoints, at each level of the upsampling chain. This is done by not only generating a heatmap after the final upsampling level, but by applying the proces from Fig. 7 after each upsampling layer. This leads to a set of progressively larger heatmaps for each image, instead of one. The heatmaps start at size $(14, 14)$ up to $(224, 224)$. The sizes of the heatmaps are the same as the sizes of the feature maps at that position to better preserve the mapping between the features and the heatmaps. A full overview of the neural network is given in Fig. 8.

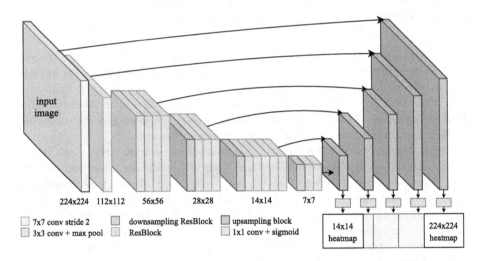

Fig. 8. A full overview of the neural network used to generate heatmaps [22].

The loss function is the weighted sum of the Mean Squared Error between the heatmap generated at each level and their corresponding ground truth heatmap generated by Eq. 1.

$$L = \sum_k w_k \left(\frac{1}{n} \sum_n (f_k(X_n) - Y_{k,n}) \right) \qquad (2)$$

Here f_k is the output of the k-th upsampling block, X_n the n-th image and $Y_{k,n}$ the ground truth heatmaps for the n-th image, downscaled to the size of the k-th output. The surface of the smallest heatmap is 256 times smaller than the largest heatmap, giving it less importance in the final loss. The weighting paramter w_k is therefore introducted, normalizing the loss of each heatmap respective to its surface. The weight of the k-th heatmap is equal to: s_5/s_k, with s_i the surface area of the ith heatmap:

$$\left(\frac{224}{2^{5-i}} \right)^2 \tag{3}$$

224 being the size of the final heatmap and 5 the number of upsampling levels.

5   Results

To show the effectiveness of the proposed data generation strategy in combination with the intermediate supervision and training techniques, a dataset of real tools is assembled to test our trained models on. Our approach has been compared to two other methods for keypoint detection: Stacked Hourglass Networks (SH) [15,25] with two stacks and Simple Baselines (SB) [24]. Stacked Hourglass is chosen for comparison as it is used often, achieves great accuracy and also employs a form of intermediate supervision. Since this method does not use transfer learning, we also use Simple Baselines for validation, as transfer learning might give an advantage when training on synthetic data. To know the impact of the intermediate supervision scheme, a comparison is also made to a model trained without the intermediate supervision.

The Percentage of Correct Keypoints (PCK) metric is used to validate performance. A keypoint is considered to be correct when its distance from the ground truth is below a certain fraction of the largest side of the objects bounding box: $\alpha \cdot max(w, h)$, with α usually at 0.1.

In the experiments described below, we train a separate neural network for each object, as opposed to one network that can predict the keypoints of each object. It is assumed that the system knows which tools keypoints need to be found. This approach has the added benefit new objects can easily be introduced into the system by simply training a new network for only that tool. Although training one large network for all objects could also have benefits such as potentially requiring less training images per object, as feature learning would be shared, and features could be learned from each object. Additionally this approach could decrease sensitivity to false positives, as the network sees different types of tools during training.

5.1   Tool Dataset

To validate our models performance and abilities to generate to real unseen data we have constructed a dataset of real tool images. We have selected four categories of tools: Screwdriver, Hammer, Wrench and Combination Wrench. For each category we collected four physical objects belonging to that category while still varying in appearance. Those objects were photographed in numerous

Table 1. Comparison of accuracy the Intermediate Heatmap Model, Heatmap Model, Simple Baselines and Stacked Hourglass Networks on the four different tool categories. Accuracy is expressed as PCK values with $\alpha = 0.1$

Model	IHM (Ours)	HM (Ours)	SB	SHN
Screwdriver	**86.1**	78.0	74.0	46.0
Wrench	**88.9**	86.1	67.6	66.7
Combination wrench	**86.1**	82.6	68.6	55.8
Hammer	**84.4**	68.8	63.5	45.8

different poses, lighting conditions, camera angles and backgrounds. Occlusions and truncations are introduces by hands or other objects. For each tool category, 50 different photographs are taken using a mobile phone camera. The keypoint locations and bounding boxes of the tools are manually labeled. The screwdriver has only one keypoint, the wrench has two keypoins belonging to the same class, and the hammer and combination wrench have two keypoints belonging to different classes.

To train the models, a dataset for each tool is constructed as described in Sect. 3. For each of the tool categories we source six different textured 3D models from the internet. The models from the internet sometimes resemble the physical objects from the real dataset, but are always different in some way. These models are then used to generate 20.000 images for each tool.

5.2 Comparison to Other Methods

For this experiment we train an IHM model for each of the four tools on their respective synthetic dataset. We also train a model that does not use the Intermediate supervision (HM) to check what the impact of the intermediate supervision is. Additionally, we also train a Simple Baselines and Stacked Hourglass network on the tool datasets to compare our performance to that of existing works. Figure 9 shows some images of correct detections made by the IHM model. Figure 10 shows some cases in which the model was wrong, by either not predicting a keypoint, or predicting the wrong location.

For each of these trained models we then computed the PCK value with an alpha of 0.1 for each tool on the validation set of real images, the results are shown in Table 1. From these results we can conclude that our proposed method generalizes well to the unseen real validation data, as it manages to get very high PCK values. We did not use the exact 3D model of any of the tools from the real world set, yet our proposed method can still detect keypoints for these unseen objects.

Furthermore, the model outperforms the Simple Baselines and Stacked Hourglass methods. The Stacked Hourglass is outperformed by quite a large margin, this indicates the importance of transfer learning for synthetic data. We can also see that our Heatmap Model (HM) that does not use intermediate supervision

(a) Correct detections on the real screwdriver dataset.

(b) Correct detections on the real wrench dataset.

(c) Correct detections on the real combination wrench dataset.

(d) Correct detections on the real hammer dataset.

Fig. 9. Some correct detections made by the IHM model on each class.

Fig. 10. Some incorrect predictions made by the IHM model.

does not perform as well as the IHM, clearly showing the benifits of using intermediate supervision.

5.3   Impact of Generalization Techniques

In this experiment the impact of the different techniques we applied to improve generalization towards real data are investigated described in Sect. 4.2. The techniques we have applied are: transfer learning, data augmentation and intermediate supervision. We have already shown the usefulness of the intermediate supervision in the previous experiment, this is not included in this experiment. In this experiment we will however investigate the impact of the weighting parameter we introduced in the loss function.

Table 2. The results of the IHM model being trained using different generalization techniques. The values are PCK values measured on the real test set.

Model	D	TL	TL + DA	TL + DA + BL
Screwdriver	4.3	68.0	84.9	**86.1**
Wrench	34.7	86.1	86.1	**88.9**
Combination wrench	30.2	70.9	84.9	**86.1**
Hammer	19.8	52.1	**85.4**	84.4

For each of the four tool categories we train the following four models: a default model with none of the techniques applied (D), a model in which transfer learning is applied by initializing its weights with ImageNet trained weights (TL), a model with transfer learning and data augmentation (TL + DA) and finally a model with the previous techniques applied as well as the balanced loss (TL + DA + BL). These models were all trained as described in Sect. 4 on the synthetic tools dataset. After training these models, the PCK values were computed over the real tool test set with an alpha value of 0.1, the results are shown in Table 2. In Sect. 4.2 we suspected that initializing the feature detector with weights trained on real images and freezing those helps the network generalize to real images while being trained on synthetic ones. This suspicion is confirmed by this experiment, as the transfer learning method leads to large increases of accuracy in each of the four categories. In that section we also hypothesised that data augmentation would add extra variation to the dataset which would make the final model more robust, which would translate to better generalization on real images. From Table 2 we can see that this is true, adding the data augmentation leads to a large performance increase in almost all categories. Finally, we consider whether balancing the weight of each heatmap in the loss function according to their surface area has any impact on the final result. This seems to lead to a small increase in performance except in the case of the Hammer.

6   Conclusion

In this paper we set out to develop and end to end method for detecting tool keypoints via deep learning. To avoid the strenuous labor of manual labelling, we have designed a system that can synthetically generate the images needed to train the deep learning model.

The data generator constructs random 3D scenes, renders these, and exports the 2D keypiont locations. To do so, a detailed 3D model of the target object is required. We show that this is not necessary when using a set of similar objects, causing the network to generalize towards the unseen target object.

When training a CNN on synthetic images its performance on real images can suffer due to the domain gap. To avoid this we designed our data generator to generate realistic looking images, but also to maximize the randomness of the rendered scenes as this improves robustness. Additionally, the data generator can render images reasonably fast, to be able to generate the large quantities of images needed for deep learning.

Furthermore, we designed a neural network for generating probability maps to localize tool keypoints. This network is adapted via intermediate supervision to boost the learning of higher level features, which should lead to a higher performance on real test images. Some other techniques such as transfer learning and data augmentation were also applied to further improve generalization.

To test our end to end solution, a dataset of real tool images was collected and labeled. For each of these four tools, a synthetic dataset was also rendered. To check if the proposed method works, models were trained on these synthetic datasets and subsequently tested on their real counterparts. The models managed to achieve high accuracy, indicating that our method generalizes well towards unseen real data. A model trained without the intermediate supervision performed worse than the model with intermediate supervision, highlighting its importance in synthetic training. Two existing models, Stacked Hourglass and Simple Baselines were also outperformed by our method. Finally, we investigated the usefulness of techniques such as data augmentation and transfer learning for synthetic training data. We concluded that both these practices lead to a significant increase in performance on real testing images.

Acknowledgements. This study was supported by the Special Research Fund (BOF) of Hasselt University. The mandate ID is BOF20OWB24. Research was done in alignment with Flanders Make's PILS and FAMAR projects.

References

1. Bay, H., Tuytelaars, T., Van Gool, L.: SURF: speeded up robust features. In: Leonardis, A., Bischof, H., Pinz, A. (eds.) ECCV 2006. LNCS, vol. 3951, pp. 404–417. Springer, Heidelberg (2006). https://doi.org/10.1007/11744023_32
2. Chang, A.X., et al.: Shapenet: an information-rich 3D model repository (2015)
3. Chen, W., Yu, Z., Wang, Z., Anandkumar, A.: Automated synthetic-to-real generalization (2020)

4. Deng, J., Dong, W., Socher, R., Li, L.J., Li, K., Fei-Fei, L.: Imagenet: a large-scale hierarchical image database. In: 2009 IEEE Conference on Computer Vision and Pattern Recognition, pp. 248–255. IEEE (2009)

5. Dwibedi, D., Misra, I., Hebert, M.: Cut, paste and learn: surprisingly easy synthesis for instance detection, pp. 1310–1319 (2017). https://doi.org/10.1109/ICCV.2017.146

6. Fischler, M.A., Bolles, R.C.: Random sample consensus: a paradigm for model fitting with applications to image analysis and automated cartography. Commun. ACM **24**(6), 381–395 (1981). https://doi.org/10.1145/358669.358692

7. Hagn, K., Grau, O.: Improved sensor model for realistic synthetic data generation. In: Computer Science in Cars Symposium. CSCS 2021. Association for Computing Machinery, New York (2021). https://doi.org/10.1145/3488904.3493383

8. He, K., Zhang, X., Ren, S., Sun, J.: Deep residual learning for image recognition (2015)

9. Hinterstoisser, S., Lepetit, V., Wohlhart, P., Konolige, K.: On pre-trained image features and synthetic images for deep learning. CoRR abs/1710.10710 (2017). http://arxiv.org/abs/1710.10710

10. Hodaň, T., et al.: Photorealistic image synthesis for object instance detection. In: 2019 IEEE International Conference on Image Processing (ICIP), pp. 66–70 (2019). https://doi.org/10.1109/ICIP.2019.8803821

11. Ioffe, S., Szegedy, C.: Batch normalization: accelerating deep network training by reducing internal covariate shift. CoRR abs/1502.03167 (2015). http://arxiv.org/abs/1502.03167

12. Kingma, D.P., Ba, J.: Adam: a method for stochastic optimization (2017)

13. Law, H., Deng, J.: CornerNet: detecting objects as paired keypoints. Int. J. Comput. Vision **128**(3), 642–656 (2019). https://doi.org/10.1007/s11263-019-01204-1

14. Lowe, D.: Distinctive image features from scale-invariant keypoints. Int. J. Comput. Vision **60**, 91–110 (2004). https://doi.org/10.1023/B:VISI.0000029664.99615.94

15. Newell, A., Yang, K., Deng, J.: Stacked hourglass networks for human pose estimation. In: Leibe, B., Matas, J., Sebe, N., Welling, M. (eds.) ECCV 2016. LNCS, vol. 9912, pp. 483–499. Springer, Cham (2016). https://doi.org/10.1007/978-3-319-46484-8_29

16. Pavlakos, G., Zhou, X., Chan, A., Derpanis, K.G., Daniilidis, K.: 6-dof object pose from semantic keypoints. In: 2017 IEEE International Conference on Robotics and Automation (ICRA), pp. 2011–2018 (2017). https://doi.org/10.1109/ICRA.2017.7989233

17. Peng, S., Liu, Y., Huang, Q., Zhou, X., Bao, H.: Pvnet: pixel-wise voting network for 6dof pose estimation, pp. 4556–4565 (2019). https://doi.org/10.1109/CVPR.2019.00469

18. Srivastava, N., Hinton, G., Krizhevsky, A., Sutskever, I., Salakhutdinov, R.: Dropout: a simple way to prevent neural networks from overfitting. J. Mach. Learn. Res. **15**(56), 1929–1958 (2014). http://jmlr.org/papers/v15/srivastava14a.html

19. Toshev, A., Szegedy, C.: Deeppose: human pose estimation via deep neural networks. In: 2014 IEEE Conference on Computer Vision and Pattern Recognition, pp. 1653–1660 (2014). https://doi.org/10.1109/CVPR.2014.214

20. Tremblay, J., et al.: Training deep networks with synthetic data: bridging the reality gap by domain randomization. In: Proceedings of the IEEE Conference on Computer Vision and Pattern Recognition (CVPR) Workshops (2018)

21. Tripathi, S., Chandra, S., Agrawal, A., Tyagi, A., Rehg, J.M., Chari, V.: Learning to generate synthetic data via compositing (2019)

22. Vanherle., B., Put., J., Michiels., N., Van Reeth., F.: Real-time detection of 2D tool landmarks with synthetic training data. In: Proceedings of the 2nd International Conference on Robotics, Computer Vision and Intelligent Systems - ROBOVIS, pp. 40–47. INSTICC, SciTePress (2021). https://doi.org/10.5220/0010689900003061
23. Wei, S., Ramakrishna, V., Kanade, T., Sheikh, Y.: Convolutional pose machines. In: 2016 IEEE Conference on Computer Vision and Pattern Recognition (CVPR), pp. 4724–4732 (2016). https://doi.org/10.1109/CVPR.2016.511
24. Xiao, B., Wu, H., Wei, Y.: Simple baselines for human pose estimation and tracking. In: Ferrari, V., Hebert, M., Sminchisescu, C., Weiss, Y. (eds.) ECCV 2018. LNCS, vol. 11210, pp. 472–487. Springer, Cham (2018). https://doi.org/10.1007/978-3-030-01231-1_29
25. yuanyuanli85: Stacked_hourglass_network_keras (2018). https://github.com/yuanyuanli85/Stacked_Hourglass_Network_Keras
26. Zhang, J., Taiet al.: Vr-goggles for robots: real-to-sim domain adaptation for visual control (2019)

Generating Versatile Training Samples for UAV Trajectory Prediction

Stefan Becker[1]([⊠])[iD], Ronny Hug[1][iD], Wolfgang Huebner[1][iD], Michael Arens[1][iD], and Brendan T. Morris[2][iD]

[1] Fraunhofer Center for Machine Learning, Fraunhofer IOSB, Ettlingen, Germany
{stefan.becker,ronny.hug,wolfgang.huebner,
michael.arens}@iosb.fraunhofer.de
[2] University of Nevada, Las Vegas, USA
brendan.morris@unlv.edu
https://www.iosb.fraunhofer.de

Abstract. Following the success of deep learning-based models in various sequence processing tasks, these models are increasingly utilized in object tracking applications for motion prediction as a replacement of traditional approaches. On the one hand, these models can capture complex object dynamics while requiring less modeling, but on the other hand, they depend on a large amount of training data for parameter tuning.

Towards this end, an approach for generating synthetic trajectory data of *unmanned-aerial-vehicles* (UAVs) in image space is presented in this paper. Since UAVs are dynamical systems, they are bound to strict physical constraints and inputs for controlling. Thus, they cannot move along arbitrary trajectories. To generate executable trajectories, it is possible to apply solutions from trajectory planning for our desired purpose of generating realistic UAV trajectory data. Accordingly, with the prerequisite that UAV trajectories fulfill a smoothness criterion corresponding to a minimal change of higher-order motion, planning methods enabling aggressive quadrotor flights are applied to generate optimal trajectories through a sequence of 3D waypoints. By projecting these maneuver trajectories to image space, a versatile trajectory data set is realized. To demonstrate the applicability of the synthetic trajectory data, we show that deep learning-based prediction models solely trained on the synthetically generated data can outperform traditional reference models on a real-world UAV tracking dataset. The evaluation is done on the publicly available *ANTI-UAV* dataset.

Keywords: Unmanned-aerial-vehicle (UAV) · Synthetic data generation · Trajectory prediction · Deep-learning · Sequence models · Training data · Quadrotors

1 Introduction and Related Work

Since *unmanned-aerial-vehicles* (UAVs) are becoming more affordable, have low maintenance costs, offer high mobility and ease of deployment, they increasingly conquering the consumer market. The use of UAVs has been extended to several application fields

© Springer Nature Switzerland AG 2022
P. Galambos et al. (Eds.): ROBOVIS 2020/ROBOVIS 2021, CCIS 1667, pp. 208–229, 2022.
https://doi.org/10.1007/978-3-031-19650-8_11

including traffic and weather monitoring [22], precision agriculture [76], and many more (see for example [18, 71]). The rising numbers number of UAVs led to concerns about associated potential risks for safety, privacy and security. The potential intended or unintended misuses pertain to various areas of public life, including locations, such as airports, mass events, or public demonstrations [46]. The increased potential threats come of course along with an increased demand for ANTI-UAV (i.e., automated UAV detection and tracking) systems for anticipating UAV behavior. These ANTI-UAV systems rely on different modalities which have varying strengths and weaknesses. For a more detailed overview of different ANTI-UAV systems, the reader is exemplarily referred to this survey [41]. However, in this work, we only consider image-based or rather video-based systems. Image-based systems offer the benefit of covering large areas and are cost-effective to acquire [72]. The basic components of such an image-based approach are the appearance model and the prediction model which is traditionally realized with recursive Bayesian filters. Within the detection and tracking pipeline, the main task of the prediction model is the prediction of the tracked object behavior. Due to the success of deep learning-based models in various sequence processing tasks, these models become the standard choice for object motion prediction. One major disadvantage of deep learning models is that they require of a large amount of training data.

To overcome the problem of limited training data associated with tracking UAVs in image sequences, this paper proposes to utilize methods from planning aggressive UAV flights to generate suitable and versatile trajectories. The synthetically generated 3D trajectories are mapped into image space before they serve as training data for deep learning prediction models.

Despite the increasing number of trajectory datasets for object classes such as pedestrians (e.g., *TrajNet++* dataset [45], *Thör* dataset [63], *BIWI* dataset [58]) or vehicles (e.g., *InD* dataset [14], *nuScenes* dataset [15], *KITTI* dataset [23]), datasets with UAV trajectories and UAV in general are very limited. For the aforementioned object classes of pedestrians and vehicles, several deep learning-based models are successfully applied for trajectory prediction. The three major basic deep learning sequence models are *recurrent neural networks* (RNNs) [65] and their variants, *temporal convolutional networks* (TCNs) [5] and *transformer networks* (TFs, [78]. Probabilistic sequence models are commonly built around these three mentioned underlying neural sequence models. For probabilistic sequence models, there exist the categories of *regression*-based and *transformative* approaches [37]. Their most relevant representatives are *mixture density networks* (MDN) [12, 13] for *regression*-based models and *generative adversarial networks* (GANs) [26] and *variational autoencoders* (VAEs) [43] for *transformative* approaches. For these sequence models, there exist many task-specific adaptions. For mentioning examples in the context of trajectory prediction, the following approaches have been proposed. There are the RNN-based approaches of [2, 35, 79] which are all combined with MDNs. Based on TCNs, there are for example the approaches of [7, 55] and based on TFs, there are the approaches of [10, 25, 81]. GAN-based adaption are presented by [3, 28, 66]. From this large model pool, representative reference models are selected for evaluation. The selected adapted models and their underlying concepts are further explained in Sect. 2. For a comprehensive overview of current deep learning-based approaches for trajectory prediction, the reader is referred to these surveys [45, 60, 64].

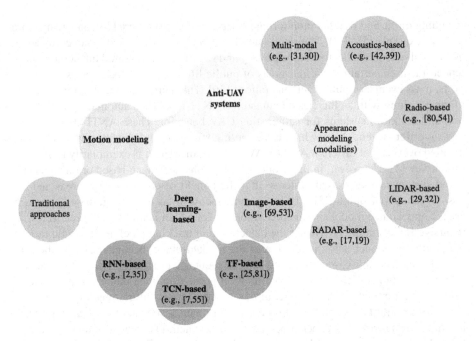

Fig. 1. Taxonomy of ANTI-UAV systems in terms of motion modeling (i.e., prediction models) and appearance modeling (i.e., utilized sensor modalities). The categorization of this paper within the taxonomy is highlighted in red. (color figure online)

The categorization of this paper within the taxonomy of ANTI-UAV systems in terms of motion modeling (i.e., prediction models) and appearance modeling (i.e., utilized sensor modalities) is visualized in Fig. 1. As highlighted in Fig. 1, the focus of this paper is on (deep learning-based) motion prediction for image-based systems and not on the appearance model. However, we throw a brief look at some of the current approaches that rely on images or use other modalities. Since the appearance model serves for generating the observed trajectory, the prediction models could in principle be modified to work with other input data, but the proposed generation method of synthetic training is not generally transferable to the other modalities. Besides image-based methods, common modalities used in ANTI-UAV systems for UAV detections are RADAR, acoustics, radio-frequencies, LIDAR and fused modalities. A general overview of different ANTI-UAV systems is given in [41]. Comparisons of key characteristics of different deep learning-based approaches on single or fused modality information are presented in [67,75,77]. Reviews with the focus on radar-based UAV detection methods are given by [17,19] and tailored to deep learning-based methods relying on radar data is presented in [24]. A review with an emphasis on Radio-based systems is given in [16]. Approaches relying on acoustic sensors to localize UAVs are, for example, introduced in the works of [39,42,51]. Utilizing their radio frequency signature is, for example, proposed in the approaches of [16,54,80]. For LIDAR, there exist, for example, the approaches of [29,32]. Image-based approaches can be divided into using electro-optical sensors or infrared sensors. Their appearance modeling, however, is very similar. A further division can be made into applying a one-stage strategy or a two-stage strategy. For a one-stage strategy, a direct classification and localization are applied. For a two-stage strategy, a general (moving) object detection is followed by a classification step. This concept of a cascaded two-stage strategy with general object detection offers an easy way to combine image-based methods with other modalities. For fixed cameras, the latter strategy is preferred. Different image-based approaches are, for example, presented in [4,53,62,68,69,72,82]. The concept of a cascaded two-stage strategy is can also be applied to combine image-based methods with other modalities. An example which uses LIDAR for low resolution range detection and an image-based system for final UAV detection are proposed in [30,31].

This paper is the extended version of our previously published conference paper [9], in which the underlying concept of utilizing UAV flight planning to generate training samples was introduced. Compared to the predecessor version, exemplarily representatives of all the above-mentioned adaptations are utilized as reference models instead of a single RNN-based model. In addition to the above more detailed overview on related work and ANTI-UAV systems in general, this version provides a more thorough evaluation, analysis and outlook.

The paper is structured as follows. Section 2 introduces the used deep-learning based UAV trajectory prediction models. Section 3 presents the proposed methods for generating realistic UAV trajectory data in image sequences. In addition to an analysis of the diversity of the synthetically generated data, Sect. 4 includes an evaluation on the real-world *ANTI-UAV* dataset [40]. After that, a discussion on limitations and failure cases is given is Sect. 5. Finally, a conclusion is given in Sect. 6.

2   Prediction Models

In this section, the utilized reference prediction models are briefly explained. Sequence prediction combines the two inference tasks of sequence encoding and synthesis by means of first encoding a given input sequence (the observation) before predicting future data points for the observed sequence. Accordingly, the task of trajectory prediction in image sequences is to predict the next N_{pred} image positions conditioned on the previous observed input sequence $\mathcal{U}$ of consecutive observed image positions $\vec{u}^t = (u^t, v^t)$ at time step t along a trajectory. When using a probabilistic sequence model instead of a deterministic model, the model generates a distribution over future positions. In order to generate either single trajectories or probabilistic predictions, each prediction models is commonly build on one of the basic sequence models of RNNs, TCNs or TFs. Due to the existence of so many similar trajectory prediction models only a few representative adaptations covering all basic models are selected.

RNN-MDN: Our first selected model is an RNN-MDN. Originated from a model introduced by [27], RNN-MDN are a popular choice where adaptations have been successfully utilized to predict pedestrian [2], vehicle [21] or cyclist [59] motions. Although these modified versions also incorporate some contextual cues (e.g., interactions from other objects), single object motion is encoded with such an RNN-MDN variant. An

RNN-MDN is a *regression*-based probabilistic model which puts out the parameters of *Gaussian mixture model*(GMM) to generate the distribution over next positions $\{\vec{u}^{t+1}, \ldots, \vec{u}^{t+N_{\text{pred}}}\}$ given $\mathcal{U}$. The model is realized as an RNN encoder. With an embedding of the inputs and using a single Gaussian component, the model can be defined as follows:

$$\vec{e}^t = \text{EMB}(\vec{u}^t; \vec{\Theta}_e),$$
$$\vec{h}^t = \text{RNN}(\vec{h}^{t-1}, \vec{e}^t; \vec{\Theta}_{RNN}),$$
$$\{\hat{\vec{\mu}}^{t+n}, \hat{\Sigma}^{t+n}\}_{n=1}^{N_{\text{pred}}} = \text{MLP}(\vec{h}^t; \vec{\Theta}_{MLP}) \tag{1}$$

Here, RNN($\cdot$) is the recurrent network, $\vec{h}$ the hidden state of the RNN, MLP($\cdot$) the multilayer perceptron, and EMB($\cdot$) an embedding layer. $\vec{\Theta}$ represents the weights and biases of the MLP, EMB, or respectively of the RNN. The model is trained by maximizing the likelihood of the data given the output Gaussian distribution. This results in the following loss function:

$$\mathcal{L}(\mathcal{U}) = \sum_{n=1}^{N_{\text{pred}}} -\log \mathcal{N}(\vec{u}^{t+n} | \hat{\vec{\mu}}^{t+n}, \hat{\Sigma}^{t+n}). \tag{2}$$

Implementation Details: The RNN hidden state (d_{RNN}) and embedding dimension (d_{EMB}) are set to 64. For the experiments, the *long short-term memory* (LSTM) [33] RNN variant is utilized.

An example prediction of the RNN-MDN on a synthetically generated UAV trajectory in image space is depicted in Fig. 2. On the left, the predicted distribution for 12 steps into the future is shown in yellow. The corresponding ground truth position is marked as a blue star. On the right, a zoomed-in detail is shown.

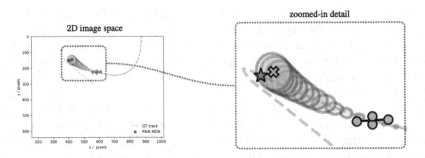

Fig. 2. Visualization of the predicted distribution of an RNN-MDN on a synthetic UAV trajectory in image space for 12 steps into the future (on the left). A corresponding zoomed-in detail is shown on the right. The corresponding position of the ground truth (GT) track is highlighted with a blue star.

TCN: The second chosen reference model is a TCN-based model. TCNs are a special variant of *convolutional neural networks* (CNN, [47]) for sequential data. In contrast to RNNs, TCNs utilizes convolution layers to handle temporal dependencies. To capture long distance dependencies *dilated convolutions* [34] are incorporated and *causal* *convolutions* [56] to ensure that the temporal order is taken into account. TCNs offer compared to RNNs the benefit of inherent parallelism, but TCNs are less flexible in processing variable length sequences. The memory of the model is limited by the filter kernel's width and the dilation rate, whereas RNNs can theoretically establish dependencies up to the first sequence element [37]. TCNs are able to outperform RNN-based models on different sequence modeling tasks [5] and in the context of trajectory prediction, TCN-based approaches have also been successfully applied [7,55].

Here, the TCN-based reference model is realized as a sequence-to-sequence deterministic model as in [55]. Thus, the model is trained by minimizing the L2-loss in the form of the mean squared error between the ground truth trajectories ($\vec{u}^{t:t_{N_{\text{pred}}}}$)and the estimated trajectories ($\hat{\vec{u}}^{t:t_{N_{\text{pred}}}}$):

$$\mathcal{L}(\mathcal{U}) = \sum_{n=1}^{N_{\text{pred}}} \|\hat{\vec{u}}^{t+n} - \vec{u}^{t+n}\|_2. \tag{3}$$

After an input embedding layer, the convolutions layers are stacked. Lastly, the encoded information of the final convolution layer is passed through a fully connected layer to output all future positions at once.

Implementation Details: The kernel size d_{kernel} is set to 3 with symmetric padding. The model is designed for a default input length of 8. By choosing a four-layered convolutional network ($n_{\text{layers}} = 4$), the context of all eight inputs is captured. In order to not lose any temporal information on the small observation time horizon, no *dilated convolution* is used. The embedding dimension is 32. Processing variable length inputs can be achieved by sliding the convolutional kernels.

TF: In addition to the aforementioned approaches, one TF-based model is selected. TFs originated in the field of natural language modeling. Despite their success in other application domains, TF-based models have also been adapted for trajectory prediction [10,25,81]. TFs contain no recurrence and no convolution by always considering the entire input sequence. The key concepts of TFs are build around an *positional encoding* and an *attention* mechanism. While the *positional encoding* is used to inject information about the position in the input sequence, the *attention* mechanism controls the influence of parts in the input sequence for estimating the target sequence. The selected model for the evaluation consists of an encoder-decoder network very similar to the original model [78], which is adapted to trajectory prediction as in [25]. Firstly, the entire observed trajectory is encoded into a single vector, before the decoder sequentially generates one trajectory point at a time, given the encoding. Thus, the model is not probabilistic and just like for the selected TCN-based model, the L2 loss is used for training.

Implementation Details: After a grid search around the parameters provided by [25], the relevant hyperparameters for the model are set to $d_{\text{model}} = 64$ (model dimension), $d_{\text{ff}} = 256$ (dimension of the feed forward network d_{ff}). The number of attention heads n_{heads} is set to 1.

GAN: Lastly, again a probabilistic reference model is selected in the form of a GAN-based adaptation. GANs are a type of generative model which learns an *implicit* model of the unknown data generating distribution. Thereby a deterministic neural network is utilized to transform samples from a simple distribution to a more complex distribution.

To overcome solving the intractable posterior distribution, GAN training is contrived as a supervised learning problem using an interplay of two neural networks: a generative model (denoted as *generator*) and a *discriminator* network. In a two-player min-max game style training, the generator tries to generate samples from the unknown data distribution $p(\vec{x})$, which the discriminator is incapable of classifying as real or fake. The value function $V(G, D)$ for such a min-max game can be defined as follows:

$$\min_G \max_D V(G, D) = \mathbb{E}_{\vec{x} \sim p(\vec{x})} \left[\log D(\vec{x}) \right] + \mathbb{E}_{\vec{z} \sim p(\vec{z})} \left[\log \left(1 - D(G(\vec{z})) \right) \right]. \quad (4)$$

The generator's stochastic input distribution $p(\vec{z})$ is commonly defined as the multivariate standard Gaussian distribution. In order to apply a GAN in the context of trajectory prediction, a sequence processing unit must be incorporated into the model. The model used in this paper is based on the approach of Gupta et al. [28] without the components to add social cues (e.g., information from other objects in the scene), using trajectory information only. According to [28], a sequence-to-sequence LSTM is built into the generator network and another LSTM encoder is built into the discriminator network. For sequentially generating a prediction, the GAN encodes the observed trajectory and then adds a random noise vector to the encoded representation. By using different noise vectors which pass through the decoder network, a sample-based distribution of future trajectories is generated. To calculate the loss, K samples $\{\hat{\mathcal{U}}_1, ..., \hat{\mathcal{U}}_K\}$ with $\hat{\mathcal{U}}_i = \{\hat{u}_i^1, ..., \hat{u}_i^{N_{\text{pred}}}\}$ are generated. The loss function combines a variety loss

$$\mathcal{L}(\mathcal{U})_{\text{variety}} = \min_i \sum_{n=1}^{N_{\text{pred}}} \|\hat{\vec{u}}_i^{t+n} - \vec{u}^{t+n}\|_2 \quad (5)$$

with a GAN adversarial loss

$$\mathcal{L}(\mathcal{U})_{\text{adversarial}} = \mathbb{E}_{\vec{u} \sim p_{\text{data}}(\vec{u})} \left[\log D(\vec{u}) \right] + \mathbb{E}_{\mathbf{z} \sim p(\vec{z})} \left[\log(1 - D(G(\vec{z}))) \right]. \quad (6)$$

D and G denote the discriminator and generator networks, respectively. The variety loss is intended to encourage the GAN to generate diverse future trajectory predictions for the same observed trajectory.

Implementation Details: The following GAN-relevant hyperparameters are selected for experiments. The dimensionality of the noise vector d_{noise} is set to 8. The hidden state of the LSTM encoder d_{enc} and decoder d_{dec} are set to 32 and 48. Another hyperparameter is the hidden state dimension $d_{\text{discr\_enc}} = 32$ of the auxiliary LSTM encoder only active during training.

A list of chosen hyperparameters for the selected reference models is given in Table 1. The RNN-MDN is implemented using *Tensorflow* [1] and is trained using an ADAM optimizer [44] with a decreasing learning rate, starting from 0.01 with a learning rate decay of 0.95 and a decay factor of $^1/_{10}$ (see [9]). All other models are implemented using *Pytorch* [57]. For their training an ADAM optimizer variant [44,48] with a learning rate of 0.001 is used.

3   Synthetic Data Generation

In this section the proposed approach to synthetically generate realistic, versatile UAV trajectory data for the desired image-based ANTI-UAV system is presented.

Table 1. Overview of chosen hyperparameters for each selected trajectory prediction model in comparison.

Model	Hyperparameters
RNN-MDN (e.g., [2,35])	$d_{\text{RNN}} = 64$
GAN (e.g., [28,66])	$d_{\text{noise}} = 8$
	$d_{\text{enc}} = 32$
	$d_{\text{dec}} = 48$
	$d_{\text{discr\_enc}} = 32$
TCN (e.g., [7,55])	$d_{\text{kernel}} = 3$
	$n_{\text{layers}} = 4$
TF (e.g., [25,81])	$d_{\text{model}} = 64$
	$n_{\text{heads}} = 1$
	$d_{\text{ff}} = 256$

Minimum Snap Trajectories (MST): Since UAVs are dynamical systems with strict constraints on achievable velocities, accelerations and inputs, they can not fly arbitrary trajectories. In conjunction with control inputs, these constraints determine optimal trajectories with a series of waypoints in a set of positions and orientations [49]. Trajectory planning generates inputs for the motion control in a way that the planned trajectory can be executed. For enabling aggressive complex quadrotor flights, we apply an explicit optimization method introduced by Mellinger et al. [50]. In the remainder of this paper, the terms quadrotor and UAV are used interchangeably, although there exist various other UAV concepts. The principle procedure can be adapted to all other designs. Since we are only interested in the trajectory data, the actual control design can, to some extent, be neglected as long as the planned target trajectory is executable and suitable for control.

Minimum snap trajectories (MST) have proven very effective as quadrotor trajectories since the motor commands and attitude accelerations of the UAV are proportional to the snap, or the fourth derivative, of the path [61]. The actual difference between planned and executed trajectory depends on the actual controller and physical limitations (e.g., maximum speed) of a UAV. First of all, it is possible to consider physical constraints in planning. Furthermore, in most cases, a well-designed controller can closely follow the target trajectory. For the intended purpose of generating trajectory data for training prediction models, the actual flight trajectory can, in a way, be seen as only a slight variation of the target trajectory. The basis for all development of input controlling and planning are the dynamic equations of a UAV. They link the net thrust forces and the net moments to the inputs. For nested feedback control (inner attitude control loop and outer position control loop, see for example [52]), Mellinger and Kumar [50] showed that quadrotor dynamics can be linearized in a way that the corresponding four control input $(i_1, \cdots, i_4)$ are differential flat. Accordingly, the states and the inputs can be written as functions of four selected *flat outputs* and their derivatives. The *flat outputs* are given by $p = [\mathbf{r}^{\mathsf{T}}, \psi]^{\mathsf{T}}$, where $\mathbf{r} = [x, y, z]^{\mathsf{T}}$ are the coordinates of the center of mass in the world coordinate system and ψ is the yaw angle. Since any smooth trajectory (with reasonably bounded derivatives) in the space of *flat outputs* can be followed by the quadrotor, this facilitates the automated generation of trajectory data. The *flat outputs* at a given time t are given by $p(t)$, which defines a smooth curve. Trajectory planning specifies navigating through m waypoints at specified times by staying in a safe corridor. Thereby a waypoint denotes a position in space along a yaw angle. Due to the fact that trivial trajectories such as straight lines lead to discontinuities in higher-order motion resulting in infinite curvatures at waypoints, such trajectories are undesirable. Since such solutions would force the quadrotor to stop at each waypoint, it is insisted that the trajectories the UAV follows are smooth. The order (n) of dynamical systems determines the input where we have boundary conditions on the $(n-1)^{\text{th}}$ order and lower derivates. Therefore, the differentiability of polynomial trajectories makes them a natural choice for use in a differentially flat representation of the quadrotor dynamics. Thus, for following a specific trajectory $p_T(t) = [\mathbf{r}_T^\mathsf{T}, \psi_T(t)]^\mathsf{T}$ (with controller for a UAV), the smooth trajectory $p_T(t)$ is defined as piecewise polynomial functions of order n over m time intervals:

$$p_T(t) = \begin{cases} \sum_{i=0}^{n} p_{T_{i1}}(t^i) & t_0 \leqslant t \leqslant t_1 \\ \sum_{i=0}^{n} p_{T_{i2}}(t^i) & t_1 \leqslant t \leqslant t_2 \\ \quad\vdots \\ \sum_{i=0}^{n} p_{T_{im}}(t^i) \; t_{m-1} \leqslant t \leqslant t_m \end{cases} \tag{7}$$

The goal is to find trajectories that minimize functionals which can be written using these basis functions. These kinds of problems can be solved with tools from the calculus of variations and are standard problems in robotics [20]. Hence, in order to find the smooth target trajectory $p_T(t)_{tar}$, the integral of the k_r^{th} derivative of position squared and the k_ψ^{th} derivative of yaw angle squared is minimized:

$$p_T(t)_{tar} = \arg\min_{p_T(t)} \int_{t_o}^{t_m} c_r \left\| \frac{\mathrm{d}^{k_r} \mathbf{r}_T}{\mathrm{d}t^{k_r}} \right\|^2 + c_\psi \frac{\mathrm{d}^{k_\psi} \psi_T}{\mathrm{d}t^{k_\psi}}^2 \mathrm{d}t \tag{8}$$

Here, c_r and c_ψ are constants to make the integrand non-dimensional. Continuity of the k_r derivatives of $\mathbf{r}_T$ and k_ψ derivatives of ψ_T is enforced as a criterion for smoothness. In other words, the continuity of the derivatives determines the boundary conditions at the waypoints. As mentioned above, some UAV control input depends on the fourth derivative of the positions and the second derivative of the yaw. Accordingly, $p_T(t)_{tar}$ is calculated by minimizing the integral of the square of the norm of the snap ($k_r = 4$), and for the yaw angle, $k_\psi = 2$ holds.

The above problem can be formulated as a quadratic problem QP [11]. Thereby, $p_{T_{ij}} = [x_{T_{ij}}, y_{T_{ij}}, z_{T_{ij}}, \psi_{T_{ij}}]^\mathsf{T}$ are written as a $4nm \times 1$ vector $\vec{c}$ with decision variables $\{x_{T_{ij}}, y_{T_{ij}}, z_{T_{ij}}, \psi_{T_{ij}}\}$:

$$\min \vec{c}^\mathsf{T} Q \vec{c} + \vec{f}^\mathsf{T} \vec{c}$$

$$\text{subject to } A\vec{c} \leq \vec{b}. \tag{9}$$

Here, the objective function incorporates the minimization of the functional while the constraints can be used to satisfy constraints on the flat outputs and their derivatives and thus constraints on the states and the inputs. The initial conditions, final conditions, or intermediate conditions on any derivative of the trajectory are specified as equality constraints in 9. For a more detailed explanation on generating MSTs, how to incorporate corridor constraints, and how to calculate the angular velocities, angular accelerations, total thrust, and moments required over the entire trajectory for the controller, the reader is referred to the work of [50]. [61] presented an extended version of MST generation, where the solution of the quadratic problem is numerically more stable.

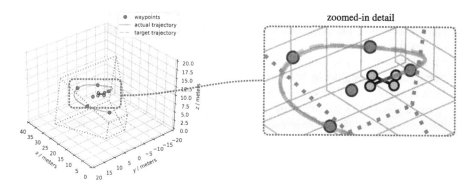

Fig. 3. Visualization of a generated MST (target trajectory) along waypoints in the viewing frustum of a camera. The MST is highlighted in blue. The sampled waypoints in the viewing frustum of the camera are shown in purple. The corresponding UAV flights with a PD controller as proposed from [52] are shown in red. (Color figure online)

Training Data Generation: With the ability to calculate MSP trajectories through specified waypoints, we have basically everything in our hand to generate trajectories that are suitable for aggressive maneuver flights for UAV control in a 3D environment. For generating a full, versatile training set with trajectory data in image space, further steps are required. The overall generation pipeline is outlined in the following. Firstly, a desired camera model with known intrinsic parameters is selected. The selection depends on the targeted sensor set-up of the detection and tracking system. In our case, we choose a pinhole camera model without distortion effects loosely orientated on the *ANTI-UAV* dataset [40] with regard to an intermediate image resolution (in pixels) (1176×640) between the infrared (640×512) and electro-optical camera (1920×1080) resolutions of the *ANTI-UAV* dataset. In case all camera parameters are known, the corresponding distortion coefficient should be considered. In the experiments the focal length (in pixels) is set to 1240, the principle point coordinates (in pixels) are set to $p_x = 579, p_y = 212$. For setting up the external parameters, the camera is placed close to the ground plane uniformly sampled from $Uni(1\,m, 2\,m)$ to set the height above ground. The inclination angle is sampled from $Uni(10°, 20°)$. Given the fixed camera parameters, the viewing frustum is calculated for a chosen near distance to the camera center ($d_{near} = 10\,m$) and a far distance to the camera center ($d_{far} = 30\,m$). For generating a single MST, a set of waypoints inside the viewing frustum is sampled. The number of waypoints is randomly varied between 3 and 7. The travel time for each segment is approximated by using the Euclidean distance between two waypoints and a sampled constant speed for the UAV $Uni(1\,m/s, 8\,m/s)$. The resulting straight-line trajectory serves as an initial solution of the MST calculation. The frame rate of the camera is sampled from $Uni(10\,fps, 20\,fps)$ for every run. In our experiments, we assumed a completely free space in the viewing frustum. As mentioned, corridor constraints, which can be used for simulating an object to fly through, can be integrated with the method of [50]. For the synthetic training dataset, 1000 MSTs are generated. The main steps for the synthetic data generation pipeline of a single run are as follows:

- Selection of a desired camera model with known intrinsic parameters.
- Determination of extrinsic parameters by sampling from the height and slope angle distribution.
- Calculation of the corresponding viewing frustum with d_{near} and d_{far}.
- Sampling of waypoints inside viewing frustum.
- Estimation of the initial solution with fixed, sampled UAV speed.
- Generation of MST trajectory by using the method of [50].
- Projection of the 3D center of mass positions of the MST to image space using the camera parameters at fixed time intervals (reciprocal of the drawn frame rate of a single run).

This procedure is repeated until the desired number of samples are generated. Note that sanity checks and abort criteria for the trajectory are applied at the end and during every run. For example, requirements on the minimum and maximum length of consecutive image points. In Fig. 3, generated MSTs along sampled waypoints in a 3D-environment are visualized. The viewing frustum for a fixed inclination angle of 15° is shown as a dotted gray line. The actual flight trajectory of a UAV is realized with a *proportional-derivative* (PD) controller as is proposed by [52]. Although the controller design is relatively simple, the UAV can closely follow the target trajectory. Thus, directly using the planned MST seems to be a legitimate design choice. In Fig. 4, exemplarily generated training samples are depicted. The diversity and suitability of the generated synthetic data are analyzed in Sect. 4.

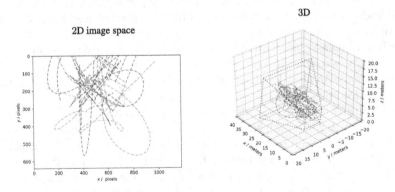

Fig. 4. Visualization of generated UAV trajectories. (Left) UAV trajectories as observed from the camera. The center of mass of the UAV along the MST is projected to image space at fixed time intervals. (Right) Visualized corresponding UAV trajectories in the world coordinate system inside the viewing frustum of the camera.

4   Evaluation & Analysis

This section analyzes the diversity of the generated synthetic data from section and the suitability for training deep-learning prediction models.

Diversity Analysis: The diversity analysis of the synthetically generated data is done using the spatial sequence alignment approach of [38]. The main idea relies on the fact that trajectories can be decomposed in sequences of basic motion patterns. For finding the basic motion patterns, the approach provides a common learned reference trajectory and removes variation due to different positions, scales and orientations. The approach learns a representation of the provided trajectory data by first employing a spatial sequence alignment, which enables a subsequent learning vector quantization (LVQ) stage. Applied on a trajectory dataset results in a small number of prototypical sub-sequences specifying distinct motion patterns, where each sample can be assumed to be a variation of these prototypes [36]. Thus, the resulting quantized representation of the trajectory data, the prototypes, reflect basic motion patterns, such as constant or curvilinear motion, while variations occur primarily in position, orientation, curvature and scale. For further details on the dataset analysis methods, the reader is referred to the work of [38]. The resulting prototypes of the generated training data are depicted in Fig. 5.

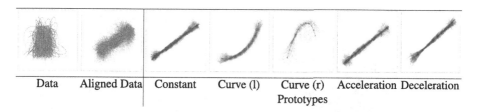

Data	Aligned Data	Constant	Curve (l)	Curve (r)	Acceleration	Deceleration
				Prototypes		

Fig. 5. Data, aligned data and learned prototypes for the synthetic UAV trajectories projected to image space. The prototypes represent different motion patterns (from left to right): Constant velocity, curvilinear motion (left and right curve), acceleration and deceleration (images taken from [9]).

The learned prototypes show that the generated synthetic data includes several different motion patterns. Besides, the diversity of the learned prototypes is visible. The dataset consists of, for example, distinguishable motion patterns reflecting constant velocity motion, curvilinear motion, acceleration, and deceleration. It can also be seen that the resulting trajectory data has a reasonable relevance distribution. This means, that there is no significant bias in the sample to cluster association. From the basic principle, sampling from basic motion patterns could also be used to generate trajectory data. But it is very hard to determine useful sampling policies and strategies to get such a well-balanced distribution of prototypes as shown in Fig. 5. Further, excluding physical implausible trajectories is inherently given with the method described in Sect. 3.

Suitability Analysis: In order to analyze the suitability of the generated trajectory data, the selected reference models are trained according to Sect. 2. For evaluation, the real-world *ANTI-UAV* dataset [40] is used. The dataset consists of 100 high-quality, full

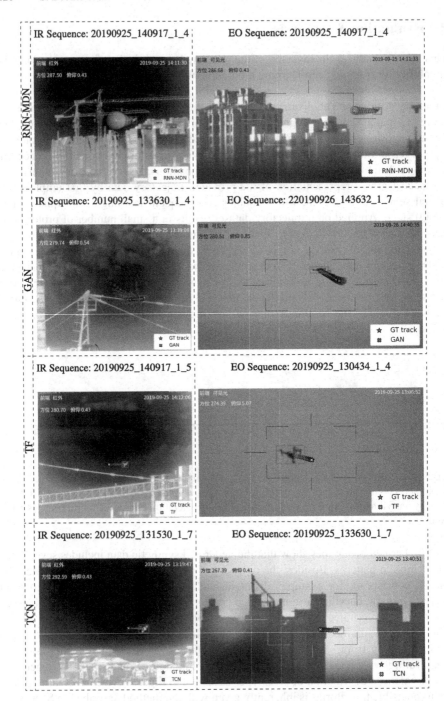

Fig. 6. Example predictions for the *ANTI-UAV* dataset [40] from the selected models. The left images show samples from the IR sequences. The right images depict samples from the EO sequences.

HD video sequences (both electro-optical (EO) and infrared (IR)), spanning multiple occurrences of multi-scale UAVs, annotated with bounding boxes. As inputs for the prediction models, the center positions of the provided annotations are used. For comparison with the deep learning-based models, two traditional models are utilized. The chosen models are a Kalman filter with a constant velocity (CV) motion model and linear interpolation. For the Kalman filter, the observation noise is assumed to be a white Gaussian noise process $\vec{w}^t \sim \mathcal{N}(0, (1.5 \, pixels)^2)$. Thereby, the uncertainty in the annotation is considered. The process noise is modeled as the acceleration increment during a sampling interval (white noise acceleration model [6]) with $\sigma^2_{CV} = 0.5 \, pixels/frame^2$. For dealing with the minor annotation uncertainty, a small white Gaussian noise is added to the generated trajectory positions corresponding to the assumed observation noise. Since neural models are able to generalize from noisy inputs up to an extent (see for example [7]), the noisy trajectories are used for conditioning during training. The performance is compared using the *final displacement error* (FDE) as metric. This metric is commonly used to assess trajectory prediction performance (see for example [2,7,25,28]). The FDE is defined as

$$\text{FDE} = \frac{1}{M} \sum_{i=1}^{M} \|\hat{\vec{u}}_i^{N_{\text{pred}}} - \vec{u}_i^{N_{\text{pred}}}\|_2. \tag{10}$$

Hence, the FDE is calculated as the average Euclidean distance between the predicted final positions $\hat{\vec{u}}_i^{N_{\text{pred}}}$ and the ground truth positions $\vec{u}_i^{N_{\text{pred}}}$. M is the number of trajectory samples for evaluation and i the sample index. The comparison is done for three different time-horizons, in particular, 8 frames, 10 frames, and 12 frames into the future.

Table 2. Results for a comparison between a selection of deep learning-based prediction models trained on the synthetic generated data, a Kalman filter with CV motion model, and using linear interpolation. The prediction is done for 8, 10, and 16 frames into the future.

	EO (1920 × 1080)					
	8/8		8/10		8/12	
Model	FDE/pixels	σ_{FDE}/pixels	FDE/pixels	σ_{FDE}/pixels	FDE/pixels	σ_{FDE}/pixels
RNN-MDN	60.304	35.202	82.780	46.124	121.453	55.489
GAN	75.732	48.587	100.481	52.363	166.584	56.451
TF	59.403	36.101	81.401	46.981	119.401	56.238
TCN	61.403	35.943	83.562	47.465	123.563	58.391
Kalman filter (CV)	81.061	60.333	110.041	84.530	179.459	104.408
Linear interpolation	86.998	67.113	119.106	89.067	183.558	108.522

	IR (640 × 512)					
	8/8		8/10		8/12	
Model	FDE/pixels	σ_{FDE}/pixels	FDE/pixels	σ_{FDE}/pixels	FDE/pixels	σ_{FDE}/pixels
RNN-MDN	20.849	18.604	41.378	21.100	61.459	24.490
GAN	22.120	22.568	43.011	24.351	67.359	26.433
TF	20.820	18.701	41.236	21.283	61.397	24.978
TCN	20.952	18.737	41.839	21.703	61.941	25.010
Kalman filter (CV)	22.340	24.630	43.172	32.522	68.012	37.047
Linear interpolation	24.235	26.517	45.434	35.837	69.665	37.714

The results for the EO and the IR video sequences are summarized in Table 2. Although the neural models are solely trained on the synthetically generated UAV data, the models could outperform the traditional reference models on the EO and the IR sequences of the *ANTI-UAV* dataset. The results are achieved without any camera motion compensation. Thus, the results of all considered prediction models can be further improved, but for such low texture backgrounds, it is very hard to find good feature correspondence. For longer prediction horizons, all errors are relatively high due to the maneuvering behavior of the UAVs. Among others, these factors lead to very similar performance for the evaluated model and that by relying only on image information the models with an image-based system are close to the maximum achievable performance on this dataset. These failure cases and limitations are further discussed in the next sections. However, in case the prediction model is utilized to bridge detection failures for supporting the appearance model of the detection and tracking pipeline, the number of subsequent failures should be lower than the shown 12 frames time horizon. Since all deep-learning models relying on synthetic data achieved better performance than the traditional reference models, they are better suited to anticipate the short-term UAV behavior. In addition, these results show the potential to utilized methods from flight planning in order to overcome the limited amount of UAV trajectory data. In Fig. 6, exemplarily predictions of the models explained in Sect. 2 are visualized for the EO sequences or respectively IR sequences. The ground truth future positions are highlighted as blue stars. The RNN-MDN predicts a distribution of future positions. The covariance ellipses around the predicted position are shown in blue. The GAN model produces a sample- based predictive distribution where the sample trajectories are shown in orange. Since the TCN-based and TF-based models are realized as deterministic models only a single (maximum-likelihood) trajectory is predicted. The final predicted positions of each model are marked with a cross.

5   Discussion

This section provides a brief discussion on limitations, failure cases and future research directions.

Limitations and Failure Cases: Although image-based ANTI-UAV systems might not be optimal for long-range detection and early behavior anticipation, efforts made for such systems are still worthwhile, as image-based systems offer a cost-effective way of covering large areas. As mentioned before, when only relying on observed image positions, the achieved prediction results on the *ANTI-UAV* dataset are possibly close to an achievable maximum due to the fact that the data includes strong camera motion and the UAVs show a highly maneuverable behavior. Of course, there are further ways to address both problems. Firstly, compensating camera motion is a well-known problem in computer vision and there exist several methods to tackle this problem (see for example [74]), but the low textured background showing in many cases a clear and dark sky makes this particularly difficult for the *ANTI-UAV* dataset. However, for closed systems with access to the camera motor control, it is possible to counter the camera motion. Secondly, generating suitable long-term predictions is always difficult in maneuver scenarios and especially when considering UAVs, because of their high maneuverability.

Following this, a prediction model's ability to react quickly to abrupt changes in motion becomes more relevant. Thus, sequential deep learning-based models provide a reliable approach. The strongest failure cases for high prediction errors are exemplarily depicted for an RNN-MDN model in Fig. 7.

IR Sequence: 20190925_101846_1_1   EO Sequence: 20190925_131530_1_4
          Maneuvering UAV   Camera motion

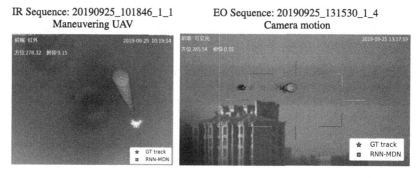

Fig. 7. Visualization of failure cases leading to high prediction errors. On the left, a UAV is shown which suddenly changes its motion. The example on the right depicts strong camera motion.

Future Research Directions: Besides being applied for trajectory prediction, deep learning-based models are also successfully utilized to classify specific maneuver types or motion states (see for example [8,21]). Thus, these models can be considered when attempting to discover motion states beneficial for an ANTI-UAV system. Such potentially useful motion states would for example be hovering or following a planned patrol route. Thereby, it is again possible to find solutions by looking at methods from trajectory planning in order to generate training data. In this paper, appearance and motion modeling are treated separately. However, current hardware-in-the-loop simulators such as *AIRSIM* [70] or *Flightmare* [73] provide the option to physically and visually simulate UAV flights. These systems, together with trajectory planning methods, could be modified to work for generating training data for joint appearance and motion modeling of UAVs. Due to our general problem definition by only taking UAV location estimates as inputs, the concept can in principle be adapted to other modalities. For example, models directly trained on the generated 3D MST trajectory could potentially be used together with a LIDAR-based UAV detector. The growing amount of newly proposed neural sequential models, introduced datasets, and alternative planning methods also offer many possibilities to exploit in future research.

6   Conclusion

This paper presents an approach for generating synthetic trajectory data of UAVs in image space. To generate minimum snap trajectories along a sequence of 3D waypoints methods, we utilize methods from planning maneuvering UAV flights. By selecting the desired camera model with known camera parameters, the trajectories can be projected to the observer's perspective. To demonstrate the applicability of the synthetic trajectory data, we show that several deep learning-based prediction models solely trained on the synthetically generated data are able to outperform traditional reference models on a real-world UAV tracking dataset.

References

1. Abadi, M., et al.: TensorFlow: large-scale machine learning on heterogeneous systems (2015). https://www.tensorflow.org/
2. Alahi, A., Goel, K., Ramanathan, V., Robicquet, A., Fei-Fei, L., Savarese, S.: Social LSTM: human trajectory prediction in crowded spaces. In: Conference on Computer Vision and Pattern Recognition (CVPR), pp. 961–971 (2016)
3. Amirian, J., Hayet, J.B., Pettre, J.: Social ways: learning multi-modal distributions of pedestrian trajectories with GANs. In: Conference on Computer Vision and Pattern Recognition (CVPR) Workshops (2019)
4. Ashraf, M.W., Sultani, W., Shah, M.: Dogfight: detecting drones from drones videos. In: Conference on Computer Vision and Pattern Recognition (CVPR), pp. 7067–7076. Computer Vision Foundation/IEEE (2021)
5. Bai, S., Kolter, J., Koltun, V.: an empirical evaluation of generic convolutional and recurrent networks for sequence modeling. arXiv preprint abs/1803.01271 (2018). http://arxiv.org/abs/1803.01271
6. Bar-Shalom, Y., Kirubarajan, T., Li, X.R.: Estimation with Applications to Tracking and Navigation. John Wiley & Sons Inc, New York (2002)
7. Becker, S., Hug, R., Hübner, W., Arens, M.: RED: a simple but effective baseline predictor for the *TrajNet* benchmark. In: Leal-Taixé, L., Roth, S. (eds.) ECCV 2018. LNCS, vol. 11131, pp. 138–153. Springer, Cham (2019). https://doi.org/10.1007/978-3-030-11015-4_13
8. Becker, S., Hug, R., Hübner, W., Arens, M.: An RNN-based IMM filter surrogate. In: Felsberg, M., Forssén, P.-E., Sintorn, I.-M., Unger, J. (eds.) SCIA 2019. LNCS, vol. 11482, pp. 387–398. Springer, Cham (2019). https://doi.org/10.1007/978-3-030-20205-7_32
9. Becker, S., Hug, R., Hübner, W., Arens, M., Morris, B.T.: Generating synthetic training data for deep learning-based UAV trajectory prediction. In: Proceedings of the 2nd International Conference on Robotics, Computer Vision and Intelligent Systems - ROBOVIS, pp. 13–21. INSTICC, SciTePress (2021). https://doi.org/10.5220/0010621400003061
10. Becker, S., Hug, R., Huebner, W., Arens, M., Morris, B.T.: MissFormer: (In-)attention-based handling of missing observations for trajectory filtering and prediction. In: Bebis, D., et al. (eds.) ISVC 2021. LNCS, vol. 13017, pp. 521–533. Springer, Cham (2021). https://doi.org/10.1007/978-3-030-90439-5_41
11. Bertsekas, D.: Nonlinear Programming. Athena Scientific, Belmont (1999)
12. Bishop, C.M.: Mixture Density Networks. Tech. rep, Microsoft Research (1994)
13. Bishop, C.M.: Pattern Recognition and Machine Learning (Information Science and Statistics), 1st Edn. Springer-Verlag, Heidelberg (2006)
14. Bock, J., Krajewski, R., Moers, T., Runde, S., Vater, L., Eckstein, L.: The IND dataset: A drone dataset of naturalistic road user trajectories at German intersections. In: 2020 IEEE Intelligent Vehicles Symposium (IV), pp. 1929–1934 (2020). https://doi.org/10.1109/IV47402.2020.9304839
15. Caesar, H., et al.: Nuscenes: a multimodal dataset for autonomous driving. In: Conference on Computer Vision and Pattern Recognition (CVPR), pp. 11618–11628. IEEE (2020). https://doi.org/10.1109/CVPR42600.2020.01164, https://doi.org/10.1109/CVPR42600.2020.01164

16. Chiper, F.L., Martian, A., Vladeanu, C., Marghescu, I., Craciunescu, R., Fratu, O.: Drone detection and defense systems: survey and a software-defined radio-based solution. Sensors **22**(4) (2022). https://doi.org/10.3390/s22041453, https://www.mdpi.com/1424-8220/22/4/1453

17. Christnacher, F., et al.: Optical and acoustical UAV detection. In: Kamerman, G., Steinvall, O. (eds.) Electro-Optical Remote Sensing X, vol. 9988, pp. 83–95. International Society for Optics and Photonics, SPIE (2016). https://doi.org/10.1117/12.2240752, https://doi.org/10.1117/12.2240752

18. Coluccia, A., et al.: Drone vs. bird detection: deep learning algorithms and results from a grand challenge. Sensors **21**(8) (2021)

19. Coluccia, A., Parisi, G., Fascista, A.: Detection and classification of multirotor drones in radar sensor networks: a review. Sensors **20**(15) (2020). https://doi.org/10.3390/s201541720, https://www.mdpi.com/1424-8220/20/15/4172

20. Craig, J.: Introduction to Robotics: Mechanics and Control, 2nd edn. Addison-Wesley Longman Publishing Co., Inc, Boston (1989)

21. Deo, N., Trivedi, M.M.: Multi-modal trajectory prediction of surrounding vehicles with maneuver based LSTMs. In: 2018 IEEE Intelligent Vehicles Symposium (IV), pp. 1179–1184 (2018). https://doi.org/10.1109/IVS.2018.8500493

22. Elloumi, M., Dhaou, R., Escrig, B., Idoudi, H., Saidane, L.A.: Monitoring road traffic with a UAV-based system. In: 2018 IEEE Wireless Communications and Networking Conference (WCNC), pp. 1–6 (2018). https://doi.org/10.1109/WCNC.2018.8377077

23. Geiger, A., Lenz, P., Stiller, C., Urtasun, R.: Vision meets robotics: the KITTI dataset. Int. J. Rob. Res. **32**(11), 1231–1237 (2013). https://doi.org/10.1177/0278364913491297, https://doi.org/10.1177/0278364913491297

24. Geng, Z., Yan, H., Zhang, J., Zhu, D.: Deep-learning for radar: A survey. IEEE Access **9**, 141800–141818 (2021). https://doi.org/10.1109/ACCESS.2021.3119561

25. Giuliari, F., Hasan, I., Cristani, M., Galasso, F.: Transformer Networks for Trajectory Forecasting. In: International Conference on Pattern Recognition (ICPR) (2020)

26. Goodfellow, I., et al.: Generative adversarial nets. In: Ghahramani, Z., Welling, M., Cortes, C., Lawrence, N., Weinberger, K.Q. (eds.) Advances in Neural Information Processing Systems. vol. 27. Curran Associates, Inc. (2014), https://proceedings.neurips.cc/paper/2014/file/5ca3e9b122f61f8f06494c97b1afccf3-Paper.pdf

27. Graves, A.: Generating sequences with recurrent neural networks (2014)

28. Gupta, A., Johnson, J., Fei-Fei, L., Savarese, S., Alahi, A.: Social GAN: Socially Acceptable Trajectories with Generative Adversarial Networks. In: Conference on Computer Vision and Pattern Recognition (CVPR). IEEE (2018)

29. Hammer, M., Borgmann, B., Hebel, M., Arens, M.: UAV detection, tracking, and classification by sensor fusion of a 360° lidar system and an alignable classification sensor. In: Turner, M.D., Kamerman, G.W. (eds.) Laser Radar Technology and Applications XXIV, vol. 11005, pp. 99–108. International Society for Optics and Photonics, SPIE (2019). https://doi.org/10.1117/12.2518427, https://doi.org/10.1117/12.2518427

30. Hammer, M., Borgmann, B., Hebel, M., Arens, M.: A multi-sensorial approach for the protection of operational vehicles by detection and classification of small flying objects. In: Kamerman, G.W., Steinvall, O. (Eds.) Electro-Optical Remote Sensing XIV, vol. 11538, pp. 53–64. International Society for Optics and Photonics, SPIE (2020). https://doi.org/10.1117/12.2573620, https://doi.org/10.1117/12.2573620

31. Hammer, M., Borgmann, B., Hebel, M., Arens, M.: Image-based classification of small flying objects detected in LiDAR point clouds. In: Turner, M.D., Kamerman, G.W. (eds.) Laser Radar Technology and Applications XXV, vol. 11410, pp. 1–9. International Society for Optics and Photonics, SPIE (2020). https://doi.org/10.1117/12.2557246, https://doi.org/10.1117/12.2557246

32. Hammer, M., Hebel, M., Laurenzis, M., Arens, M.: Lidar-based detection and tracking of small UAVs. In: Buller, G.S., Hollins, R.C., Lamb, R.A., Mueller, M. (eds.) Emerging Imaging and Sensing Technologies for Security and Defence III; and Unmanned Sensors, Systems, and Countermeasures, vol. 10799, pp. 177–185. International Society for Optics and Photonics, SPIE (2018). https://doi.org/10.1117/12.2325702, https://doi.org/10.1117/12.2325702

33. Hochreiter, S., Schmidhuber, J.: Long short-term memory. Neural Comput. **9**(8), 1735–1780 (1997). https://doi.org/10.1162/neco.1997.9.8.1735

34. Holschneider, M., Kronland-Martinet, R., Morlet, J., Tchamitchian, P.: A real-time algorithm for signal analysis with the help of the wavelet transform. In: Combes, J.M., Grossmann, A., Tchamitchian, P. (eds.) Wavelets, pp. 286–297. Springer, Berlin Heidelberg, Berlin, Heidelberg (1990)

35. Hug, R., Becker, S., Hübner, W., Arens, M.: Particle-based pedestrian path prediction using LSTM-MDL models. In: 21st International Conference on Intelligent Transportation Systems (ITSC), pp. 2684–2691 (2018). https://doi.org/10.1109/ITSC.2018.8569478

36. Hug, R., Becker, S., Hübner, W., Arens, M.: A short note on analyzing sequence complexity in trajectory prediction benchmarks. In: Workshop on Long-term Human Motion Prediction (LHMP) (2020)

37. Hug, R.: Probabilistic parametric curves for sequence modeling. Ph.D. thesis, Karlsruher Institut für Technologie (KIT) (2022). https://doi.org/10.5445/IR/1000142503

38. Hug, R., Becker, S., Hübner, W., Arens, M.: Quantifying the complexity of standard benchmarking datasets for long-term human trajectory prediction. IEEE Access **9**, 77693–77704 (2021). https://doi.org/10.1109/ACCESS.2021.3082904

39. Jeon, S., Shin, J., Lee, Y., Kim, W., Kwon, Y., Yang, H.: Empirical study of drone sound detection in real-life environment with deep neural networks. In: European Signal Processing Conference (EUSIPCO), pp. 1858–1862 (2017). https://doi.org/10.23919/EUSIPCO.2017.8081531

40. Jiang, N., et al.: Anti-UAV: a large multi-modal benchmark for UAV tracking (2021)

41. Jurn, Y.N., Mahmood, S.A., Aldhaibani, J.A.: Anti-drone system based different technologies: architecture, threats and challenges. In: 2021 11th IEEE International Conference on Control System, Computing and Engineering (ICCSCE), pp. 114–119 (2021)

42. Kartashov, V., et al.: Use of acoustic signature for detection, recognition and direction finding of small unmanned aerial vehicles. In: 2020 IEEE 15th International Conference on Advanced Trends in Radioelectronics, Telecommunications and Computer Engineering (TCSET), pp. 1–4 (2020). https://doi.org/10.1109/TCSET49122.2020.235458

43. Kingma, D.P., Welling, M.: Auto-encoding variational Bayes. In: International Conference on Learning Representations (ICLR) (2014)

44. Kingma, D., Ba, J.: Adam: a method for stochastic optimization. In: International Conference on Learning Representations (ICLR) (2015)

45. Kothari, P., Kreiss, S., Alahi, A.: Human trajectory forecasting in crowds: a deep learning perspective. IEEE Trans. on Intell. Transp. Syst. pp. 1–15 (2021). https://doi.org/10.1109/TITS.2021.3069362

46. Laurenzis, M., Rebert, M., Schertzer, S., Bacher, E., Christnacher, F.: Prediction of MUAV flight behavior from active and passive imaging in complex environment. In: Laser Radar Technology and Applications, vol. 11410, pp. 10–17. International Society for Optics and Photonics, SPIE (2020). https://doi.org/10.1117/12.2558561, https://doi.org/10.1117/12.2558561

47. LeCun, Y., Bengio, Y.: Convolutional Networks for Images, Speech, and Time Series, pp. 255–258. MIT Press, Cambridge (1998)

48. Loshchilov, I., Hutter, F.: Decoupled weight decay regularization. In: International Conference on Learning Representations (ICLR) (2019)

49. Mellinger, D.: Trajectory generation and control for quadrotors. Ph.D. thesis, University of Pennsylvania (2012)

50. Mellinger, D., Kumar, V.: Minimum snap trajectory generation and control for quadrotors. In: International Conference on Robotics and Automation (ICRA), pp. 2520–2525 (2011). https://doi.org/10.1109/ICRA.2011.5980409

51. Mezei, J., Molnár, A.: Drone sound detection by correlation. In: 2016 IEEE 11th International Symposium on Applied Computational Intelligence and Informatics (SACI). pp. 509–518 (2016). https://doi.org/10.1109/SACI.2016.7507430

52. Michael, N., Mellinger, D., Lindsey, Q., Kumar, V.: The grasp multiple micro-uav testbed. IEEE Rob. Autom. Mag. **17**(3), 56–65 (2010). https://doi.org/10.1109/MRA.2010.937855

53. Müller, T., Erdnüß, B.: Robust drone detection with static VIS and SWIR cameras for day and night counter-UAV. In: Counterterrorism, Crime Fighting, Forensics, and Surveillance Technologies, vol. 11166, pp. 58–72. International Society for Optics and Photonics, SPIE (2019). https://doi.org/10.1117/12.2537940, https://doi.org/10.1117/12.2537940

54. Nguyen, P., Ravindranatha, M., Nguyen, A., Han, R., Vu, T.: Investigating cost-effective RF-based detection of drones. In: Workshop on Micro Aerial Vehicle Networks, Systems, and Applications for Civilian Use, DroNet 2016, pp. 17–22. Association for Computing Machinery, New York, NY, USA (2016). https://doi.org/10.1145/2935620.2935632, https://doi.org/10.1145/2935620.2935632

55. Nikhil, N., Morris, B.T.: Convolutional neural network for trajectory prediction. In: Leal-Taixé, L., Roth, S. (eds.) ECCV 2018. LNCS, vol. 11131, pp. 186–196. Springer, Cham (2019). https://doi.org/10.1007/978-3-030-11015-4_16

56. van den Oord, A., et al.: WaveNet: a generative model for raw audio. In: 9th ISCA Speech Synthesis Workshop, pp. 125–125 (2016)

57. Paszke, A., et al.: PyTorch: An imperative style, high-performance deep learning library. In: Advances in Neural Information Processing Systems (NeurIPS), pp. 8024–8035. Curran Associates, Inc. (2019)

58. Pellegrini, S., Ess, A., Schindler, K., van Gool, L.: You'll never walk alone: Modeling social behavior for multi-target tracking. In: International Conference on Computer Vision (ICCV), pp. 261–268. IEEE (2009). https://doi.org/10.1109/ICCV.2009.5459260

59. Pool, E., Kooij, J.F.P., Gavrila, D.M.: Crafted vs. learned representations in predictive models - a case study on cyclist path prediction. IEEE Trans. Intell. Veh. **4**, 747–759 (2021). https://doi.org/10.1109/TIV.2021.3064253

60. Rasouli, A.: Deep learning for vision-based prediction: a survey. arXiv preprint arXiv:2007.00095 (2020)

61. Richter, C., Bry, A., Roy, N.: Polynomial trajectory planning for aggressive quadrotor flight in dense indoor environments. In: Inaba, M., Corke, P. (eds.) Robotics Research. STAR, vol. 114, pp. 649–666. Springer, Cham (2016). https://doi.org/10.1007/978-3-319-28872-7_37

62. Rozantsev, A., Lepetit, V., Fua, P.: Detecting flying objects using a single moving camera. IEEE Trans. Pattern Anal. Mach. Intell. **39**(5), 879–892 (2017). https://doi.org/10.1109/TPAMI.2016.2564408

63. Rudenko, A., Kucner, T.P., Swaminathan, C.S., Chadalavada, R.T., Arras, K.O., Lilienthal, A.J.: ThÖr: Human-robot navigation data collection and accurate motion trajectories dataset. IEEE Rob. Autom. Lett. **5**(2), 676–682 (2020). https://doi.org/10.1109/LRA.2020.2965416

64. Rudenko, A., Palmieri, L., Herman, M., Kitani, K.M., Gavrila, D.M., Arras, K.O.: human motion trajectory prediction: a survey. Int. J. Rob. Res. **39**(1), :027836492091744 (2020)

65. Rumelhart, D.E., Hinton, G.E., Williams, R.J.: Learning Representations By Back-Propagating Errors, pp. 696–699. MIT Press, Cambridge (1988)

66. Sadeghian, A., Kosaraju, V., Sadeghian, A., Hirose, N., Rezatofighi, H., Savarese, S.: Sophie: an attentive GAN for predicting paths compliant to social and physical constraints. In: Conference on Computer Vision and Pattern Recognition (CVPR), pp. 1349–1358. Computer Vision Foundation/IEEE (2019). https://doi.org/10.1109/CVPR.2019.00144

67. Samaras, S., et al.: Deep learning on multi sensor data for counter UAV applications-a systematic review. Sensors **19**(22) (2019). https://doi.org/10.3390/s19224837, https://www.mdpi.com/1424-8220/19/22/4837

68. Schumann, A., Sommer, L., Klatte, J., Schuchert, T., Beyerer, J.: Deep cross-domain flying object classification for robust UAV detection. In: International Conference on Advanced Video and Signal Based Surveaillance (AVSS), pp. 1–6 (2017). https://doi.org/10.1109/AVSS.2017.8078558

69. Schumann, A., Sommer, L., Müller, T., Voth, S.: An image processing pipeline for long range UAV detection. In: Emerging Imaging and Sensing Technologies for Security and Defence III; and Unmanned Sensors, Systems, and Countermeasures, vol. 10799, pp. 186–194. International Society for Optics and Photonics, SPIE (2018). https://doi.org/10.1117/12.2325735, https://doi.org/10.1117/12.2325735

70. Shah, S., Dey, D., Lovett, C., Kapoor, A.: AirSim: high-fidelity visual and physical simulation for autonomous vehicles. In: Hutter, M., Siegwart, R. (eds.) Field and Service Robotics. SPAR, vol. 5, pp. 621–635. Springer, Cham (2018). https://doi.org/10.1007/978-3-319-67361-5_40

71. Shakhatreh, H., et al.: Unmanned aerial vehicles (UAVs): a survey on civil applications and key research challenges. IEEE Access **7**, 48572–48634 (2019). https://doi.org/10.1109/ACCESS.2019.2909530

72. Sommer, L., Schumann, A., Müller, T., Schuchert, T., Beyerer, J.: Flying object detection for automatic UAV recognition. In: International Conference on Advanced Video and Signal Based Surveillance (AVSS), pp. 1–6 (2017). https://doi.org/10.1109/AVSS.2017.8078557

73. Song, Y., Naji, S., Kaufmann, E., Loquercio, A., Scaramuzza, D.: Flightmare: a flexible quadrotor simulator. In: Kober, J., Ramos, F., Tomlin, C.J. (eds.) Conference on Robot Learning (CoRL). Proceedings of Machine Learning Research, vol. 155, pp. 1147–1157. PMLR (2020). https://proceedings.mlr.press/v155/song21a.html

74. Szeliski, R.: Computer Vision: Algorithms and Applications, 1st edn. Springer-Verlag, Heidelberg (2010). https://doi.org/10.1007/978-1-84882-935-0

75. Taha, B., Shoufan, A.: Machine learning-based drone detection and classification: State-of-the-art in research. IEEE Access **7**, 138669–138682 (2019). https://doi.org/10.1109/ACCESS.2019.2942944

76. Tokekar, P., Hook, J.V., Mulla, D., Isler, V.: Sensor planning for a symbiotic UAV and UGV system for precision agriculture. IEEE Trans. Rob. **32**(6), 1498–1511 (2016). https://doi.org/10.1109/TRO.2016.2603528

77. Unlu, E., Zenou, E., Riviere, N., Dupouy, P.-E.: Deep learning-based strategies for the detection and tracking of drones using several cameras. IPSJ Trans. Comput. Vis. Appl. **11**(1), 1–13 (2019). https://doi.org/10.1186/s41074-019-0059-x

78. Vaswani, A., et al.: Attention is all you need. In: Guyon, I., et al. (eds.) Advances in Neural Information Processing Systems 30: Annual Conference on Neural Information Processing Systems 2017, 4–9 December 2017. Long Beach, CA, USA, pp. 5998–6008 (2017). https://proceedings.neurips.cc/paper/2017/hash/3f5ee243547dee91fbd053c1c4a845aa-Abstract.html

79. Vemula, A., Muelling, K., Oh, J.: Social attention: Modeling attention in human crowds. In: International Conference on Robotics and Automation (ICRA), pp. 1–7 (2018). https://doi.org/10.1109/ICRA.2018.8460504, https://doi.org/10.1109/ICRA.2018.8460504

80. Xiao, Y., Zhang, X.: Micro-uav detection and identification based on radio frequency signature. In: International Conference on Systems and Informatics (ICSAI), pp. 1056–1062 (2019). https://doi.org/10.1109/ICSAI48974.2019.9010185
81. Yuan, Y., Weng, X., Ou, Y., Kitani, K.: Agentformer: Agent-aware transformers for socio-temporal multi-agent forecasting. In: Proceedings of the IEEE/CVF International Conference on Computer Vision (ICCV) (2021)
82. Zhang, X., Kusrini, K.: Autonomous long-range drone detection system for critical infrastructure safety. Multim. Tools Appl. **80**(15), 23723–23743 (2021). https://doi.org/10.1007/s11042-020-10231-x

Author Index

Printed in the United States
by Baker & Taylor Publisher Services